"*Untamed* is a desperately needed shot of spiritual adrenaline into our mild-mannered and mediocre attempts at following Christ."

—from the foreword by Rick Warren,
author of *The Purpose Driven Life*

"You may find yourself uncomfortable with this book. If so, the Hirsches have succeeded. . . . Live a life that has stories to tell. Be untamed in your faith and pursuit of the wild Savior, Jesus."

—from the afterword by Neil Cole,
author of *Organic Leadership*

"This dynamic duo gives prophetic voice to what it means to become missional, outwardly-focused followers of Jesus. This is a book to be read and wrestled with—a much needed resource for the church today."

—Margaret Feinberg, MargaretFeinberg.com; author of
Scouting the Divine and *The Organic God*

"*Untamed* is a vision of life with Jesus that goes beyond what other authors have covered. Alan and Debra courageously tackle even taboo subjects to show that life with Christ is more than we often imagine it to be."

—Skye Jethani, author of *The Divine Commodity*;
managing editor of *Leadership Journal*

"Depending on who you read, Jesus has been represented as (and reduced to) a social activist, a tortured reformer, or a cavalier teacher. Against this background, *Untamed* is refreshing, grounded, thoughtful . . . tantalizing."

—Reggie McNeal, missional specialist, Leadership Network, Dallas, Texas; author of *The Present Future* and *Missional Renaissance*

"The demand for an intelligible path toward discipleship is one of the greatest needs of the post-Christendom church. In *Untamed*, Alan and Debra deliver beautifully."

—Gabe Lyons, founder of *Q* and co-founder of *Catalyst*; coauthor of *unChristian*

"*Untamed* is like *Where the Wild Things Are* applied to faith. The Hirsches encourage us to live life as a holy, messy adventure in the land of a loving God."

—Sally Morgenthaler, author of *Worship Evangelism* and "Leadership in a Flattened World" in *An Emergent Manifesto of Hope*

"*Untamed* . . . is the fruit of a significant and penetrating analysis of American culture, candid conversations with key ministry leaders all over the U.S., and sheer gumption in holding up a flag for a radical, uncompromising discipleship. . . . *Untamed* is the best book I have read this year."

—Andrew Jones, developer, Church Mission Society; TallSkinnyKiwi.com

"In this bold, compelling, and inspiring work, Alan and Debra Hirsch . . . share with readers a captivating vision of the true Messiah. All who are unsatisfied with the boring safety of their tame Christianity need to read this book!"

—Greg Boyd, senior pastor, Woodland Hills Church, St. Paul, Minnesota; author of *Seeing Is Believing* and *Repenting of Religion*

Shapevine

untamed

reactivating a missional form of discipleship

alan hirsch and debra hirsch

BakerBooks

a division of Baker Publishing Group
Grand Rapids, Michigan

Published by Baker Books
a division of Baker Publishing Group
P.O. Box 6287, Grand Rapids, MI 49516-6287
www.bakerbooks.com

Printed in the United States of America

Library of Congress Cataloging-in-Publication Data
Hirsch, Alan, 1959 Oct. 24–
    Untamed : reactivating a missional form of discipleship / Alan Hirsch and Debra Hirsch.
        p.   cm. — (Shapevine)
    Includes bibliographical references.
    ISBN 978-0-8010-1343-0 (pbk.)
    1. Christian life. 2. Church. 3. Missions. I. Hirsch, Debra, 1963– II. Title.
BV4501.3.H58 2010
248.4—dc22   2009040137

10   11   12   13   14   15   16   7   6   5   4   3   2   1

Dedication

To our two brothers, Dean Duerkop and Lawrence Hirsch, for being passionate, consistent followers of Jesus—men after God's own heart!

Special Thanks

To Michael and Rita Warren for their extravagant generosity to two orphaned Aussies in America.

To the zany Jonny Birch of asbojesus.wordpress.com for the wonderful cartoons that spice up the text.

122805

contents

foreword

A generation ago a well-known English bishop ruefully admitted, "In the New Testament, everywhere Paul went he sparked a revolution. But today, everywhere I go, they just serve tea and crumpets!" Sadly, this expresses a fundamental problem in many churches. We've become tamed by tradition, captivated by culture, and controlled by our desire to fit in, not make waves, and never offend anyone. We've been domesticated instead of being discipled.

In the Great Commission Jesus commands us to "go and make disciples of all nations," but we can't make disciples until we *are* disciples. We can't make a difference until *we* are different. This requires us to return to the Jesus model of disciple making. Over a three-and-a-half-year period Jesus repeatedly defined the term "disciple" by saying, "You are my disciple if . . ." and "You cannot be my disciple unless . . ." As time passed he continually turned up the heat and called for deeper and deeper commitment.

Thirty years ago, when Kay and I planted Saddleback Church, we began imitating the intentional and sequential discipleship process Jesus used with his Twelve. Like Jesus, we move people from "come and see," through all of the same stages Jesus used, to "come and die." Because of our emphasis on radical discipleship, we have baptized over 28,000 new adult followers of Christ, grown them to maturity, and sent over 10,000 of them to serve in all 195 nations of the world. You can't improve on Jesus!

Surveys and polls reveal that in many countries, the life-styles of believers are not very different from those of non-believers. Too many Christ followers have settled for living a nice, comfortable, moral, and decent life instead of following the radical and wild adventure of trusting God's promises and obeying his commands. Fortunately, Alan and Debra have written just what needs to be said. *Untamed* is a desperately needed shot of spiritual adrenaline into our mild-mannered and mediocre attempts at following Christ.

The starting point is to get a new vision of who God is, how he acts, and what he expects from us. In *Untamed* you will discover a wild God, a God who loves us so much he dove into humanity headfirst. He didn't play it safe, and he expects you to take risks in faith also.

In these pages you are about to read, Alan and Debra will carefully and clearly lead you to truly transforming disciple-ship. They lay out the path, expose the pitfalls and obstacles, and show how to stay on the road until you reach the finish line. As you get serious about following an untamed God, you will begin to enjoy the untamed lifestyle of being radically committed to Christ's mission in the world. Your Father in heaven created you for this, Jesus saves you for this, and the Holy Spirit empowers you for this! This is your destiny.

In C. S. Lewis's Narnia stories, the children were worried about their first encounter with Aslan, the great lion who represents Jesus. Susan asks, "Is he safe?" Mr. Beaver replies, "Who said anything about being safe? 'Course he isn't safe! But he's good, and he is the King." Aslan was far from being tamed and housebroken. But he was good, and just, and strong enough to defeat evil. Once the children met Aslan, they began the adventure of their lives.

It is my prayer that the same will happen to you as you read this book. Jesus loves you just the way you are, but he loves you far too much to let you stay that way.

Rick Warren
www.radicalis.com

about the shapevine missional series

The key purpose of Shapevine the organization is to bring the various elements of missional Christianity—namely, church planting movements, urban mission, the emerging church, the missional church movement, the organic/simple church, and marketplace ministries—into meaningful dialogue around the truly big ideas of our time. Consistent with this purpose, the Shapevine Missional Series in partnership with Baker Books seeks to bring innovative thinking to the missional issues of church planting, mission, evangelism, social justice, and anything in between.

We seek to publish both established authors as well as others who have significant things to contribute but have operated largely under the radar.

The series will focus on three distinctive areas:

- **Living—Practical Missional Orthopraxy**
  Orthopraxy is what makes orthodoxy worth having. We yearn for the experience and continual flow of living out the gospel message in our day-to-day lives for the sake

of others. The stories and ideas in the Shapevine Missional Series are aimed at providing practical handles and means to wrap our readers' minds around the idea of living as the people of God, sent into the world with the Spirit and impulse of Jesus himself.

- **Learning—Solid Missional Orthodoxy**

  Jesus both lived and proclaimed a theology of a missional God. His was and is a message of mercy, justice, and goodness toward others. It was this message that erupted into the greatest movement in the history of humankind. The same God who sent his only Son now sends those who follow his Son, in the same manner and with the same message. This is at the heart of a missional theology.

- **Leading—Tools for Missional Leadership**

  Our aim is for the books in this series to serve as tools for pastors, organizational leaders, and church members throughout the world to equip themselves and others as they travel the path of faithfulness in the missional life.

As a global interactive forum, Shapevine allows anyone to both learn and contribute at whatever level suits. To learn more, go to www.shapevine.com or contact us at info@ shapevine.com.

Alan Hirsch and Lance Ford

series editor's preface

The Shapevine series seeks to highlight the missional significance of its various contributors; this book fits admirably
in the purpose of the series. The fact that I am one of the
authors of this particular work should not distract from the
sheer strategic significance involved in the rediscovery of a
vigorous and explicitly missional form of discipleship.

The fact that discipleship in the church is considered a
somewhat lost art ought to disturb us profoundly. On the
odd occasions we have actually managed to engage in some
form of discipleship, we have tended to limit it to issues of
personal spirituality (prayer times, Bible study, God's leading, tithing, etc.) and not conceive of it as something that
has direct ramifications beyond the individual's privatized
religious sensibilities. But discipleship in the way of Jesus is
surely much more comprehensive than that. That we have
cultivated an attenuated form of "designer" discipleship, a
do-it-yourself spirituality that has little to say beyond the
confines of the Christian community itself, only highlights
the need to recover something a whole lot more vigorous
than what we currently have. Again, this unnerves those of
us concerned with the health and impact of Christianity in

the twenty-first century because if we fail in this most fundamental of tasks, we must surely fail in whatever ministry that
should build upon it. Discipleship—our capacity to lovingly
embody and transmit the life of Jesus through the lives of
his followers—is the internal "quality control" mechanism
inherent in Christianity itself. It is an absolutely foundational
activity.

As Dietrich Bonhoeffer warned in the years leading up to
the Second World War, a Christianity without discipleship is
a Christianity without Christ. And a Christless Christianity
is surely an abomination that is likely to do much damage to
the world in which it appears. The rise of Nazism within Ger-
many, even among German Christians, only proves his point.
We do well to heed the lessons of history in this regard.

This might be the first book in the series that will focus on
recovering the loving art of a rigorous, missional discipleship,
but it won't be the last.

Alan Hirsch, series editor

why write this book?

We have both walked with Jesus for many years now and know personally just how difficult the path of missional discipleship can be. Following Jesus has a very clear cost. And the cost includes living a life that sometimes runs contrary to the culture around us. Serious believers who want to go deeper in their discipleship must be willing to constantly critique both personal and cultural assumptions for the sake of becoming more like Jesus. This book is about just that. Simply stated, we write to help disciples of Jesus become better and deeper disciples. In order to do this, we have selected from both our personal and ministry experience a number of "obstacles" that, more than others, seem to trip up the people of God. It is these that we write about.

In the course of writing this book, we celebrated our twentieth wedding anniversary *and* our twentieth year of being in "official" ministry, for we started pastoral ministry four days after we were married. In fact we were so keen to get started that we cut our honeymoon short to move into the pastor's house next door to the church where we were to be the ministers—not something we would now recommend! For us, serving God has always been a partnership. And we see ourselves and our ministries as richer for the different perspectives and passions we each bring. No doubt you will feel something of these passions as you read through the text and some of the stories we've included. In light of this, and in case you'd like to know a little more about us, we thought we'd share something of our story and some of those passions with you.

Deb's Passion

For as long as I (Deb) can remember, I have identified with the "other," those that have been deemed different or "outsiders," those society has generally struggled to accept. Most of my early memories involve my sister (Sharon) and my cousin (Mark), neither of whom quite fit the norm. My sister was born with a physical disability, and my cousin had a distinctly "effeminate" nature; neither were really acceptable in the rough, working-class area we grew up in. At our school, being different or standing out in any way ensured you were the object of ridicule, or even abuse. I can still remember the fights I would get into defending and protecting them from constant bullying. No doubt these experiences were to lay a foundation within me of deep sensitivity to issues of marginalization and injustice, a theme that continues to run through my life.

I found Jesus (or rather, he found me) many years later along with that same sister and cousin. We were in our early twenties, living reckless lives of drugs, sex, and partying. We were active members of the GLBT[1] community and proudly identified ourselves as "gay." We were seekers, but didn't realize just how lost we were until one of our friends (and drug dealer) became a Christian and shared the message of the gospel with us. In Jesus we found not only great relief from the existential angst we carried, but experienced deep liberation for our souls. Our lives were literally turned around, and all those old clichés became for us a profound reality: we were the lost and now found, we were the blind who could now see.

Part of this "seeing" for me was a realization that my sensitivity for the "other" was actually a gift from God. God loves the outcast, those society has for whatever reason pushed to the edges. Here my passion met with God's heart. I cannot read the Scriptures without seeing the truth of this. It is to "the least of these," in whatever shape or form—whether transsexual, gay, prostitute, or poor—that I believe I am called, in order that somehow they can come to know that same amazing, transforming grace I experienced all those years ago. And along with that comes the deep burden that we as a church would be better equipped to help these people walk the path of discipleship.

Al's Passion

I (Alan) grew up in a Jewish family and was born and raised in apartheid South Africa until age twenty-two. Having a seemingly natural affinity with black people, I became politically active against apartheid as early as age thirteen. Nothing too hotheaded, but I had already decided that apartheid was profoundly wrong and morally reprehensible. After spending a mandatory two-year stint in the military, where I was first introduced to drugs and then to Jesus, I attended university in Cape Town. I then eventually immigrated to Australia with my family in 1983, shortly after I met my wonderful wife and partner.

Although I was not an observant Jew by any stretch of the imagination, I can honestly say I don't remember a time when I ever doubted God's existence, and I can remember moments of ecstatic worship, even as a very young boy, where God seemed more real to me than my own self. My journey to explicit Christian faith started early, with what seemed to a young Jewish teenager as an illicit fascination with Jesus. As far as I can recall, I had never met a real Christian until I was about twenty, when one of my drug buddies was born again and began to share the gospel with me. For me, coming to Jesus was coming home in every way. I had an overwhelming encounter with God and was totally and absolutely won over. It was the defining moment of my life: I gave my life fully to Jesus and I have never looked back.

As for my passion and my reasons for writing this text, it is important for the reader to know that this book is set within the context of this great love affair that I have with God's people. I really believe in the church: when it is true to its identity and purpose, it is far and away the most transformative force for good in society. It must be, because when it is faithful, it is the most concentrated expression of the liberating kingdom of God.

My calling, and my passion, is to reawaken the missional capacities of the church in the West. In *The Shaping of Things to Come*, and especially in *The Forgotten Ways*, I have attempted to set forth this positive, transformative, and distinctly *apostolic* vision of the church as a Jesus movement. If this book seems somewhat more critical (dare I say prophetic) in tone, then it must be understood that it is set within the broader context of an apostolic (a missionary perspective and drive) vision for the church as a missional movement that can, and will, change the world. I believe that *this* is exactly the form of the church that can reestablish the vitality of Christianity in the West. But through my own struggles and other forms of personal experience and observation, I have come to believe we are never going to be the movement Jesus wants unless we *first* get the issues of discipleship right. This is because the health and growth of transformative Jesus movements are directly related to their capacity to make disciples. No disciples, no movement—it's that simple.

Going South: Submerging into Our City

South Melbourne Restoration Community, the church where we began our first "official" ministry (affectionately called South), was located in an inner-city context and made up largely of people who, in one way or another, were on the fringes of society. From the homosexual to the prostitute, the schizophrenic to the drug addict, our community was full of people who didn't quite fit the norm. And even though there were some "normal" people (thank God), this was no regular church. Many said of us that we were the first port of call for those on their way into the church and the last port of call for those on their way out. If they couldn't make it with us, they weren't going to make it anywhere!

We led this wonderful community for fifteen years. We lived, loved, cried, and laughed with this bunch of people; and they, more than most, helped define who we are as people. This collection of "freaks" became our family, one little microcosm of the greater family of God. We learned so much throughout these years, and, as is often the case, much more through our mistakes—and they were many!

Forging New Paths

Throughout our time at South, we were privileged to be able to plant other communities of faith, and help in initiating various outreach agencies and missional orders. On top of this, Al was also involved in leadership of our denomination and Deb led a ministry to gays, lesbians, and transsexuals, and also served the poor through her work with the Salvation Army.

Our passion to see others come to know Jesus has always been a constant throughout our ministry. The outworking of this passion, among other things, was pioneering Forge Mission Training Network, an agency devoted to developing missional leaders for incarnational forms of mission in Western cultural contexts. Forge now has networks in Australia, Canada, and the USA, with the possibility of a European one in the future. One of our great joys has been to see Forge become a significant grassroots movement God has used to influence the way the church both sees itself and responds to its context.

We say this here not from any notion of personal achievement, rather because we have a great sense of having been graced to be able to experience firsthand what missional church in the untamed way of Jesus can be. But we can say this: looking back on our various experiences, particularly our many failures, most could, at root, be traced back to failures in discipleship. If discipleship involves our life in Christ and his life in and through us, then we think that many problems can be traced to breakdowns in this connection. For whatever reasons (and we now have a few clues about this) Jesus's "software" was not properly downloaded into our lives. This applies to issues from deformed Christian identity to narrow understandings of the family, and everything in between. If we failed at mission, it was because we failed to ground a sense of obligation to Jesus's lordship in everything we did. If we failed in generosity, it was because we hadn't rooted out the love of money and status that forms the basis of our consumerist culture. Likewise, if we failed in areas of personal morality and social responsibility, it was because we didn't pay enough attention to what it means to walk in the radical way of Jesus.

We believe our own experience only mirrors the experience of so many in the Western church: these various issues present significant cultural and theological fault lines in Western expressions of Christianity, and given the strategically significant situation of the church in the West, we must find a way to once again become the robust, untamed, transformative movement God has designed the church to be.

In writing this book, we not only hope to identify some of these flaws in our scripting, but also to provide some lively clues as to how we may, in the power of the Spirit, overcome them. And we write not as judges (God forbid), but rather as fellow travelers personally committed to increasingly becoming the untamed people we are called to be. We do believe that whatever direction you or I should take, we should somehow be taking it with Jesus. And so it is our deep hope that we can, with you, authentically live out the radical, grace-saturated life of Jesus and become more like the One we love.

the first word

(introduction)

The disciple must face the world fully aware of the desire of the Darkness to pervert and destroy the witness of the Light.

—Gene Davenport

To believe means to be so rooted in Christ that he becomes the foundation of one's existence, the beginning and end of the movement known as life, its measure and source and strength. The extent to which we succeed depends on our loyalty and on our power of sacrifice. Hence the believer does well to say not that he is a Christian, but that he is becoming one.

—Romano Guardini

For the disciple of Jesus the stage of discipleship is not the first step towards a promising career. It is in itself the fulfillment of his destiny.

—David Bosch

One day long ago, over the hot sands of a Middle Eastern country, a white skylark flew in joyous loops about the sky. As she swooped near the earth, she heard a merchant cry out, "Worms! Worms! Worms for feathers! Delicious worms!" The skylark circled about the merchant, hungry at the mention of worms, but puzzled about what the merchant meant. Little did the skylark know that the merchant was the devil. And seeing that the skylark was interested, the devil motioned her nearer. "Come here, my little friend. Come! See the lovely worms I have!"

Cautiously, the skylark landed and cocked her head to the merchant. "Come! Taste the juicy worms!" The skylark became aware that she was, indeed, quite hungry. And these worms looked bigger and tastier than any she had ever dug for herself out of the hardscrabble ground of the desert. The skylark hopped closer and put her beak up close to the worm. "Two worms for a feather, my friend. Two worms for merely one!"

The skylark was unable to resist. And she had, after all, so many feathers. So, with a swift motion she pulled out a feather—just a small one—from beneath her wing and gave it to the merchant. "Take your pick, my little friend . . . any two, your heart's desire!" The skylark quickly snatched up two of the plumpest worms and swallowed her meal with delight. Never before had she tasted such wonderful worms. With a loud chirp, she leapt into the air and resumed her joyful flight.

Day after day the skylark returned. And always the merchant had wonderful worms to offer: black ones and blue ones, red ones and green ones, all fat and shiny and iridescent. But one day, after eating her fill, the skylark leapt again into the air—and to her horror, she fell to the ground with a thud. She was unable to fly!

All at once with a shock she realized what had happened. From eating the delicious worms she had grown fatter and fatter; and she had plucked her feathers one by one, first her body, then her tail, and finally her very wings had grown balder and balder. Horrified, she remembered how, slowly, imperceptibly, day by day, it had been getting harder and harder to fly, and how she had told herself it was no matter. She could always stop before it was too late. Now suddenly here she was, trapped on the ground. She looked up and saw the merchant looking at her. Was that a small, sly grin spreading across his face? He grabbed the now helpless bird, put her in a cage, and walked away laughing.[1]

The Cage of a Thousand Compromises

We start with this parable because, like all bargains with the devil, it mirrors so many processes that make up human life and, for the purposes of this book, the nature of the Christian walk gone wrong. Tragically, like the formerly wild skylark, little by little we give up our freedoms in Christ, only to end up in a cage made of a thousand little compromises. This of course need not be so. A way is set out for us that not only delivers us freedom to be who God has made us to be, but also helps us to maintain our freedom.

When we try to take shortcuts to costly discipleship, we end up with a domesticated existence that is far from the liberated, untamed life Jesus calls us to. Much of what we write here is about exposing some of the personal and cultural issues, and the idolatry so often associated with them, that in the end undermine our capacity to experience full, Christlike lives. If some of what is set forth in these pages seems strange to us, then it might well be because we have become too domesticated, accustomed to being featherless, and have now lost the

> ### Slip Sliding Away
>
> In C. S. Lewis's *The Screwtape Letters*, Wormwood commits the novice tempter's error of being overeager to report "spectacular wickedness." But Screwtape reminds him that the only thing that matters is to "separate the man from the Enemy [God]." In fact, "murder is no better than cards if cards can do the trick. Indeed, the safest road to Hell is the gradual one—the gentle slope, soft underfoot, without sudden turnings, without milestones, without signposts."

art of flight. Perhaps it is because we have forgotten what it really means to follow the untamed, revolutionary Jesus. We must now remember in order to reactivate the journey.

In your hands is a book on what we call "missional discipleship." In many ways it contains ideas and a call to live a lifestyle that should be normative for Jesus's people. But *we* know all too well from personal experience and observation that following Jesus doesn't always come easy. And being involved in various expressions of missional Christianity has given us an appreciation for just how hard it is to be consistent followers of our Lord and Savior. To be a truly radical disciple does require a relentless evaluation of life's priorities and concerns, together with an ongoing, rigorous critique of our culture, to ensure we are not adopting values that subvert the very life and message we are called to live out.

We sincerely believe discipleship has become a frontier issue for the people of God at this time in history. And most commentators would agree that in sincerely seeking to appeal to the prevailing consumerist culture, the Western church has all but lost the art of discipleship.[2] This causes, for instance, Southern Baptist prophet Reggie McNeal to conclude that "church culture in North America is a vestige of the original [Christian] movement, an institutional expression of religion that is in part a civil religion and in part a club where religious people can hang out with other people whose politics, worldview, and lifestyle match theirs."[3]

If this is indeed the case, we should be clear this is *not* what the church is called to be, and is, in fact, a failure in discipleship. And it must be addressed if we are to give faithful witness to our century. Therefore, rediscovering what it means to radically follow Jesus is an area of strategic, *missional* concern. The gospel is the power of God for the salvation of the world (Rom. 1:16), and God wants to redeem the broken and lost world around us. He has chosen to do this through us. Our lives, individual and corporate, play a vital role in the unfolding of the grand purposes of God. More is at stake in discipleship than our own personal salvation. The gospel cannot be limited to being about my personal healing and wholeness, but rather extends in and through my salvation to the salvation of the world. To fail in discipleship and disciple making is therefore to fail in the primary mission (or "sent-ness") of the church. And it does not take a genius to realize that we have all but lost the art of disciple making in the contemporary Western church. No wonder Dallas Willard calls our systematic failure to disciple "the great omission" in his book by that name.

The Structure of *Untamed*

We have divided the book into four sections. Following our approach of removing impediments to discipleship, we have identified three areas where problems in discipleship locate themselves: theology, culture, and personal issues.

Section one: Untaming (our idea of) God

The church has always believed that our most fundamental problems in discipleship have their roots in faulty views of God. If not properly addressed, these distorted views deeply impact our effectiveness as disciples and missionaries in our world. The first section therefore will look at some foundational theological issues related to our understanding of God, Jesus, and the Holy Spirit. Although we have tried to write this in a very accessible manner, some readers might find this section somewhat abstract and feel impatient to get to the "practical" issues. But nothing is more important than a right perception and experience of God. So, our advice is to slow down, and seriously examine your heart and engage your mind here. In probing issues relating to God, it is hard to avoid dealing with concepts in one form or another. But real theology is more than a series of ideas; rather, we are dealing with what must be our most defining Reality—something that must not be avoided.

Section two: Untaming our culture

Culture is the context we all swim in. We can't help but be deeply informed by it at every level of our human life— individual as well as social. Culture is a complex jungle of ideas, history, language, religious views, economic systems, political issues, and the like. Culture forms the basic way in which human beings communicate and share life and meaning together. But not all of it fits nicely with reality as God defines it. The problem is that most of us are unaware of these issues because we simply assume that our culture is right. If we are not careful, then, the culture rather than God actually gets to define reality. This is the core of many problems in discipleship.

This section will explore the power of money and status, our understanding of the family, and (yes) the church. We put issues of church here because the church, as a human agency, must always express faith culturally. But it is often more conditioned by culture than it is by the gospel. For instance, how does the culture of consumerism affect our experience of the church? Is the church challenging society here, or are we being co-opted to a larger cultural agenda?

Section three: Untaming the self

On a more distinctly personal level, there are numerous obstacles to discipleship that are part of our own scripting (or software) as individuals. While theology and culture do impact us personally, the issues explored here are felt *within* our own psyches. How we understand who we are (self-image) and how we understand sexuality has everything to do with how we follow Jesus and engage the world. We cannot avoid these issues. In this section we will explore the discipleship implications of what it means to be made in the image of

God and how sexuality connects with our spirituality . . . or doesn't.

Section four: Untaming the mission

As people captivated by the incarnation, we couldn't finish the book without suggesting some practical ways of implementing untamed discipleship based on the life of Jesus. And so the final chapter is exactly that: a simple guide to incarnational mission. This chapter, based on six principles of incarnational living, includes a number of examples of individuals and communities doing just that in their local contexts. Nothing too heady, just some simple clues to going deep into culture based on the life and example of Jesus.

Practices and group discussions

At the end of every chapter is a set of practices along with some questions for group discussion. The practices are designed to be suggestions the reader can adopt in order to activate a more untamed version of following Jesus. By applying them you can *act* your way into a new way of thinking. As for the group discussion, we really do believe that community is the best context for discipleship and the right place for accountability and the pursuit of truth. Don't do this alone. Discipleship is never a purely individual quest: we suggest that a few friends read each chapter together and discuss possible outcomes.

Signature Themes

If the book is structured around theology, culture, psychology, and mission (in that order), the reader will also discern that consistent themes pervade the entire book. Each chapter is spiced with four distinctive motifs or themes that, taken together, will create a certain vibe, or atmosphere, in the book. They are . . .

Jesus-shaped discipleship

It seems crazy to say it, but the first thing we can say about missional discipleship is that it must take Jesus with utmost seriousness. Whatever place "Yahweh is Lord" had/has for Israel, "Jesus is Lord" has for us as disciples. Every single aspect of the way we live out our lives needs to be re-aligned around the person of Jesus and his lordship. A dynamic, vital, living reality and response to Jesus in every moment of our lives is *our most fundamental truth*, and we have forgotten it to our great peril.

N. T. Wright notably states that the longer you look at Jesus, the more you will want to serve him—that is, of course, if it is the real Jesus you are looking at.[4] Because Jesus defines our concepts of God, getting it wrong *here* means getting it wrong *everywhere* (as we shall see in chapters 1 and 2). And because Jesus defines and models for us a perfected humanity, he shows us the way of true holiness. We will present to you a holiness more akin to a gutsy, inclusive, gritty faith than to the moralistic, exclusive, sterile version Christians have come to be known for.

Shema spirituality

The Shema (Deut. 6:4–9) is considered the most important confession in the Old Testament and in Judaism, and is confessed three times a day by every orthodox Jew. The word *shema* itself stems from the first word of this text and simply means "listen!" or "take heed." "*Hear*, O Israel: The LORD our God, the LORD is one. Love the LORD your God with all your heart and with all your soul and with all your strength."

But its defining influence extends through the New Testament to each one of us. Jesus confirms the absolute truth of the Shema:

One of the teachers of the law came and heard them debating. Noticing that Jesus had given them a good answer, he asked him, "Of all the commandments, which is the most important?"

"The most important one," answered Jesus, "is this: 'Hear, O Israel, the Lord our God, the Lord is one. Love the Lord your God with all your heart and with all your soul and with all your mind and with all your strength.' The second is this: 'Love your neighbor as yourself.' *There is no commandment greater than these.*" (Mark 12:28–31, italics ours)

Jesus explicitly places the Shema at the epicenter of what it means to be a true disciple—to love God, to love others, and to live this out authentically in God's world. We believe that we must simply take Jesus at face value here; he is saying that "Shema spirituality" is core to the outworking of our discipleship—our life under God. Actually, when we look into this, there are thoroughly good reasons for it. We suggest that Shema spirituality helps us do the following:

- Rediscover the true nature of worship (we must love one God, not many—no idols and images, please)
- Learn what it means to love God in and through the whole of life (with intellect, passion, family, culture, money, sexuality, and so on)
- Understand our relationship to the world and our obligation to "the other" (we can never come to a true discipleship in isolation from the love of people)
- Recover an authentically monotheistic worldview, out of which we can rightly interpret our world (operating with a unified worldview around the kingship of God)

Loving the one true God with all that we are, and loving others as ourselves, is as simple as it is profound. We have discovered that this core truth can indeed provide the answer to the obstacles we encounter on the road. In its simple but

profound summation of the law and prophets, we find something of an antidote to the various forms of deceptive thinking and living. We have, therefore, coined the phrase "Shema
spirituality" and use it consistently throughout the book.

No mission, no discipleship

We take the missional agenda of the church with utmost
seriousness. You simply cannot be a disciple without being a
missionary—a *sent one*. For way too long discipleship has been
limited to issues relating to our own personal morality and
worked out in the context of the four walls of the church with
its privatized religion. In doing this, we have severely neglected
our biblical mandate to *go* and "make disciples." We have narrowed the gospel message to just being about us. Please hear
us here: we don't want to neglect issues of personal morality.
To strive for holiness and maturity in our own personal lives is
extremely important, but it is only half the picture; the other
half is our God-given responsibility to the world around us. The
fact is that you can't be a disciple without being a missionary:
no mission, no discipleship. It's as simple as that.

The mission we are all called into will, to varying degrees,
involve an active engagement with the poor and the marginalized. The Scriptures are clear about this. One cannot read the
Bible without being confronted with God's heart for outcasts
of all varieties. While we have no specific chapter that deals
explicitly with this, issues of justice and care for the poor
will be found in many of the stories we share and are implied
throughout the whole book. We are also conscious of the fact
that many books have been written on this very subject, and
we encourage the reader to explore them.

Of prophets and idols

We don't believe what we are saying is in any sense new,
but rather that it represents a contemporary restatement of
the ancient, *prophetic*, call to faithfulness that has been a

constant part of the church's calling in every age. In many ways, the prophetic challenge to the church is part of the ongoing work of the Holy Spirit in seeking to sanctify the people of God, and the world through them. The Nicene Creed rightly states that Christians believe that the Holy Spirit spoke through the prophets. We sometimes fall into thinking that the prophets were simply speaking into a past era, but the truth is that the same Spirit still speaks through the prophets and those called to extend their challenge in the life of God's people. And because we as humans are prone to sin, safety, and self-concern, we need the prophetic ministry in order to be true to our calling. For a whole host of reasons, we all stray from our radical calling to change our world by *working out* the life of Christ in us (Phil. 2:12–13). In fact, at least a third of Scripture is dedicated to the ongoing integrity of God's people. God's people in every age need correction—ours no less. Without claiming to be prophets ourselves, we hope to draw deeply from this abidingly relevant prophetic tradition, of which Jesus is the complete and most perfect representative.

So Here We Go . . .

Join with us now as we journey into issues of discipleship. And please know that when addressing the issues we cover in this book, we do not do so dispassionately. We are deeply involved with this material. We struggle with every element on a daily basis, and our stories, which are woven throughout the text, are as yet incomplete. We, like you, have sold some of our feathers, and we yearn to retrieve them. We yearn to be more and more like Jesus because we believe the purpose of our lives can only be found in becoming eternally conformed to the image of God's Son (Rom. 8:29). It must become something of a holy obsession! We invite you to join us in being obsessed with becoming more like the One we love.

the untamed god

1

jeebus made me do it

The great Christian revolutions came not by the discovery of
something that was not known before. They happen when
someone takes radically something that was always there.

—H. Richard Niebuhr

To be a Christian means to participate in the life of Christ—
all of it; only the whole brings peace.

—Romano Guardini

To look at something as though we had never seen it before
requires great courage.

—Henri Matisse

In a hilarious episode of *The Simpsons* called "Missionary
Impossible," Homer pledges ten thousand dollars to PBS
and is generally credited for saving the television network.
However, it quickly becomes apparent that Homer does not
have the money, prompting a mob of characters and per-
sonalities from various PBS shows to chase him through the

streets. He hides out in the First Church of Springfield and bargains with Reverend Lovejoy who, despite Homer's obvious lack of Christian faith or understanding, packs him off as a missionary to the South Pacific. Just as the plane is about to take off, Homer shows his utter ignorance when he anxiously exclaims, "Jeebus? Jeebus? But I don't know Jeebus! Helllp me Jeebus!"

Homer arrives on the island where he meets the natives. At first he is so fearful that he's about to be eaten for dinner, he drops to the ground crying "Oh God!" repeatedly. The natives take him for a religious mystic and so they too fall to the ground crying out to God. Emboldened by his new status as spiritual guru, Homer begins trying to teach them about religion, but realizing that he knows nothing about it, he tries something new. While the natives were noble savages ignorant of and unspoiled by civilization, Homer decides to build a casino on the island, which he names "The Lucky Savage." This introduces alcohol, gambling, and violence to the island and totally ruins the natives' previously virtuous way of life.

We start the chapter with this story because it highlights the impact of how ignorance of Jesus by those who claim his name is toxic to both the believer as well as those around him or her. Following "Jeebus," Homer wreaked utter havoc on the population, and we are left wondering if this does not describe large tracts of Christian history equally well. Now we of all people do not want to say that God doesn't use the odd Homers of this world (we think the church *should* be a freak collection and that God does use weirdos of all sorts), but it does highlight the fact that the missional disciple must know God in a real way or else bear false witness. And given our previously mentioned commitment to a distinctly missional form of Christianity, this chapter will highlight some of the ways ignorance of Jesus (willful or otherwise) creates a toxic religion that is not only *not* worth spreading, but detrimental to the cause of Christ.

God Is Like Jesus

The first and absolutely most foundational thing we can say in a book about missional discipleship is that it must be based squarely on the founder of the Christian faith—Jesus the Messiah. And while this might seem obvious, one can easily be excused for not being able to recognize anything approximating Jesus in some of the people who claim his name. This discontinuity between Jesus and the religion that claims his name, what Jacques Ellul calls the "subversion of Christianity," has led countless people to say with political humorist Bill Maher, "I don't know anyone less Jesus-like than most Christians." It also prompted researchers David Kinnaman and Gabe Lyons to write a book called *unChristian*, which is based on what most non-Christian twenty-somethings said about so-called Christians.[1]

Jesus is the key not only because Christian discipleship is about becoming more like Jesus but also because it is only in and through Jesus that we can get the proper, truly *Christ*-ian understanding of God. In other words, Jesus gets defining rights in relation to life, discipleship, theology, and everything in between. Not only is he the mediator between God and humanity (1 Tim. 2:5), he is the prism through which we can and must understand God (Col. 1:9–21, Heb. 1:1–3). New Testament scholar Albert Nolan is quite right when he states,

> By his words and practice, Jesus himself changed the content of the word "God." If we do not allow him to change our image of God, we will not be able to say that he is our Lord and our God. To choose him as our God is to make him the source of our information about divinity and to refuse to superimpose upon him our own ideas of divinity.
>
> This is the meaning of the traditional assertion that Jesus is the Word of God. Jesus reveals God to us; God does not reveal Jesus to us. . . . We cannot deduce anything about Jesus from what we think we know about God; we must deduce

everything about God from what we do know about Jesus. . . .
To say that Jesus is divine does not change our understanding
of Jesus; it changes our understanding of divinity.[2]

Reclaiming the centrality of Jesus will help us avoid the
perennial mistake of superimposing upon the life and personality of Jesus our preconceived ideas of what God is supposed
to be like. N. T. Wright affirms this when he says,

> My proposal is not that we know what the word "god" means,
> and manage somehow to fit Jesus into that. Instead, I suggest
> that we think historically about a young Jew, possessed of a
> desperately risky, indeed apparently crazy, vocation, riding
> into Jerusalem in tears, denouncing the Temple, and dying
> on a Roman cross—and we somehow allow our meaning for
> the word "god" to be recentered around that point.[3]

Jesus is, and must be, the central reference point for the
Christian because God looks like Jesus and Jesus does what
God wants to do! (See John 10:38, 12:49–50.) We love Greg
Boyd's wonderful description of this:

> Jesus spent his ministry freeing people from evil and misery.
> *This is what God seeks to do.* Jesus wars against spiritual
> forces that oppress people and resist God's good purposes.
> *This is what God does.* Jesus loved people others rejected—
> even people who rejected him. *This is how God loves.* Jesus
> had nothing but compassion for people who were afflicted
> by sin, disease, and tragedy. *This is how God feels.* And Jesus
> died on the cross of Calvary, suffering in the place of sinful
> humanity, defeating sin and the devil, because he passion-
> ately loves people and wants to reconcile them to God. *This
> is how God saves.*[4]

It is true that Jesus is like God, but the greater truth, one
closer to the revelation of God that Jesus ushers in, is that
God is like Jesus! As Michael Ramsey, the former Anglican
archbishop, noted, "God is Christlike and in him is no un-

36

Christlikeness at all."[5] Or as Jesus says when asked to show his credentials, "Anyone who has seen me has seen the Father. How can you say, 'Show us the Father'?" and "I and the Father are one" (John 14:9; 10:30).

We Become What We Worship

Focusing our discipleship on Jesus forces us to take seriously the implications of following him, of *becoming like him* . . . like God. The spiritual agenda for discipleship is thus set: Jesus is our primary model, teacher, guide, savior, and Lord. He is the standard by which we assess discipleship and spirituality. And we must become living versions of him—little Jesuses.[6]

So, if we want to know what God is like, we need to look no further than the person of Jesus Christ. Now while this may seem like an incredibly obvious thing to say, it is staggering how few of us really integrate this most fundamental of truths into our lives. Recently one of us was reminded of this reality when attending a local Bible study. The group was studying a book on the character and attributes of God. The leader of the group was asking whether God was knowable, and if so, how we can really know him. The participants were caught up by the "otherness" and "awesomeness" of God experienced in worship, and seemed to sit more comfortably talking about this. When the leader pushed for more specifics, one person mentioned creation and then another the Scriptures, but no one seemed to be able to go further. It wasn't until the study leader stated that it was Jesus who shows us who God is, and that we know God in and through him, that the people seemed to make the connection. What is interesting is that these highly intelligent, mature men and women had been going to church most of their lives, and yet they missed this primary fact—the Jesus factor.

That there is a radical disconnect between God and Jesus for many believers, as illustrated in the story above, shouldn't surprise us. For most people it is far easier to sit with the "otherness" of God—we prefer our divinity at a safe distance. But while God's transcendence does, and should, instill feelings of awe and a desire to worship within us, it does not immediately show us a way to *follow*. We see God or read about him and stand in awe. But what then are we supposed to do besides worship and adore him? When confronted with the reality of God in Jesus, God in human flesh, God is no longer beyond and unfathomable, but immediate and present. He has come close to us, and his claim on our lives becomes somewhat more unavoidable. That was the whole point of the incarnation.

Jesus or Jeebus?

Voltaire once noted that God created us in his image . . . and that we returned the favor. Following this logic, we say, "Show us your Jesus, and we'll show you who you are." This challenge poses quite a shocking reality check for all of us, for the sad fact is we have made Jesus look a lot more like us than we would care to admit. We have cut Jesus down to size, made and repackaged him into an image of ourselves on a good day and at our best. Now to be fair, it is hard for any of us not to do this to some degree. We all do and will struggle to discover just who Jesus really is. This struggle is, and should be, intrinsic to our discipleship. The fact is, we *need* Jesus to be like us, for if he isn't, we doubt whether he can possibly understand who we are and what our human experience is like. An example of this is a crucifix we purchased in Africa which hangs on one of our walls. It portrays Jesus as a black man. All of us have a deep need to know that Jesus identifies fully with us. But to be honest, we can easily overbalance this identification and end up with an image of Jesus that is a far cry from who he really is.

38

Whenever we visit a European city, we usually do three things. Like most Christians, we visit some churches. We also visit, because of our respective backgrounds, the Jewish and the gay areas which, strangely enough, coexist in the same areas of most cities. One of the interesting things we have noted is the contrast between the churches and synagogues. They are strikingly different. The synagogues are usually sparse and unadorned, with absolutely no icons or images; the churches, on the other hand, are usually overly adorned, with icons and images on every wall and altar. It seems to us, historically at least, that Christians have a propensity to create icons and images of God, even though the very creation of an image of God (mental or metal) limits him and can easily become an attempt to control him.[7] The Jewish people seem to have learned the lesson of the second commandment better than us (Exod. 20:4).

On a recent trip to Vienna, we followed our normal pattern, visiting churches et cetera, when we happened across a very big painting of Jesus hanging in the oldest church in Vienna. What struck us about this particular portrait was that Jesus looked strikingly like the average Austrian male, albeit a somewhat more emaciated one (we can't have Jesus too chubby can we?). The artist made a deliberate and successful attempt to connect his depiction of Jesus with the nationality of the people. Like we said, that is kind of a good thing—he *does* lovingly identify with Austrians—but image-making comes at a cost. We left the church wondering, *What if this Jesus on the cross looked more like the all-too-Jewish carpenter he really was?* Would the Austrians in World War II have so eagerly participated in the slaughter of Jewish people in the Holocaust if their Jesus looked more explicitly historical, and therefore Jewish? And if, in this case, he has simply become a purely Aryan Jesus, was this the real Jesus at all or simply an idealization of Austrian religious values—a quasi-religious, nationalist idol?

These are probing questions that should highlight for us the inherent risk in making any image of God and, by extension, Jesus. It seems we often end up with some sort of "Jeebus" who simply affirms our many cultural blind spots and engenders dangerous bigotry. Jesus is reinterpreted in the light of my image and thus becomes a symbolic representation of me/us when we are at our best. We are projecting our self-concern onto God, and it ends in co-opting God to serve our agendas. He becomes a national god, a projection of our collective or individual hopes, a focal point of our narrow concerns, or simply a projection of "me" on a good day. Not a good look! And certainly not worth worshiping.

In *ReJesus*, Alan and Michael Frost spend a lot of time dealing with this very issue: our need and propensity to create Jesus in our own image. The early chapters of that book are dedicated to freeing Jesus from the stained-glass prisons and domesticated images we have locked him in. A few are pertinent:

- Spooky Jesus: the bloodless alien with an aura and his pumping heart in his hand, which, it should be noted, violates the very meaning of the incarnation—all humanity is bleached out
- Bearded-lady Jesus: portrays Jesus in an overly sentimental and feminine way, kinda like he's just been done over by the *Queer Eye for the Straight Guy* gang just before he gets on the cross
- Little baby Jesus: made famous in the movie *Talladega Nights*, drawn from the harmless stereotype rolled out at Christmastime to make us feel all schmaltzy about our families
- Jesus is my boyfriend: the over-romanticized understanding of Jesus typified in much of the contemporary, touch-me-Lord-type songs we sing
- Jesus the celebrity rock star: typified in Andrew Lloyd Webber's musical *Jesus Christ Superstar*, in which Jesus

doesn't quite know what he's doing, but he loves to sing about it

There are many ways we have re-created Jesus in our own image, and the above parodies are but a few. Even the artistry of icons focuses on an aspect of Jesus and thus limits who he is. Did he really have a blazing aura around his head and assume the hand gestures of a kung fu master? Just a little probing will identify that we all have the capacity to create our own version of Jeebus.

In much of our image-making, we have sought to domesticate Jesus and make him a much more manageable lowercase-"l" lord that comfortably legitimates our lifestyle. Let's be honest: for many Christians, Jesus has come to look and behave like a nice, regular, high-conformity, somewhat-morally upright/uptight churchgoer. Is this really the wild Messiah we encounter in the Gospels? Is this the One we love, follow, and seek to be like? Really? Surely not! It is us who must become like him, not he like us.

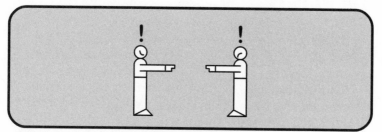

"Wow, Jesus! You look and sound just like me!"

It is important for each and every one of us to be able to access Jesus, and feel that he can identify with us and us with him. But we have to tread carefully indeed so we do not end up with an idolatrous predicament—a "Jeebus" of our own making—very far from the God in Jesus as revealed in the Scriptures. The world would reap the consequences of our false witness.

Limp-wristed versus ultimate-fighting Jesus

As we can see, getting to grips with Jesus is not an easy task. As soon as we try to "image" him, we limit him. In fact, many attempts to make an image of God are actually a way of trying to control him—it's that annoying second commandment again! And we believe this commandment always applies to God, the three persons of the Trinity—it is not just limited to the God of the Old Testament. How is it that we so easily disregard it? If we can learn anything from the story of Israel, we discover that any attempt to limit or stereotype him will fail because image-making always fails (see footnote for an explanation of what we think about art and image).[8]

A recent example of reimaging Jesus was supplied by Seattle pastor Mark Driscoll. He has become somewhat infamous for his portrayal of Jesus as some sort of ultimate fighter. But in attempting to "butch up" Jesus and make him appeal to "real men," has Driscoll come close to creating Jesus in his own image? Consider this from one of his sermons:

> Latte-sipping Cabriolet drivers do not represent biblical masculinity, because real men—like Jesus, Paul, and John the Baptist—are dudes: heterosexual, win-a-fight, punch-you-in-the-nose dudes. In other words, because Jesus is not a limp-wristed, dress-wearing hippie, the men created in his image are not sissified church boys; they are aggressive, assertive, and nonverbal.[9]

Now we don't believe Mark's original intention was bad. What he was trying to do is rescue Jesus from the overly feminized ways in which Jesus has been portrayed. We would agree and also want to rescue the image of Jesus from this. In fact, in *ReJesus*, Alan and Michael talk about this exact issue, the over-feminization of Jesus.[10] But the problem with Driscoll's ultimate-fighting Jesus is that Jesus has been freed from one distortion only to be captured by another.

It cannot but be a distortion. Is Jesus really some "punch-you-in-the-nose-type dude"? And is that really the model and type of Christlike masculinity to which every man should aspire? We think not. Is this parody of masculinity not actually the source of so much gratuitous violence in the world? Besides, if Driscoll is right, then the incarnate God-Man's capacity to identify with the human race, most of whom are *not* variations of Arnold Schwarzenegger, nor want to be, is severely limited (and quite honestly—no offense, Arnie—that would be repulsive). *Christianity Today* commentator Brandon O'Brien rightly says, "I don't gauge my masculinity by the girth of my neck, and I'd rather not sweat for a living. I'm happiest when I'm reading and writing. I like lattes."[11] And as for Jesus being "nonverbal," we find this statement difficult to reconcile with the fact that Jesus is called the "living Word." The Gospels are filled with conversations Jesus had with people in his path. Not to mention the fact that God has been communicating with us through the use of language since the beginning of creation.

Let's tease this out a bit to probe how stereotyping Jesus seriously damages the church's life, mission, and witness. As mentioned in the introduction, our community became a home for many homosexually oriented men and women. Many of the men were more "effeminate" in their mannerisms—what Driscoll mockingly calls "limp-wristed." Our question is, Where is the space for men who, through no fault of their own, are more effeminate than Driscoll's adaptation of Jesus? Dare we say there isn't any—they simply get the message that they are unacceptable to Jesus as they are. But this strikes a blow against the gospel itself! Does Jesus not love these people unconditionally and accept them into his family? Or does his love require that they should become macho and straight *before* they can become believers? All this highlights our point that Jesus must not be made into something he is not. How does a gay-oriented, effeminate man relate to a "punch-you-in-the-nose-type dude"?

A story of a close friend who became a vital part of our community comes to mind. Matt (not his real name) was a gay man actively involved in the gay community. He was, like many of his friends, going out to parties and clubs, living a pretty reckless life full of drugs, sex, and rock 'n' roll (or in his case, *disco!*). And, like his friends, he was searching for "the perfect man" who would fulfill all of his hopes and dreams. Fortunately for Matt, he did eventually find that perfect man, but it certainly was not the man he thought he would find. Matt found Jesus!

At the time, Matt was a waiter and worked with other gay men in an inner-city restaurant in Melbourne, Australia. He encountered Jesus at Eastertime. He recalls going back to work after the Easter break and being questioned by his gay friends about why he was not at the gay bars and out partying with them over the holiday. They assumed he had found a guy and were full of questions about the new man in his life. When asked to tell them about him, Matt replied, "Well he is Jewish, he is a carpenter, he's really spiritual," and so on, at which point the guys excitedly asked, "Well then, what's his name?" Matt said at this point he knew he was in trouble. When he replied "Jesus," their jaws dropped; they were stunned.

We tell this story because in Jesus, Matt, living as a gay man, had found the perfect "lover." He used to say, "Jesus will never use and abuse me nor will he ever leave me." Jesus became for him, as he is for all of us, *the perfect man*. Of course, it wasn't sexual; it was a relationship about receiving love and loving in return. Through his relationship with Jesus, Matt was able to experience true, unconditional love from a man in a way he had never experienced before.

If we want to insist on portraying Jesus as a kind of violent, gun-toting trucker, then we should consider not only the impact on the gay community, and on the many other men of a different ilk, but also on women. And how the church has historically treated women is nothing less than shameful!

To get the right view of Jesus is profoundly important both for mission and discipleship, particularly when ministering to those who don't fit our cultural stereotypes. Jesus must be freed in order to relate to all people; if he isn't freed, the incarnation fails to make sense. Jesus refuses to be put into any of our boxes. He doesn't—and never will—represent one individual over another, or the majority of the population over the minority. As the Archetypal Human, he represents us all. And we all need to be able to identify with Jesus. That's the whole point of the incarnation: he became a human in order to fully identify with each and every one of us.

What Kind of Holiness Is This?

We must now come to the question of how we understand Jesus missionally. And to do this, we simply have to recover the sheer power of his *humanity*. We must again be surprised by the amazing capacity of Jesus to break religious stereotypes and embody a kind of holiness that embraces the seriously weird and the wonderful along with those considered "mainstream" or "normal."

A question we pose is this: What is it about the holiness of Jesus that caused "sinners" to flock to him like a magnet and yet managed to seriously antagonize the religious people? This question begs yet another, even more confronting question: Why does our more churchy form of holiness seem to get it the other way around—to comfort the religious and antagonize the sinners? Jesus's brand of holiness (the true form) didn't seem to deter the sinners from wanting to get up close and personal with him. The Gospels are full of stories of sinners, the bungled, the broken, and the bent clamoring to be near Jesus. Jesus was different. He wasn't like the other holy rollers, the religious folk of his day. There was something magnetic about his person that caused even the most desperate to do the unthinkable and violate not only

45

social etiquette of the day, but risk further marginalization by being close to him. Think of the story of the woman with the issue of blood (Mark 5:25–30). She knew, as did everybody else, that her particular condition required a strict separation from the community and that "holy" ones should avoid all contact with people like her. And yet *this* holy man exuded something that caused her to reach out and touch him. She wasn't frightened or repelled by his form of holiness, for his holiness was inviting, alluring, enticing.

No doubt about it, Jesus's holiness was compelling. The Gospels clearly show us that social rejects loved to be around Jesus. Think of prostitutes, lepers, tax collectors, adulterers, Roman soldiers, Samaritans, Gentiles, and the list goes on. They couldn't get enough of him. By hanging out with people like these, Jesus shows us that one cannot achieve holiness by separation from the unclean. As previously mentioned, our community at South became something of a refuge for similar types of people—prostitutes, schizophrenics, and the like—and we know from personal experience that they *don't generally like Christians*. How can they love Jesus and so dislike his followers? Surely if we were Christlike they would like to be around us as well. That they don't should disturb us.

The even more amazing thing is that not only did the social outcasts and sinners want to be around Jesus, but Jesus wanted to be around them! This was the whole purpose of Jesus's mission, to save "sinners" (Luke 19:10), and he practiced active *proximity* with them (more of this in another chapter). Jesus the Holy One often went out of his way to connect with, or be seen with, those who the "holy ones" of the day would never have even thought of entertaining. The holiness of Jesus, it seems, is a redemptive, *missional*, world-embracing holiness that does not separate itself from the world, but rather liberates it.

And it wasn't that Jesus was simply "a nice inclusive guy." Everyone loves a nice guy, but nice guys don't end up murdered on crosses. Actually, as Ben Witherington notes, "It is no surprise, in view of his teachings and actions, that Jesus was crucified. What is surprising is that it did not happen sooner."[12] His radically embracing brand of holiness was thoroughly confrontational to all, especially the religious elite, the "separate ones." The term *prophetic* captures what we mean here because it called for a radical, redemptive holiness that went way beyond mere morality. But make no mistake, Jesus wasn't willing to just accept a sinful "status quo"; he was deeply concerned with both personal liberation and social transformation.

Untamed holiness

One of the greatest counterfeits for following the untamed Jesus comes from the substitution of morals and decency for Jesus's untamed kind of holiness. One of the standard attempts to stereotype, and therefore domesticate, Jesus is to make him into a moral teacher, someone who taught us how to live decent, rule-based lives. He was much more dangerous and subversive than that. He was more of a prophetic nonconformist than a tame ethics teacher. And whatever "ethics" might be gleaned from his teachings must be radically reinterpreted through his person, his wildness. We cannot separate the person from what he taught without seriously distorting what he was about. He calls people to throw everything away to follow him (Matt. 13:44), to a cross (Matt. 10:38; 16:24), to a love for God that will make all other loves seem like hatred (Matt. 10:35–37). This was no divine ethics lecturer speaking! His was a wild holiness that called to account all those who refused to deal with God—those who preferred instead to follow the lame dictates of a religion of ethical codes and pious rituals. Greg Boyd is correct in his assessment:

> The church as a whole does not look like the body of Christ, whose outrageous love attracted people who would otherwise have had nothing to do with a "religious establishment" or "ethical system." We don't generally have tax collectors, prostitutes, and other sinners (not *former* tax collectors and *former* sinners)

47

in our company (Mark 2:16). Rather, despite our own insistence that it is not so, we often look like a body of Pharisees whom sinners—people with *certain kinds* of sin we've identified as more serious than our own—avoid at all costs.[13]

Deb tells the story of when she was preaching on John 8, where Jesus encounters the woman caught in adultery. Her point was that Jesus has a certain way, or order, in which he communicated to this woman, the "sinner" of the story. In his remarkably inclusive and gentle way, he spoke words of acceptance *first*, not condemnation. It was only after his acceptance of her that he then exhorted her to go sin no more, understanding that it is God's acceptance of us that will ultimately lead us to repentance. For Jesus, acceptance *must* precede repentance. Grace must be introduced into the equation from the very beginning of the relationship and we, being his followers, should do likewise in our relationships with non-Christian "sinners." Deb then went on to explain that we Christians tend to reverse the equation: we will accept people only once they repent. At the end of the sermon, a woman came up to her and thanked her for the message, but indicated very quickly she was glad that Deb mentioned Jesus did say to the woman, "Go and sin no more." She had missed the whole point! In fact, she actually demonstrated what Deb was saying. We so easily focus on the sin-morality side without the grace-love side of the equation. Truly did Stanley Hauerwas say that our ethics derive from what we have seen of God.[14] To experience the radical grace of God in Jesus *is* to change—to miss grace is to miss the whole point! Love, and not detached morality, is the fulfillment of the law (Rom. 13:8).

We believe many Christians likewise tend to regard sin simply as acting immorally or unethically, and see an ethical life as the highest goal for a human being. But this is not the biblical view of discipleship because it substitutes duty to ethics in place of our primary duty to God. It is about relationship, not rules and regulations. It is far more convenient (and safe) to deal with rules than with God. Morality unconnected to the source of morality yields the cold, sad, judgmental self-righteousness of moralism.

Rules = conformity

Following rules generally requires high levels of conformity, be it to the state, the community, or even the church. But conformity to these necessary social institutions does not necessarily equate to faithfulness to God. One can live a morally upright life while leaving God entirely out of the equation. This is a dangerous and idolatrous shift because, once we are at this point, any idea that there really is a duty to God simply evaporates, and all we are left with is the oppressive idols of rules and law-keeping.[15] The Pharisees of the New Testament are a case in point: they were rule keepers who, for the most part, were far from having a personal relationship with God. Paul also constantly warns us about self-righteousness and teaches us to see ourselves as ones who receive our righteousness as a gift from God. He tells us to live in conformity to God, not to rules. We should be clear about the New Testament teaching on this: any attempt to live a self-righteous life based on morality ("the law" in Paul) always ends in religious despair because it can't save us. Conforming to Jesus in discipleship *will* make us godly and upright people, but let's keep first things first.

In fact, if we are going to be genuinely Christlike, we will not be conformists! For one, our Lord can hardly be called a conformist. He disturbed the status quo, railed against injustice and lack of mercy, hung out with highly questionable people, and fomented a revolution that called for the overthrow of religious oppression. He put Rome on notice that its time was coming. How can we who model ourselves after Jesus be any different?

Peter Vardy, a British philosopher who has studied the writings of that wild disciple Søren Kierkegaard, says,

All too often the domains of society and conformity, the social expectations that come from raising children, setting up home and the like, become a substitute for individuality in the God relationship. This [Kierkegaard] sees as a travesty of the Christian demand. He blames this on priests and the general wish for mediocrity. There is a demand by "the crowd," the mass of people, to live an ordinary, unexamined and passionless life in which God is essentially irrelevant, and yet they want this life to be regarded as Christian.[16]

As uncomfortable as this makes us feel, we should listen to what is being said. Groupthink is not necessarily a Christian virtue, and we should not mistake a crowd for a community of Christ followers! People can easily hide from God in a crowd; crowds are great for dodging God. In truth there is real potential for evil in masses of people—witness a mob, for instance. If we are not careful, churches can easily develop a herd mentality, a crowd instinct that will tend to penalize dissenting voices and actions. The church, however, is destined for an individual and corporate responsibility to God that will almost inevitably put us at prophetic odds with society around us.

The Christian Thought Police

Dirty Jesus?

Darryl Gardiner (our good friend from New Zealand) doesn't mince words. While he is a brilliant communicator and missional activist, he is not exactly known for being polite or well mannered! One year, at our Forge "Dangerous Stories" summit, he spoke about connecting with the "Dirty Jesus." In his usual hard-hitting style, Darryl worked his way through some of the Gospels, "dirtying" Jesus up as he went. He unapologetically claimed that the more tame and sanitized our Jesus is, the less he resembles the Jesus of the Gospels, and this in turn has a big impact on the way Christians live out their faith. A sanitized Jesus is a misrepresentation of him and leads us to live sterile lives. Both of us confess to having been mildly uncomfortable at times with his message, and the audience even more so. But the more we thought about his words, the more we realized that what he was saying was actually exactly right. The fact is, there was not much about the birth, life, and death of Jesus that was particularly "clean" or "nice." We have such a sanitized view of Jesus that we confuse him with a polite, clean, super-spiritual, otherworldly sort of guy. But he is much more gritty and hard to handle. He is the Lord, after all. Jesus had an in-your-face kind of holiness, and he reserves his harshest judgments not for the standard old sinners, but for the religious people of his day. And he had some extremely hard words to say about them—he called them things like unkosher dogs, snakes, whitewashed tombs, hypocrites, unfaithful stewards, greedy, cheats, just to name a few! (See Matt. 22:24–39.) And in his sermon, as well as in his life, Darryl is actually a very Christlike person— somewhat offensive and very provocative—and it is us who have generally misunderstood the nature of what it means to be Christlike.

Summing Up . . .

We have only grazed the surface of what happens when we supplant a form of "Jeebus" for the real, gutsy, untamed, intoxicating Jesus of the Gospels. In our desperate attempts to control him, we limit him and therefore box him into our own self-serving images. We are prone time and time again to a morality that is more about observing rules and regulations than trusting in a living relationship of holiness that thrusts us into the world, rather than separates us from it.

Recovering the centrality of Jesus in discipleship is not only essential to a resurgence of authentic Christianity and the mission of the church; it is essential to the healing of historical Christianity, period! Jesus not only shapes and defines on our idea of God, but also shows us what kind of people we ought to be in the world. We are to be, and increasingly become, like him. Recovering a love for and focus on Jesus leads to a recovery of the grand themes of the church of Jesus Christ: salvation, justice, mercy, faithfulness, redemptive holiness, righteous anger at brokenness and evil, and that marvelous central fact that God is indeed *love*. Whatever else we might know about God, these must never be marginalized, or else we end up with a very dangerous religion. To this we turn in the next chapter.

Suggested Practices

- *Focusing faith on, in, and through Jesus*: Jesus said, "I am the way and the truth and the life. No one comes to the Father except through me" (John 14:6), and he is called the Mediator and High Priest (1 Tim. 2:5; Heb. 4:14–16; 9:15; 12:24). This means that whatever, and whenever, we think of God, it must be somehow qualified by the person of Jesus. Any approach to God must recognize the unique role of the second person of the Trinity. Make a discipline of focusing your faith through the prism of Jesus. For instance, when you pray to the Father, focus your prayer *through* Jesus.
- *Cycling through the Gospels*: One of the most basic things that needs to be done is for Christians to commit to constantly reading, and rereading, the Gospels. The

Gospel accounts of Jesus fill out our understanding of him. In the Bible, revelation is given through actual history. And so we must be committed to understanding Jesus *as he was* . . . God with skin on, a person who inhabited a time, culture, and geography. If we fail to take the historical Jesus seriously, we will tend to make him into who we want him to be.

- *Relate to him through the various characters in the Gospels*: This is related to the practice above. Every time you reread the Gospels, try seeing them with fresh eyes, as if you have never heard any of it before. This is especially important for people who have been Christians for a long time. By being overfamiliar with the Gospels, we think we know what they (and therefore Jesus) are about, whereas they should always surprise us. For instance, try to see Jesus through the eyes of the religious people of his day—the Pharisees.

- *Practice St. Ignatius's* Examen: This is a very old and useful way of including Jesus into your everyday world.[17] Essentially, it involves keeping a journal where you ask yourself several questions every day (or every week). They include such questions as (1) where did I work with Jesus today, and (2) where did I resist Jesus today? Be specific and prayerful about the conclusions.

- *Desanitize Jesus*: Churches tend to want to domesticate and sanitize Jesus. In part, sanitizing Jesus will mean humanizing him. But also it means debunking the overly "churchy" images of "Sunday school Jesus" and putting him back in the context of real life. Allow him to offend you again!

Discussion Starters

1. Discuss the concept that it is not so much that Jesus is like God, but that God is like Jesus.

2. To what degree have you (and your community) domesticated Jesus by re-creating him in your own (or
collective) image? How is Jesus unlike you and your
community?
3. What would happen if the radical Jesus turned up at
your church?
4. What would happen to your faith and life if Jesus and
his influence were entirely removed?
5. If you were around in Jesus's day, how would you personally have reacted to him? What aspects of Jesus's
life and teachings and type of holiness offend your
sensibilities?
6. Research and try practicing creative problem-solving
or strategic thinking approaches when reading biblical texts (for example, try the "six thinking hats" of
Edward de Bono, or simulation games).[18]

2

your god is too sick

If your conception of God is radically false, then the more devout you are, the worse it will be for you. You are opening your soul to be molded by something else. You had much better be an atheist.

—William Temple

If a man does not love the Lord with all his mind, he does not thereby become pure reason with no loves; he simply loves something else with all his heart, soul, strength and mind. One's loves are always deeper than his reason; and reason is always in the employment of some love.

—Paul Ramsay

The most important aspect of faith is our mental picture of God.

—Greg Boyd

Recently we couldn't make it to our community worship, so we decided to go to TV church instead. Quite honestly, we wish we hadn't. We ended up thoroughly disturbed by the sheer garbage the TV preacher was dishing out. But there we were, transfixed and horrified at the distortions being foisted upon the doting audience. We became part of a massive, translocal audience of viewers who, for whatever reason, were not part of a local church, subjecting ourselves to dangerous religious twaddle. A weekly diet of this could seriously damage a person's spiritual and social health.

One thing that has always perplexed us is how so many of us can be so taken in by people who parrot back to us simply what we want to hear, and then somehow still manage to call it Christianity. Paul calls this having "itching ears" (2 Tim. 4:3), and if it didn't have such tragic consequences, it would be really funny. We do actually know people who watch this stuff for its sheer comedic value! But trawling through the "God channels" ought to be an experience that unnerves any disciple of Jesus. How can so many sincere folk be so fooled by people who appear, to us at least, to be obvious charlatans? There can be no question of the sincerity and zeal with which both the deceived and the deceivers adhere to their beliefs. But the bond between them seems to lie in their common desire for the same thing. Cults, of course, are built on the same phenomenon. And it is not at all new, for deception reaches as far back as Eden.

We should never be fooled by mere sincerity: it has never been a particularly good test for truth—as is clearly seen in the case of our TV "evangelists." False prophecy has always plagued spirituality because, as Martin Buber rightly notes, in most cases

> false prophets are not godless. Rather, they adore the god "success." They themselves are in constant need of success and achieve it by promising it to the people. But they do honestly want success for the people. The craving for success governs their hearts and determines what rises from them. That is what Jeremiah called the "deceit of their own hearts." They do not deceive; they *are* deceived, and can only breathe in the air of deceit.[1]

We begin this chapter with this rather disconcerting reflection on the nature of false prophecy and deception because it provides us with the right platform to be able to explore how apparently earnest religious people can get it so wrong. This in turn allows us to raise questions of how we can keep ourselves in the way of Jesus and not fall prey to similarly deceptive impulses in our own hearts and those of other apparently sincere people. To do this we have to explore issues relating to the right knowledge of God.

A book on missional discipleship must first get the basics right in relation to God. If we get the fundamental notions of God wrong, it will negatively impact our personal discipleship and damage the very people we are trying to reach, as we saw in the previous chapter with Homer and "Jeebus." The truth is that all of us entertain false notions of God to some degree. None of us gets all of it right—even the most insightful. But if we get it fundamentally wrong and then get passionate about the untruth we have come to believe, then all hell breaks loose—*literally!* History amply bears out the truth that we Christians are dangerous people when we are wrong. And this highlights for us the reason why it is critical to constantly readjust and examine ourselves in relation to Truth . . . to God himself.

Idolatry: The Rebel's Religion

If God is not the defining center of our faith, life, and identity, then who or what is? This is a question that should disturb each and every one of us. This is particularly true considering the fact that we are compulsive idolaters and rebels who, rather than take our cues from a God who demands our all, seek to fit reality into something far more convenient and self-referential. In the Bible, to refuse God's definition of reality and subsequently construct our own is called idolatry—and it is the religion of the rebel who renounces the kingdom for the more cozy alternatives. C. S. Lewis says it in his characteristically brilliant way:

> What Satan put into the heads of our remote ancestors was the idea that they could "be like gods," that they could set up on their own as if they had created themselves—be their own masters—invent some sort of happiness for themselves outside God, apart from God. And out of that hopeless attempt has come nearly all that we call human history—money, poverty, ambition, war, prostitution, classes, empires, slavery—the long terrible story of men trying to find something other than God which will make him happy.[2]

This is *exactly* why the Bible is so consistent in its condemnation of idolatry and the creation of images of God—be they physical or conceptual. William Temple notes that "it is as much idolatry to worship a false mental image as by means of a false metal image. The mental image misrepresents God and has the same disastrous effects on character." And he concludes with this pithy comment, "If your conception of God is radically false, then the more devout you are, the worse it will be for you. You are opening your soul to be molded by something else. You had much better be an atheist."[3]

We easily lose focus on what is essential. We miss the fact that discipleship has to do with becoming like Jesus, living the Shema, and not forgetting that the "more important matters

And on the eighth day man re-created God . . .

. . . In his own image he made him.

of the law," namely love, mercy, forgiveness, justice (Matt. 23:23–24), are nonnegotiables in the equation.

As hard-line religious fundamentalists (the contemporary Pharisees?) amply illustrate, simply replacing these central aspects of discipleship with a whole lot of religious zeal does not make up for getting the basics wrong. In fact, zeal without proper understanding of God can actually result in sincerely opposing what God represents, and all in the name of God. Consider what Paul has to say about the Pharisees of his day:

> Brothers, my heart's desire and prayer to God for the Israelites is that they may be saved. For I can testify about them that they are zealous for God, *but their zeal is not based on knowledge.* Since they did not know the righteousness that comes from God and sought to establish their own, they did not submit to God's righteousness. (Rom. 10:1–3, italics ours)

The truth is that religious zeal is not necessarily a sign of trust in and commitment to God; in fact it may betray a deep doubt and an insecurity that depends on self rather than on God, and on the belief that whatever is lacking in God's grace must be compensated for by one's own virtue.

Religion can either make us good or very, very bad. As C. S. Lewis explains, religion

> opens us to new possibilities of both good and evil. From that point on the road branches: one way leads to sanctity,

humility, the other to spiritual pride, self-righteousness, and persecuting zeal. There is simply no way back to the mere humdrum virtues of the unawakened soul. If the Divine does not make us better, it will make us very much worse. *Of all the bad men, religious bad men are the worst.*[4] (italics ours)

This quote reminds us of a dangerous man we encountered in our early years of ministry. On the surface this man was attractive and charismatic, with an apparent love and respect for Jesus: he fed the poor and led Bible studies and did the things normally associated with godliness. However, over time a number of things began to alert us that something wasn't right about him. He began to consistently and subtly undermine the leadership team, particularly Al, who was the team leader at that time. Over the months he became more overt and started directly challenging the leadership. He sent letters to everyone in the church with false accusations against us. He was basically trying to take over leadership and split the community. We then discovered he was sleeping with several of the women in our church, including married women. He was also drawing people into his life and seriously messing with their heads. This was in many ways more serious than the illicit sex. He was creating a little cult. When confronted with these issues, his true colors really surfaced.

After many months of trying to negotiate with him, we were unable to reach any resolution. Eventually we had to ask him to leave, and even once had to have him physically removed from the church building by our local law enforcement. He responded to this by sitting outside our church every Sunday for six months with placards and accosting everyone who came along. He also tried to get the media involved. It really was an awful time for us. In the end we discovered, through some of his family members, that his dad was a cult leader in South America and had a history of splitting churches. This guy was following in his footsteps. Of course we were thrilled that he thought to try it on us!

It is interesting that around that time, Deb was reading M. Scott Peck's book *People of the Lie*, which powerfully describes the anatomy of evil. Peck suggests that it is a form of pathological narcissism that imbibes people and uses things, including theology, to draw people into its orbit. Peck says that real evil is deceptive because it looks more upright and attractive than what we might initially expect. This was certainly the case with our accuser; on the surface all was well polished, but underneath there were not only deep psychological scars but profound theological errors in his understanding of God. We were dealing with one sick puppy.

The reality is that what we believe about God *does* have consequences. History is full of people who have wreaked enormous damage and even killed for what they believe in. Historian George Weigel rightly notes,

> How men and women think about God—or don't think about God—has a great deal to do with how they envision a just society and how they determine the appropriate means by which to build that society. This means taking theology seriously—which includes taking seriously other's concepts of God's nature and purposes, and the commitments to the beliefs arising from these concepts.[5]

He explains how theology is worked out within the context of the radical Islamist threat. At its core, the jihadist idea of God is a sick one. "The power of jihadism, and the distinctive character of the threat it poses, derives from its theological roots." And the key theological idea that underwrites today's jihadist ideology and practice is the identification of God as Absolute Will.[6] When God is viewed in this way, there can be no pathos, no possibility of sacrificial *love* (agape) in the relation of God toward his creation. This deeply distorted understanding of the God of Abraham leads jihadists into grave error: for instance, mercy comes to be understood as weakness, and the concept of justice is reduced to sheer revenge—a process vividly on display when terrorists, for example, set bombs off among innocent people. "These social malignancies can be traced back to one source, namely that of a defective understanding of God."[7]

But before we are tempted to simply point out defects in Islam, let us remind ourselves that it was so-called European Christendom that produced the Crusades, the Inquisition, numerous genocides, and systematic anti-Semitism. It also kept slavery very much alive until a few brave followers of Jesus decided it was time to take it out over eighteen hundred years after Jesus arrived on the scene! How was this possible? We suggest that all these are generated by a sick and distorted view of God—certainly not the same God we find in the sacrificial life, teachings, and death of Jesus. It is utterly inconceivable to us how people can supposedly love Jesus and yet burn tens of thousands of people for not agreeing with some theological ideas or conforming to some bizarre ecclesial practice (as in the Inquisition)!

One Love—Shema Spirituality

In light of all this, how can we ensure we have a true understanding of God? Or even better, how can we *know* God? We believe Jesus is the answer and points us in the right direction when he says,

> "Hear, O Israel, the Lord our God, the Lord is one. Love the Lord your God with all your heart and with all your soul and with all your mind and with all your strength" [and] "Love your neighbor as yourself." There is no commandment greater than these. (Mark 12:29–31)

The power of Shema spirituality, or what Scot McKnight creatively calls "the Jesus Creed," sums up the central revelation of God in Scripture and provides us with a *worldview in a sentence.* In other words, it is not just a simple description of what true worship means (and it is that), but also a description of a disciple's basic orientation to the world.

- The Shema contains the revelation that God is one.
- The Shema shows us that God wants to be loved and worshiped in every aspect of life and with all of our being. The clear implication is that nothing in life, culture, and the human experience lies outside of this all-encompassing claim. No false dualisms, no sacred-secular splits—all of our lives, including our sexuality, work, play, home, politics, and economics, can, and indeed must, become aspects of our worship to the One True God.
- The Shema is expanded by Jesus to explicitly include the love of people, for it has always been a temptation of "religious" people to see religion as purely devotion toward God. Jesus will not allow this. Discipleship in the way of Jesus must include the love of people.

The Ten Commandments show us this truth. The first three of the ten have to do with one God and the prohibition of idolatry. The fourth has to do with the sanctification of *time*, thereby safeguarding the God-relationship. The rest of the commandments move straight into what it means to live together without killing each other—straight into ethics, or *lifestyle!* No grand philosophies, no eloquent speeches . . . just holy living in the whole of life-under-God.

In contrast, the Western spiritual tradition has tended to limit discipleship to issues relating to our personal morality, thereby neglecting our missional involvement in the world. But discipleship must include both and everything in between. We would argue that if we truly understood Shema spirituality, we wouldn't even have to talk about mission because it is all contained in the primal confession—loving God and loving others as ourselves! To worship God involves loving God in all and every arena of life. Mission is implicit throughout the creed. And discipleship in the way of Jesus is all about living out the Shema. It is missional to the core! Hence, no mission, no discipleship.

The Shema as Jesus restates it provides the disciple with the best approach to a true biblical understanding of God. As we have noted in the introduction, the Shema is *the* central, most important confession in the Bible. When Christians confess that "Jesus is Lord," understood in the light of the Shema, we have together a distillation of monotheism, an ethos, and a worldview in a sentence.[8]

The School of Love

So what does it mean to love God? If we were to design a school or training program for loving God, what would it look like? We think such a school would have three areas of focus: right feeling, right acting, and right thinking. These three can be said to converge in a sweet spot called discipleship. Let's unpack this a bit.[9]

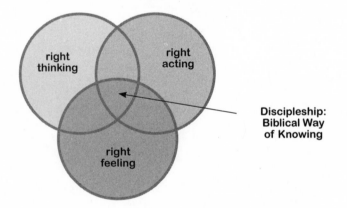

Feelin' alright . . .

In the biblical worldview, in order to truly *know* something (*yada* in Hebrew), one cannot merely observe it but must come into contact with it. There must be mutuality and personal involvement. That's why this word is used for knowledge of God and also for the act of sex. Leanne Payne makes the insightful point that "we come to know ultimate reality, not by theological ideas about it, even though these are valid and necessary, but by union with it—by the establishing of a personal relationship between God and man."[10] To know God this way requires a passionate concern and the application of one's whole personality existentially. Therefore Søren Kierkegaard can rightly say that if passion, intense personal involvement with the truth of something, is eliminated, then faith can no longer exist.[11]

But to know God in this way, our hearts must be engaged. We can't remain passive spectators of God but rather must be active participants with him. The Bible's understanding of "the heart" is far bigger than how we usually understand it. It is not only the source of our emotions, as we tend to think, but also of our will, loyalty, and commitment. Without the heart, therefore, we cannot ever hope to understand God, because the heart (passion and will) is the source of our capacity to love.[12] To know God means to love him with "all our hearts," and loving God conveys a type of knowledge that cannot be gained by any other means. "Only to our intellect is God incomprehensible: but not to our love." So says the author of the great Christian classic *The Cloud of Unknowing*.[13]

Jonathan Edwards maintained that if the heart is left unmoved by God, no spiritually significant action can, or will, take place.

> I am bold in saying this, but I believe that no one is ever changed, either by doctrine, by hearing the word, or by the preaching or teaching of another, unless the religious affections are moved by these things. . . . In a word, there is never any great achievement by the things of religion without a heart deeply affected by those things. . . . True religion is placed in the affections.[14]

Clearly, the heart is faith's truest home.

Putting our bodies on the line

The follower of Jesus broadens his or her knowledge of God through living truth, not just believing in it. True knowledge of God must be expressed in practice or action—that's why the Bible is one-third ethics. Obedience—body and soul—is part of the condition of God's covenant (for example, Exod. 24:7; Jer. 11:3) as well as the momentous parting words of commission under which we live (Matt. 28:18–20). As C. S. Lewis says, "Obedience is the 'holy courtesy' required for entering into the divine relationship."[15]

In the Bible, the real test of what you know is how you live your faith. Something goes seriously wrong with our capacity to integrate or even comprehend Scripture if we just study but do not obey it. "As you have lived, so have you believed," said Kierkegaard.[16] It is not a person's words, but an individual's life, that is the best picture of faith.

Think of Christians whom you admire, and you can be sure they are not simply devout people who got their theology or devotional lives right, but rather people who actually *did* something significant in their worlds. We think of St. Patrick, Martin Luther, John Wesley, William Booth, Corrie ten Boom, Dietrich Bonhoeffer, Mother Teresa, Jackie Pullinger, as well as countless other known and anonymous saints who have made a difference in their own unique ways.

Thinking thoughts after God

With our hearts open to God, and a commitment to obey, it's time to seriously engage God with our minds. Intellectual laziness is simply not an option for disciples. This doesn't mean that God expects all of us to be intellectual giants, but he does require that we love him with our minds. As the poet Percy Bysshe Shelley rightly said, "The mind becomes that which it contemplates." This has both negative and positive consequences, for if we think about nothing, our minds become nothing. But if we think thoughts after God, we become more like him. Besides, for many it can be a pathetic and dangerous cop-out to just "feel" God in worship and prayer—this is necessary but not sufficient for a fully fledged Shema spirituality. The same is true for simple obedience alone, because apart from the other aspects of Shema, it can easily terminate in the dead end of dry activism or legalism.

A Mature Community

To be mature disciples, we need to engage with knowing and loving God on all three levels: our minds, our hearts, and our actions. And because we are all wired differently, we will tend to prefer one over the other, which is why real *knowledge* of God is reached in the context of the community of faith where people can learn from one another. The activists learn from the theologians, who learn from the pastors, and so on. This way we can complement each other's strengths and compensate for the more underdeveloped areas. The local and broader church community also provides for us a form of accountability, where we can measure our "knowledge of God" against historical witness as well as that of other brothers and sisters. We do not arrive at truth alone.

Another One Bites the Dust

Leading a community of faith for over fifteen years has not only been a great privilege and an incredibly enriching experience, but at times it has been a source of great anxiety and heartbreak. One of the sources of heartbreak is to look back and see how many have left the way of discipleship. It's like *The Pilgrim's Progress* gone wrong—where way too many are not pilgrims and so they do not progress. Sadly, our experience has seemed to correlate more with the parable of the sower (Matt. 13:1–23), where only one in four remains faithful and becomes fruitful in the end! Many of these friends have redefined Christian discipleship to suit their respective lifestyles, or have reframed God in some way, or have simply ditched the faith altogether—and in so doing have sold their feathers for worms, only to have lost the capacity to fly.

Much of this book is an exposition of the inner dynamics of the parable of the sower, or, to return to our parable of the skylark, of why so many sell their feathers. People leave the path for reasons such as spiritual shallowness, status anxiety, pursuit of wealth, fear of persecution, or because of many other, sometimes even demonic, anti-discipleship forces that are at work in our world.

Dealing with the complex, sexually charged (often in a very broken way) community at South that emerged largely from fringy, non-Christian backgrounds has forced us to come to grips with the actual motives of *why* people choose to leave the path of following Jesus. We think we are given a vital clue in Ezekiel 14, where Ezekiel narrates the situation of some of the elders of Israel coming to him to get a prophecy. At this point he is given an insight into the nature of their inquiring. God says to him:

> Son of man, these men have set up idols in their hearts and put wicked stumbling blocks before their faces. Should I let them inquire of me at all? Therefore speak to them and tell them, "This is what the Sovereign LORD says: When any Israelite sets up idols in his heart and puts a wicked stumbling block before his face and then goes to a prophet, *I the LORD will answer him myself in keeping with his great idolatry*." (14:3–4, italics ours)

In verse 7 he continues, "When any Israelite or any alien living in Israel separates himself from me and sets up idols in his heart and puts a wicked stumbling block before his face and then goes to a [false] prophet to inquire of me, I the Lord will answer him myself. . . . And if the [false] prophet is enticed to utter a prophecy, I the Lord have enticed that prophet" (vv. 7–9).

It appears that what is being said here is if someone is pre-committed to falsity and will not pursue God with pure heart and motives, they will hear only what they want to hear. (We do well to remember that it is only the pure in heart that will see God [Matt. 5:8].) The horrifying result of impure motives is that people sincerely believe it is God who has spoken, when all along it was their own lying hearts! Isaiah agrees when he utters this chilling warning:

> Let him who walks in the dark, who has no light, trust in the name of the Lord and rely on his God.
>   But now, all you who light fires and provide yourselves with flaming torches, go, walk in the light of your fires and of the torches you have set ablaze. But this is what you shall receive from my hand: You will lie down in torment. (Isa. 50:10–11)

When we deliberately turn our hearts from the love of truth and redefine it to suit ourselves, we will experience the anguish of our choices. God's truth can be for me a guiding light, something that gives me direction, only if it has been revealed to me in my encounter with God—not if I have somehow selected it for myself from among many existing options. The heresy in this act is nothing other than the clinging to a particular thought or idea simply because it is one's own. And the result is, as Charles Williams wrote, "the disintegration of the intellect, the justification to oneself of error and evil."[17]

In Romans, Paul draws directly on this prophetic understanding of idolatry in his sharp (and always current) exposé on the inner nature of unbelief. He reminds us that although all can discern God, they suppress this knowledge (and therefore their conscience) in order that they might engage in immorality (1:18). He ends up describing well the dark sides of twenty-first-century culture. The constant catchphrase throughout the rest of the passage is that because of this act of dodging truth, God "gives them over" (vv. 24, 26, 28) to spiritual dullness, existential futility, and moral darkness.

This "handing over" is what is meant in both Ezekiel's as well as Isaiah's prophecies above. The judgment we receive is this: as we ignore God, we are handed over to our sins, to ungodly rationalizations, and ultimately to self-deception.[18]

Witness the profound deception of the Nazis in Albert Speer's testimony (see sidebar).[19] It is because of the all-too-human propensity for rationalization and self-deception that we fail in discipleship. For disciples, God provides the light (the truth) by which we must walk. It requires real integrity (purity of heart) to stay true to God and self in this way. The Christian community is called to walk in this light. A biblical

> ### The Hall of Mirrors
>
> "In normal circumstances people who turn their backs on reality are soon set straight by the mockery and criticism of those around them, which makes them aware they have lost credibility. In the Third Reich there were no such correctives, especially for those who belonged to the upper stratum. On the contrary, every self-deception was multiplied as in a hall of distorting mirrors, becoming a repeatedly confirmed picture of a fantastical dream world which no longer bore any relationship to the grim outside world. In those mirrors I could see nothing but my own face reproduced many times over."
>
> —The testimony of Albert Speer, one of Hitler's henchmen

spirituality collapses when we refuse to walk in the light of the God revealed in Jesus, and thereby fail to have fellowship with one another (1 John 1:5–10). Any attempt to demarcate and restrict God's truth leads eventually into a darkness we will be deceived into thinking is actually light. Truth, and the disciple's commitment to truth *no matter what*, plays a vital role in keeping us walking in the way of Jesus (2 Thess. 2:9–10). And to do this we must constantly, as well as comprehensively, repent of our idolatry! (See Ezek. 14:6; 1 Thess. 1:9.)

Here are a few ways we idolatrously attempt to redefine God and confine discipleship.

Theology of the little head

We hope the reader will excuse the slightly risqué heading, but we believe this humorous little phrase captures the very point we want to make here. Again, this comes from tons of experience with sexually charged young adults of both the heterosexual and the homosexual variety.

We once heard Tony Campolo tell of a time when he was head of the department in a secular university. Being Tony Campolo, he was well-known as a follower of Jesus and became something of a mentor to many Christian students on the campus who would seek his advice on various issues they were facing. He tells a story of a young man he was mentoring who, after six months of being at the university, declared that he now had significant intellectual problems with his faith. As a result, he was undergoing a serious existential crisis. Tony wryly asked the question, "When did you start sleeping with your girlfriend?" The student, now somewhat taken aback, asked why this had anything to do with his deep existential crisis, but eventually confessed that he had started having sex with his girlfriend two months prior to this conversation. Tony, speaking from his vast experience as a mentor, apologist, and evangelist, noted that the main reason why people develop so-called "intellectual problems" with Christianity usually stems from a moral issue.

Psychology has a great name for this—it's called *cognitive dissonance*. It occurs when a person's beliefs, knowledge, and values clash with persuasive information that calls them into question. This inconsistency causes psychological discomfort, and the mind adjusts to reduce the discrepancy. In ethics,

71

cognitive dissonance is important because of its ability to alter values. For example, when an admired celebrity behaves in a way his or her admirers deplore, the dissonance (stress) the fans experience will often result in the fans changing their attitudes toward the behavior rather than the celebrity (thereby alleviating the stress). "Dissonance also leads to rationalizations of unethical conduct, as when the appeal and potential benefits of a large amount of money makes unethical actions to acquire it seem less objectionable than if they were applied to smaller amounts."[20]

Making your faith fit your lifestyle.

This squares completely with our pastoral experience. Almost every time someone comes to us saying that they suddenly have serious intellectual problems with God, the real issue is that they are having sex with someone—or want to and are working themselves up to it! They have begun thinking with the little head and not with their big head. And the penis, as it has often been noted, is not known for its conscience! Although this metaphor is distinctly masculine, the exact same sexual motive lies behind the sins of many women who claim the same issues.

The reality is that disciples sometimes have to obey God simply because of the joy of doing God's will—even, and perhaps especially, when this runs up against the dictates of our passions and desire. If we wish to preserve the life-giving connection with God, we must learn the discipline of obedience to God in a world that will reward us for waywardness.

Our love of God, and hence our discipleship, is at stake in our choices, so we need to beware. We "do not fail in obedience through lack of love, but have lost love because [we] have not attempted obedience."[21]

A dishonest buck

> Mansion $2,000,000
> Ferrari $400,000
> Pool $200,000
> Private Jet $5,000,000
> Golf Club Membership $5,000
> Armani Suit $20,000
> Wife's New Breasts $50,000
> A God who knows you deserve all these things? Priceless!

People can lose integrity and focus when it comes to money. One of the clearest religious examples of this is seen in the so-called prosperity doctrine. The great danger in this prosperity doctrine is that it is *almost true*.[22] This is what makes it an even more insidious error, because there is enough truth in it to allow us to legitimize it with some "shonky" theology. But remember that deceived people are actually sincere in believing it is true. However, they believe it because it is precisely what they *want* to believe and because it tells them what their idolatry (in this case, mammon) requires them to believe. Think back to the passage in Ezekiel. The idol in their heart is money, they inquire of God with this idol firmly entrenched, God allows them to be deceived (according to their idolatry), they say, "Thus says the Lord," and *voilà*, prosperity doctrine is born. But in order to rationalize their beliefs, the adherents of prosperity doctrine must dismiss much of the critique of wealth in the Bible—especially that of Jesus and Paul. Herein lies its error, and to some degree it is endemic throughout the church in the West, not just in Pentecostal-charismatic circles. We are all wealthy, and we all have to justify it—cognitive dis-

73

sonance again. But mammon is a harsh and powerful god, as we will explore later.

A not-so-flowery use of power

One of the most dangerous rationalizations in Christian history involves false ideas of power. Jesus clearly came as a servant, not as an overpowering dictator, and those who walk in his ways must do likewise—this is an absolutely explicit teaching in the New Testament (e.g., Luke 22:25–27; Phil. 2:1–11). This is much clearer even than the New Testament teaching on homosexuality. And yet we persist in the use of worldly, un-Christlike power. The fallen desire for power over others profoundly distorts our understanding of Christian faith, and with it the revelation of God received in the incarnation of Jesus.

This has equally terrifying consequences for God's people. We see it when an overpowering leader enslaves followers of Jesus. It's ironic that when this happens, it's not just the people themselves who are enslaved to the leader, but the leader becomes enslaved to the people. "The tyrant is himself a slave" (Plato). In a situation where power is being abused, the leader will grow only to the height to which the crowd raises him, but he or she ends up in the same state of servitude as the crowd—they are transformed by the very power they exercise.[23] This is the very stuff cults are made of, and religious people are susceptible to this abuse of power. Rather than freeing people by helping them relate to Jesus as Lord, control freaks, true to the tendency of the narcissistic personality, actually feed on the needs and adulation of those they lead. And so they become, in M. Scott Peck's words, "people of the lie."[24]

Ordinate: Inordinate

We have only mentioned "the big three" (money, sex, and power), but we recognize there is a myriad of smaller, much more subtle ways we can serve or justify our sins and our idolatry. All of this highlights for us the importance of Shema spirituality for the disciple. We are called to love God with mind, heart, soul, and strength. Only by living according to the Shema can the disciple maintain the love relationship with God. And only by living according to the Shema can we maintain what theologians call *ordinate* love—the idea that loving God first and putting everything else in priority below God enables us to love everything and everyone more than if we love the lesser thing or person exclusively.

The sage advice of C. S. Lewis is that we must actively train ourselves to love God *more* than the people and things in our world. Remarkably, when we are able to do this the other things in our lives will be enjoyed and loved all the more. However, if we love these at the expense of our love of God, we will eventually not love them at all. In fact, as we have seen in "the big three" above, loving anything before God turns it into a tyrannical idol that will consume us in the end. Lewis rightly says that it is probably impossible to love any person or thing too much. But we must, says Lewis, make sure we do not "love these too much in proportion to our love for God." As he goes on to note, it is always the smallness of our love for God, not the greatness of our love for his creation, that constitutes inordinacy.[25] All things find their place in relation to God and God's scale of values. Discipleship means loving God first and foremost, and loving everything else in the light of that love.

Here we experience again some profound wisdom buried in the heart of Shema spirituality—that loving God as our *primary* or "first" love (as Rev. 2:4 puts it) actually frees us to experience his world in a far more profound and fulfilling way. "When first things are put first, second things are not suppressed but increased."[26] And again, "Aim at Heaven and you will get earth 'thrown in,' aim at earth and you will get neither."[27]

Offering Our World Back to God

We can see how, in many ways, Shema spirituality goes back to the nature of worship. Not only does the Shema demand that we forgo all forms of idolatry (there is but one God and he demands our total allegiance), it is an all-inclusive claim that extends over all of our lives. To respond to this claim with all we have is what the Bible means by the term "worship." Worship cannot, and must not, be limited to simply singing songs to God, although it should include that. Worship is nothing less than *offering our whole world* back to God. As such, it must involve and include all the elements of life and spirituality, not just religious practices—as if politics, economics, sexuality, and such are somehow excluded from God's insistence of wholeness before him.[28]

What is discipleship if not offering our lives back to God? And what is mission if not offering our world back to God? In other words, worship, in the broadest and most fundamental understanding of the term, is an adequate category in which to locate an authentic missional spirituality. Such worship is by nature world-engaging and transformative. It can be represented as follows, where all the elements of life are gathered up, unified, and directed toward God in and through Jesus our Lord.

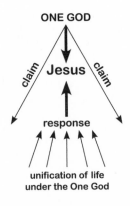

The dangerous act of worship

Worship is therefore a dangerous act, because to truly encounter the Holy in the act of worship *is to change*. God requires nothing less than our sanctification: "Be holy because I am holy"(1 Peter 1:16; cf. Lev. 11:44–45). If our encounter with God does not require something of us, we have to ask whether it was really God we encountered.

Rudolf Otto pins down the heart of the worship experience in a somewhat strange combination of Latin words— *mysterium tremendum*.

The *mysterium* component is comprised of two elements:

- God is experienced as the "wholly other"—the encounter is something truly amazing, totally outside our normal experience
- an element of fascination, which causes the subject of the experience of the encounter with the Holy to be caught up in it, enraptured, transformed—drawn into God through his grace

Tremendum, in turn, is comprised of three elements:

- awfulness (inspiring awe, a profound unease)
- a sense of being overpowered (that, among other things, inspires a feeling of humility)
- profound energy (creating an impression of immense vigor)

We see exactly this with all the experiences of the biblical saints (for example, Abraham, Moses, David, Isaiah, Jeremiah, Ezekiel, Paul, John, and Peter). All authentic God encounters should contain these two basic dimensions: holy awe (even terror) together with, and at the same time as, divine comfort and grace. While both elements must always be present to some degree, one will tend to predominate. If one of these elements is completely missing, then it's not the biblical God one is encountering. Brennan Manning profoundly captures this awe-grace dimension of the biblical God encounter when he writes (speaking for God),

> I will not leave you alone. You are mine. I know each of My sheep by name. You belong to Me. If you think I am finished with you, if you think that I am a small god that you can keep at a safe distance, I will pounce upon you like a roaring lion, tear you to pieces, rip you to shreds, and break every bone in your body. Then I will mend you, cradle you in my arms, and kiss you tenderly.[29]

It is a fearful thing to fall into the hands of the holy God (Hosea 6:1; Heb. 10:31; 12:29). And yet, he is our healing, our purest joy, our deepest longing, and our complete salvation.

We love the way Mark Labberton describes worship in his stimulating book *The Dangerous Act of Worship*: "Worship turns out to be the dangerous act of waking up to God and to the purposes of God in the world, and then living lives that actually show it."[30] It is this last, annoyingly *missional* component that we so often forget.

First and foremost, worship is a matter of allegiance: whom or what shall we deem worthy of glory, honor, and dominion? To whom shall we ascribe ultimate authority in our lives? Do we offer this to God or the gods? But worship must also lead us to become a particular kind of people, a people who reflect the ways of the God we worship. The important question Lee Camp poses is, "*Who* or *what* are we truly worshipping?"[31]

Labberton rightly notes that we have become too self-centered in our worship. Worship isn't just about singing songs to God, listening to sermons, partaking in the liturgy, or even simply praying. It must include loving our neighbor, seeking justice for the downtrodden, evangelism, and the renewal of true community. Waking up to God is "dangerous because worship is meant to produce lives fully attentive to reality as God sees it, and that's more than most of us want to deal with."[32] True worship exposes spiritual complacency in a world of suffering and injustice.

So JUST DO IT then!

Labberton's book reminds us that worship is not only about bringing together every aspect of our lives under the lordship of the one God, but also that true knowledge of God is where our heads, hearts, and bodies are put on the line for the sake of the cause of the kingdom. There can be nothing greater in all the world than to love the one true God with all of our heart, mind, soul, and strength, and to love our neighbors as we love ourselves.

If we are going to be missional disciples, we need to put our best efforts into knowing God, into the pursuit of the Holy. This is our first and foremost task. It is also our greatest joy, and to miss this is to miss the whole point of the discipleship.

In choosing God, we gain the world. In a rephrasing of monotheistic Shema spirituality, Jesus commands us to "seek first his kingdom and his righteousness, and all these things will be given to you as well" (Matt. 6:33). In choosing the kingdom of God, we become the heirs of all things. But we must choose with integrity to live under God. Lewis quotes William Law: "If you have not chosen the Kingdom of God, it will make in the end no difference what you have chosen instead." He then questions,

Will it *really* make no difference whether it was women or patriotism, cocaine or art, whisky or a seat in the Cabinet, money or science? Well, surely no difference that matters. We shall have missed the end for which we are formed and rejected the only thing that satisfies. Does it matter to a man dying in the desert by which choice of route he missed the only well?[33]

Suggested Practices

- *Regular iconoclasm*: Given that we live in a world that demands our attention, and also our loyalties, it is critical that we submit ourselves to a regular inventory of idolatry. This is best done in the context of a loving set of relationships that give us permission to ask the tough questions. Ask questions about how much time is dedicated to certain aspects of your life. What dominates your thinking? What demands your attention? Relate these to the Shema.

- *Worship beyond singing*: The heart of biblical worship is to offer your whole world back to God. Try to love God through the various aspects of your life rather than allowing them to become disassociated from your love of God; that is, see your work, play, and family as part of God's calling for your life.

- *A life of learning*: Read the writings of great and broad thinkers in the historical orthodox tradition: it is critical that we find both the depth of thinking and the broad sweep that great thinkers and saints can provide (for example, Augustine, Martin Luther, C. S. Lewis, G. K. Chesterton, Philip Yancey, etc.). Make space for reflection and thought about the big issues of life.

- *Act your way into a new way of thinking*: Our standard approach to learning in Western church circles is usually through the head. But this is not enough to ensure a right knowledge of God. Besides, it was not the way Jesus formed his disciples. He gave instructions and set tasks for the disciples, and then taught them once they had attempted them. Be brave and risk being led by God's Spirit into new things—things that will challenge you and draw you out of your comfort zones. This means there will be times when you don't know what you are doing. Then watch the learning take place.

Discussion Starters

1. Discuss the nature of false prophets, mentioned at the start of this chapter.
2. How can religion be toxic to us, our families, and the people in our social circles?
3. How does the love of truth keep us open to God? And how can the lack of it lead to problems in discipleship? (See 2 Thess. 2:10)
4. Describe instances where zeal without knowledge has damaged the world in God's name.
5. Discuss the nature of cognitive dissonance. As a group read the book *Mistakes Were Made, but Not by Me*, by Carol Tavris and Elliot Aronson.
6. Discuss our statement, "All authentic God encounters should contain these two basic dimensions: holy awe (even terror) together with, and at the same time as, divine comfort and grace."

3

the spirit's edge

God is not only the creator of earth and heaven. He is also the One who created delight and joy. . . . Even lowly merriment originates in holiness. The fire of evil can better be fought with flames of ecstasy than through fasting and mortification.

—Abraham Heschel

The work of the Spirit is to impart life, to implant hope, to give liberty, to testify of Christ, to guide us into all truth, to teach us all things, to comfort the believer, and to convict the world of sin.

—Dwight Lyman Moody

Spontaneity, total commitment, and primal responses that arise from the depths—these are the raw materials out of which a missionary church is made.

—John V. Taylor

About a week after introducing Alan to Jesus in the back of a Radio Shack store, his Christian boss thought it was time Al met with the Holy Spirit—as well as the pastor of his church. So he invited Alan and Jenny, his girlfriend at the time, over for dinner and a "chat." The clash of cultures couldn't have been more intense—Al and his girlfriend representing some shady, drug-infested planet, and the hosts from some equally wacky, but definitely "holier," world. The *very*-churched hosts happened to be boisterous, tongues-speaking, chandelier-swinging, snake-handling Pentecostals! It became quickly apparent to "unchurched Alan" that this was going to be an occasion not to be enjoyed, but rather endured. After dinner the men went upstairs to play pool and the women stayed in the lounge chatting. A while later, the men heard a commotion downstairs; the women had started praying for Jen, who experienced being "filled with the Spirit," and they were calling the men down to join in the fun.

Attention then turned to the other obvious sinner in the room: Al, who immediately had to suppress a very strong urge to run out of the house screaming. However, he managed to politely sit down and grit his teeth while they all converged to lay their hot, trembling hands on him. Their prayers were a weird mixture of cursing the devil and calling down the fire of the Spirit. All in all, pretty daunting! Then, against all expectation, *it* happened: God entered into Alan's life in such a powerful way that he still (twenty-nine years later) gets goose bumps thinking about it.

Whatever transpired there in that rather odd and incongruous setting in fact became the defining moment of his life. While still unable to fully explain what happened that night, what he does know is that he somehow encountered the Eternal One, the Creator of all things, whose nature he experienced as pure redemptive love; as a result, his life was never the same again.

The Trinitarian Framework of Discipleship

We open with this story, not because we think every Christian should have the same experience or that we should derive some definitive doctrine of the Spirit from it, but because it demonstrates some things we wish to highlight in a chapter on the Holy Spirit and being an untamed disciple—that there is a wildness, a radical immediacy, an uncontrolled element of surprise when dealing with God the Holy Spirit.

Discipleship (from spiritual awakening, to conversion, to maturity) is birthed in the Spirit, but it is also very much maintained in the Spirit. While there are other forms of learning, discipleship involves growth into the "deep things of God" (1 Cor. 2:10), and this simply cannot be achieved without the ongoing work of the Holy Spirit. As such, we partake of the divine dance that is intrinsic to the life of God, and we share in the divine life through the Spirit. In other words, Christian life must be lived for the glory of God, under the saving lordship of Jesus, and in the power of the Spirit. Biblical discipleship is trinitarian, or it is not really biblical.

In fact, without the Spirit there can be no Christianity in the Scriptural sense of the term, because there will be no real knowledge of God at all: one of the foundational works of the Spirit is to usher us into the true knowledge and experience of God. Said differently: if there was no Holy Spirit, there would be no possibility of encounter

> Many people have come to Christ as a result of my participation in presenting the gospel to them. It's all the work of the Holy Spirit.
>
> —Billy Graham

with God, because it is the Spirit who mediates the knowledge of God and thereby leads us into truth and righteousness (John 16:5–11). And because the Spirit brings us into deeper awareness of, and conformity to, the one true God, he keeps us from becoming toxic. The truth is, discipleship is not simply a human affair built with our own efforts and capacities; rather, it is birthed, developed, and completed in God.

The Tale of Two Churches

By now you will have realized that our lives were not quite "normal." Well, the same was true for our church life. In our early Christian experience, before we started our "official" ministry at South, we hung out in both a Pentecostal megachurch *and* a cessationist-fundamentalist church, which meant we got to experience life with feet on both accelerator and brake *at the same time.*

We would attend the more conservative, fundamentalist church on Sunday mornings, where we would sing the old hymns, hear the Word preached, and take the Lord's supper all in a very orderly, controlled fashion. Then we would tromp off to the Pentecostal church in the evening and partake of the *Pentecostal shuffle*—a bouncy kind of dance known only to true devotees. These two churches were poles apart in the way they expressed their faith, but we loved it because we learned things we never would have if we limited ourselves to the one church. We came to see that the same God existed in both, and in fact we loved the diversity.

The genuine spiritual vitality of the Pentecostals kept us passionate and zealous for God, and the deep love of the Bible and earnestness of the conservatives kept us grounded and deepened our understanding of our newfound faith. We used to say that Sunday mornings kept our minds engaged and Sunday evenings kept our spirits alive. We learned about the *gifts of the Spirit* from the Pentecostals and the *fruits of the Spirit* from the conservatives. (Of course it was not that clearly divided, but you get the point.)

Without doubt, this dual experience provided a solid foundation for us as young believers. However, not all that we experienced was positive: we also came to see the weaknesses. The cramped solemnity of fundamentalism could at times really quench the work of the Holy Spirit. And some of the extreme excesses of Pentecostalism made one wonder at times whether it was really the *Holy* Spirit at work.

It is important to look briefly at some of the more obvious weaknesses in both expressions of evangelical Christianity. Either of them, without being informed by the other, fails to fully represent the Holy Spirit and his work in our personal and corporate lives. And embracing only one expression, without the counterbalance of the other, can cause us to have a less-than-adequate understanding and experience of God's Spirit. Again, we say this as people who have a deep love for the things of God and know that our own experiences have caused us to look afresh at how the Spirit seeks to work in our lives. We ourselves are guilty of quenching the Holy Spirit because of our own reactions against the imbalances in either expression of God's church.

Power and control

One of the things we observed at times in our Pentecostal experience was a disconcerting kind of spiritual "engineering." Behind some of the apparent spontaneity and spiritual dynamism was a thoroughly mechanical, cut-and-dried set of techniques that (we believe unwittingly) hurt and damaged the spiritual fabric of Jesus's people. After being there for a while, we realized that it was the exact same "liturgy" every Sunday: rocking music to dance to (and we did), then D-minor chords to cry to (and we did), then singing in the Spirit, gifts of the Spirit (but not too much), a thirty-minute offering talk, forty minutes of preaching, ten minutes of communion, fifteen minutes of altar call, ending with some more emotive music. After years of being in ministry, we and many others have come to the conclusion that with enough of the right music, preaching, emotively charged atmosphere, and clever group-socialization (crowd-control) processes, you can pretty much grow a church without God! Technique is a terrible substitute for God—an idol—and it's too easy to revert to it to "grow the church" while the authentic experience of the Holy Spirit is being edged out the back door.

The other seriously problematic issue for charismatics and Pentecostals is an apparent preoccupation with power and secret knowledge—never a particularly good look for sinful humans. For all the fantastic aspects of the Pentecostal movement, it doesn't take long to discern an unhealthy obsession with power and "insider" knowledge. Much (not all—hence the need for spiritual discernment) that goes by the name "word of knowledge" and "prophecy" is actually thinly veiled attempts to control people. And many of the "dog and pony shows" that go under the name of miracle meetings are manifestations of a profoundly ungodly will to power and simple "crowd control."

To shock us into the dangers of this, we should remember that the Nazis were also good at these things—they scoured the earth for occult objects of power and used knowledge in a profoundly occult way! The Nuremberg rallies are still object studies in mass manipulation. The search for occult knowledge and magical powers goes as far back into human experience as we can tell, and when genuine Christian empowerment and the knowledge of God are distorted, they deteriorate into a mildly Christianized obsession with *magic* and *gnosis*. And these in turn draw their energies, not from God, but from some of the darkest aspects in human nature— and beyond that, from the demonic itself.

Pentecostalism needs to be very wary of uncritical understandings of the category of power. Confusing God's power with human attempts to control is very dangerous indeed and leads directly to toxic-city. If we both measure and define ourselves in relation to Jesus, then we must look to Jesus to understand authentic spiritual power and the right use of knowledge. When we see how Jesus operates, all normal notions of human power are actually inverted! The greatest becomes the

Crowd dynamics.

87

least, the child, the servant—in other words, the *powerless.* Jesus himself explicitly rejects offers of power (Luke 4:1–13) and instead reveals his true glory and power in and through the cross—hardly a normal place of power (1 Cor. 1:18–2:9; Phil. 2:1–11).

Order and control

On the other hand, we have the fundamentalists—ironically named, because to us it appeared that there was *not* a lot of fun but a whole *lot* of mental. Actually fundamentalism describes the religious mood of both movements we experienced, so perhaps we can basically say that it seemed to us that our more mainline Protestant evangelical brethren simply had a semi-pathological distaste for things disorderly and out of control. They sought order and control, and they did so in the name of maintaining "objectivity."

People really do fear the God encounter, and for good reason. "It is a dreadful thing to fall into the hands of the living God" (Heb. 10:31). The approach of the divine can present a real danger to fallen human beings. We take our own security and ways of thinking very seriously and fear the loss of control that God's sovereignty brings with it. Here lies the root of our rebellion and idolatry. In spite of what we say in our choruses about wanting to be touched and ravished by God, we don't really mean it: we generally prefer to worship and know God at a safe distance. British missiologist and theologian J. V. Taylor rightly says of our encounter with God,

> To encounter the Holy Spirit will be more like suddenly catching sight of the volcanic inferno beneath our earth's familiar crust. The Holy Spirit is totally primordial. His is the elemental force beyond all other forces, and to call it, correctly, the force of love is not to temper its intensity but to increase fearfully our estimate of love's fervor.[1]

Another problem for the more conservative mainline churches is doctrine worship. Doctrine is good, but only as a guide to the right experience of God. And make no mistake, doctrines of God can intrude into the actual God relationship. In fact, this is what we think has happened to a large portion of Christianity today. It certainly was the problem of the Pharisees: when their doctrine became too hard set, it preset their understanding of God. That meant they were unable to comprehend God as he appeared in Jesus; Jesus simply did not fit their theological categories. However, they refused to change their categories to suit the revelation of God, and so they ended up rejecting the Messiah they longed for. Much of the Gospel of John explores this tragic misapprehension, and it is called the power of darkness.

God takes a break.

We must learn from this: we must not use the Word of God as a shield against the actual presence of God. Lesslie Newbigin rightly warns, "A proper confidence in the ancient promises of God must not become an improper and eventually fatal barrier against recognizing and rejoicing in the action of God now."[2] As important as theology is in guiding our understanding of God, it must never be allowed to substitute for our relationship to God himself. God cannot be limited to ideology or theological assertions about him. This is another, very subtle form of idolatry. Truth must guide the relationship, but it is an easy slip from there into worshiping the idea of God rather than God himself. It was

89

the early church father Gregory of Nyssa who, knowing the propensities of the Hellenistic mind, warned that "every concept which comes from some comprehensible image by an approximate understanding and by guessing at the divine nature constitutes an idol of God and does not proclaim God."[3]

That this form of idolatry is prevalent in the church is beyond question. The theological rationalism of the Western church is actually another form of Gnosticism that has plagued us from the time Christianity moved into the Gentile world. This time Gnostic impulses are manifested not so much through spooky prophetic "words of knowledge" (as in charismatic circles), but by managing God and people through controlling the *ideas* that shape them. In some of the more sombre, doctrinaire circles of conservative evangelical Christianity, one can be excused for thinking that people believe in *belief-about-God* rather than believing in God himself.

The danger is that if such people desire control through objective truth, then, like all forms of deception and idolatry, their wish is simply granted (see chapter 2 on self-deception). That is exactly what they get: a whole lot of theology, but a fading experience of the God theology should point to. Author James Jones sums this up nicely: "The Bible is of little value without the sovereign work of the Holy Spirit. The Bible has no significance when ripped from the context of the experience of the Spirit. Refusing to subsume the Spirit under the Word frees the Spirit to do more than confirm the text and shut up."[4] Shutting the Spirit up, as Jones says, is a serious hindrance to untamed discipleship and should be recognized as one of the obstacles many readers need to overcome. It is the work of the Holy Spirit to usher us into a direct love and knowledge of God. Dry ideology is a dangerous and repressive idol.

The Shema calls us into a life of active love of and service to God and others. Love is the actual *means* of knowing God.

Heat and light company

Perhaps you, like us, have experienced some of these same excesses first hand. For us it meant becoming increasingly disillusioned and cynical about the negative aspects of both ends of the spectrum, and as a result we became a less Spirit-directed than we were at first. As church leaders, we now know all too well that this is the tragic story of so many new churches and moves of the Spirit, as religion and technique creep in and subvert the primal forces and more chaotic freedoms associated with the Spirit, or the "Beyond-in-Our-Midst," as J. V. Taylor calls him.

Truly we need both light and power, and thankfully the Holy Spirit provides both. In the Spirit, one need not be gained at the expense of the other—we are guided into a direct encounter with truth, but we are also baptized in a holy fire. A kind of holy burning should describe aspects of our life from that point on (John 14:16; Acts 2). The conservative evangelicals need to be willing to fly closer to the flame and cope with holy chaos in their lives and churches, while the more charismatically inclined need to learn the value of objective truth and communal accountability. It is characteristic of a flame that it brings both heat and light.

The challenge for all of us is to get to know the Holy Spirit in deeper ways and to remember that God will not be reduced to a set of ideas and beliefs. Untamed disciples must allow themselves to be drawn into the numinous and somewhat dangerous orbit of the divine if they are going to be genuine lovers of God. As the moth is drawn

> **The Holy Spirit Is Busy**
>
> There was a boy riding on his bike outside a church. The priest saw him and told him to come into the church, and the boy said, "But they'll steal my bike."
>
> The priest explained how the Holy Spirit would take care of it, so they went inside.
>
> The priest showed the boy how to make the sign of the cross and the boy repeated it "in the name of the Father, the Son ... Amen"
>
> The priest said, "What about the Holy Spirit?"
>
> The boy replied, "He's outside taking care of my bike!"

91

to the flame, believers who have made God into a system of ideas need to risk being overwhelmed by God again if they wish to be authentic disciples. Being an untamed follower of Jesus means risking ecstasy and losing control.

Whole Holiness

Before we move on to some of the many wonderful expressions of the Holy Spirit, we thought it important to address some of our misunderstandings around the issue of holiness. As mentioned in chapter 1, often our understanding of biblical holiness is one that leads us to see holiness from a negative perspective or as a list of "don'ts" and prohibitions. One of the key roles of the Holy Spirit is to oversee the change process by which we become holy, and when holiness is properly understood, it is actually an incredibly redemptive, highly missional concept.

Part of the problem with our understanding of holiness relates to the fact that we understand the word "holy" as a passive adjective when we refer to the "Holy" Spirit. But there is another, more distinctly Hebraic way of translating the original language that emphasizes other dimensions of the work of the Spirit in our lives. Rather than translating *hagia* as a passive adjective ("the Spirit who is holy") we can legitimately translate it far more dynamically as "the *Sanctifying* Spirit"—that is, it is the Spirit who is actively engaged in making the world a more holy place. Isn't this who God is, and doesn't it far better describe what he is doing all the time?

When we talk of God as being holy, or of Jesus as holy, or of the Holy Spirit, we must resist the temptation to see holiness in moralistic terms, or else we do violence to the idea of the redeeming God and end up seeing God as the ultimate moralist! That is simply bad theology. God is the model of holiness and we must become like the One we love. "As obedient children, let yourselves be pulled into a way of life shaped by God's life, a life energetic and blazing with holiness" (1 Peter 1:15 Message).

A Hebraic understanding of holiness suggests that all of life is actually in the process of being redeemed and brought into the sphere of the sacred: Holiness begins with God, flows into our own hearts and our lives, moves from there into the community, and eventually reaches every aspect of life in the world. God is extending his sanctity over ever-increasing portions of life until all is made holy. God is never a detached observer, but is deeply involved in the sanctification of the world. In fact he leads the charge!

This way of understanding holiness is far more world-engaging, and is best exemplified in the life, teachings, and ministry of Jesus. As we have seen, the biblical concept of holiness provides us with a much more active, and therefore missional, understanding of holiness than we are used to in the Western tradition. Holiness is not gained by withdrawal from the world but by active, redemptive engagement in the world.

Instead of looking at holiness as a list of "don'ts," see it as a list of "do's"; for every prohibition in Scripture actually implies its positive. In fact, positive virtue generates the prohibition. For instance, in the Ten Commandments, "do not kill" actually teaches that we should value and preserve life. "Do not commit adultery" implies we should actively pursue holiness in relationships, and so on.

Another dimension of biblical holiness is the idea of *consecration*: of being set aside to do a distinct task. True holiness involves clearing the desk, setting selfish agendas aside, and being willing to partner with God in the redemption-sanctification of the world by doing all things—the everyday things—in his name and for his glory. God is holy, therefore we consecrate ourselves to the task of being holy as he is holy (Lev. 11:44; 19:2). His holiness is redemptive. Holiness is dynamically missional, very engaged . . . profoundly untame! Being holy, therefore, is not about being a detached, judgmental, culturally colorless person; it means being like God, who is far from all these things! How we are holy either misrepresents or rightly represents who God is. When we are more like Jesus, we will be holy as God intended it. And it is the role of the Sanctifying Spirit to help us in this task.

Let There Be . . .

So much for obstacles that need to be identified and overcome in our relationship to God. Now it's time to take a good look at some things (there will naturally be more than we can list in one chapter) that should result from a truly vital experience of the Holy Spirit. Guided by the understanding that we discern the work of the Spirit by recognizing his attributes, we can say that the presence of the Spirit in our lives and in the community should be evidenced by the following characteristics.

Let there be some serious creativity

The Spirit is the agent of creation. Inconceivable power and creativity reside in him. Look at the sheer genius evident in the design of the universe, the brilliant simplicity of the subatomic world, or the intricacies of human nature: all are created by the Spirit of God. It is not too much to expect that where he is present, there will be an uprush of serious creativity. In fact, we should really question the Spirit's manifest presence in the church if there is no creativity, but simply religious ritual and rut-like habit.

The disciple's connection to the Spirit should set him or her *a'dreamin'*. We shouldn't be surprised that people in touch with the Holy Spirit get creative, artistic, and entrepreneurial. This is something we should expect and celebrate. It's not coincidental that the prophecy of Joel (fulfilled at Pentecost) says that the oldies are going to dream dreams again and the young people will get visions. In fact, creativity forms a major part of our mission in the world. Not only does it diminish suffering and beautify our world, but it plays a role in the invention of a better world to live in. A sanctified imagination is a powerful tool because the fundamental job of the imagination in life is to produce, out of the society we have to live in, a vision of the society we want to live in. This is the human expression of God's dream for the world that is normally called the kingdom of God. Bono reflects this work of the Spirit when he says, "Dream up the world you want to live in; dream out loud, at high volume!" Where the Spirit is, there will be lots of new things happening.

Let there be risky mission

Missio Dei is a term used to describe the mission of God. This sentness (*missio*) describes the nature of the Triune God himself. God sends his Son into the world. The Father is a sending God, and the Son is a sent one. And the Father and the Son send the Spirit (John 14:26; 15:26). The Spirit is a missionary—so much so that when reading Acts, it's hard to tell whether the book should be titled the Acts of the Spirit or the Acts of the Apostles. Mission is ascribed to both, and both play an essential part. But, as we have already noted, as God's people we only participate in God's prevenient grace. We follow the Spirit in mission. Mission is a spiritual quest and is very close to the heart of God. To do it well, we must be willing to deal with the Spirit, discern his ways, and align ourselves with his purposes.

> There can be no recovery of vital belief in the Holy Spirit and consequently no true . . . mission unless we are prepared to have dealings with the great deeps of an elemental energy.[5]

Where the Spirit is, there will be extension of the Jesus movement. The advance of the kingdom is a sure sign of the presence of the Spirit. The Third Wave charismatic movement in the 1980s was right to note that where the kingdom advances, there is spiritual conflict as well as signs and wonders. This much is evident in the life of Jesus and in the early church. Where the Spirit is, there will be missional church and discipleship.

Let there be communitas

Communitas is a concept Alan explores in depth in *The Forgotten Ways*.[6] It basically describes the kind of community that forms in the context of a dangerous ordeal, a demanding task, or another form of challenge that requires the members of the group to "find" each other in a new and dynamic way. It happens when people move from being friends or associates to being comrades. It describes the discipleship of the New Testament as well as movements that achieve significant impact on their surroundings. Communities of the Spirit are frontiers of the kingdom, and this means that there will always be an element of adventure inherent in them.

Discipleship clearly demands that we integrate an element of constant change and a substantial amount of risk into our lives. Following Jesus is never safe when it comes to our tamed, middle-class sensibilities. Simply encountering together the numinous Holy Spirit of God should be enough to create *communitas*; when we add the missional church dynamics described in the section above, we should *expect* this form of camaraderie-fellowship to characterize our churches. Where the Spirit is, there will be wild community adventures.

Let there be lots of little Jesuses

One of the works of the Spirit is to make us more like Jesus. Second Corinthians 3 is a passage dedicated to this concept. Paul ends with an insightful and profound reflection on the inner spirituality of discipleship when he says, "And we, who with unveiled faces all reflect the Lord's glory, are being transformed into his [Jesus's] likeness with ever-increasing glory, which comes from the Lord, who is the Spirit" (v. 18). When we grasp passages like this together with those that talk about the Spirit of Christ within us (for example, Romans 8), we can say that if we are not heading toward authentic Christlikeness, and therefore engaged in discipleship, then there is something deeply wrong with our spirituality. This is why Lyons and Kinnaman's research in *unChristian* (mentioned in an earlier chapter) is so unnerving.

If the Holy Spirit is manifestly at work, there will be a whole lot of little Jesuses hanging around. We should expect this, and when it is missing, we should be very concerned indeed. Where the Spirit is, there will be untamed, Jesus-like disciples.

Let there be love

Paul says, "God has poured out his love into our hearts by the Holy Spirit, whom he has given us" (Rom. 5:5). The giving of the Spirit is not only an act of unprecedented love, but it should also inspire love in us, because God is love. In the end, Christian discipleship and mission should be an ever-deepening exploration of the redemptive power of love.

J. V. Taylor explores this aspect of human and divine interconnectivity in his book on the Holy Spirit called *The Go-Between God*. He sees the central work of the Spirit as the "go-between"—between God and humanity, between people, and between humans and their world. In other words, he is our context, or as Taylor says, our "milieu." The Spirit is the one that brings all things together in righteousness. Where we see love, justice, mercy, and faithfulness being expressed in human affairs, in or out of the church, Taylor says we see something of the Spirit's handiwork. Reformed theologians call this phenomenon common grace, Wesleyans call it prevenient grace, comparative theology calls it theophany.

However we might conceptualize the presence of love, goodness, and grace in the world, it is the work of the Spirit of God in the world.

The work of the Spirit will call us to love and trust God's way of doing things and not to rely on any form of coercion or technique. Love is its own power. Where the Spirit is, there will be untamed, messianic love.

Let there be learning community

When Alan had his encounter with the Holy Spirit, he remembers distinctly feeling that his mind had just caught fire. It almost felt like he had never thought real thoughts before that time. That experience was accompanied by an unquenchable curiosity that exists undiminished to this day. Of course this should not be surprising when we recognize that God designed the vast intricacies of the mind in the first place. The life the Spirit brings includes a passionate drive for understanding God's magnificent creation and for ultimately exploring the mind of God himself. All who think (and teach) that we check our minds at the door when we become Christians—those who diminish the need for deep intellectual engagement—insult the Creator's purposes in designing the human mind in the first place.

A great example of passion for life, commitment to radical discipleship and risky mission, as well as a deep love of learning can be found in the Celtic movement, which played such a key role in evangelizing Europe in the dark ages. In a marvelous book, Thomas Cahill describes how the Irish monastic movement helped save civilization through their love of learning, commitment to study, and writing and storing texts for others to read.[7] If ever there was an integrated missional church empowered by the Holy Spirit, it was the Irish movement founded by Patrick and developed by Columba, Aidan, and others. Where the Spirit is, there will be an untamed and constantly adaptive learning community.

Let there be some miracles

Humbug to all the liberal theologies that disregard the clearly supernatural aspects of life in God! It is just another rationalist ploy to control God and people through ideas. There is no way we can comprehend the ministry of Jesus, experience the power of the resurrection, or even understand the dynamics of the early church unless we give significant space to the idea that God can, and does, intervene in history.

Disciples of the untamed and untamable Jesus will be open to the leading, empowering, liberating work of the Spirit. And they will surely hope for a whole lot more of those gracious interventions we call miracles. Where the Spirit is, there will be the in-breaking of God through miracles.

Let there be spiritual maturity

This might seem obvious given that holiness and spiritual maturity seem to be inextricably linked, but in a world that barely understands the meaning of holiness, it is necessary to reiterate. The Spirit nurtures us toward human wholeness by bringing us closer to the reality of holiness. In 1 Corinthians 2:10–16, Paul makes connections between the Spirit and healthy human spirituality, and the absence of the Spirit and what he calls "soulishness." The reality is that we cannot mature if we do not open our hearts to the work of the Spirit. Only the Sanctifying Spirit can usher in a true Christian spirituality. Where the Spirit is, there will be ongoing growth and maturing in the life of the disciple.

Let there be a lot more discernment

This book has to do with overcoming obstacles inherent in our thinking about God, present in our culture, and programmed into our psyches. It is a book about idolatry, false worship, deception, and the lies we tell ourselves to get off the hook. It takes a serious keenness of spirit (and purity of heart) to be able to discern these errors and problems

99

in faith—in other words, it requires spiritual discernment (Heb. 5:14; 1 Cor. 2:14–15). In fact, it is one of the gifts of the Spirit given to the church so that we might be able to faithfully negotiate our world (1 Cor. 12:10). Where the Sanctifying Spirit is, there will be godly discernment between good and evil.

Let there be unity around Jesus

One of the best vision statements we have ever seen for a community of believers was simply "to live under the Lordship of Jesus in the power of the Spirit." It rightly locates the center of the faith around Jesus and his lordship, but it recognizes that to do this we need the power and guidance of the Spirit. In fact, this is one of the functions of the Spirit in the church—to keep us on track and to maintain unity around our Lord. In Ephesians, we are called to "make every effort to keep the unity of the Spirit through the bond of peace. There is one body and one Spirit—just as you were called to one hope when you were called—one Lord, one faith, one baptism; one God and Father of all, who is over all and through all and in all" (4:3–6). It is a wonderful restatement of Shema spirituality, but it is interesting to note that faith is maintained by keeping the unity already given to the church by the Spirit. Where the Spirit of Christ is, there will be a deep and abiding oneness in Jesus.

Let there be ecstasy and intimacy

Part of the work of the Spirit is to bring the joy of God into real life. The coming of the Holy Spirit upon people in the New Testament is usually experienced as an ecstatic encounter with God (see, for example, Acts 2, 10, 19). To be enthused (literally, *en-theos*, in-dwelt by God) is part of the wonderful works of the Spirit of God. Ecstasy, literally a "going out" of oneself, is usually also accompanied by intimacy (a profound closeness) with God and also with other disciples. Similar to

100

the unity described above, the intimacy of Christian connection is described in the Bible as the "communion of the Holy Spirit" (2 Cor. 13:14), and it refers to the deep fellowship believers have with one another in the Spirit.

When referring to knowing God, the OT often uses the word *yada*. This word derives from the idea of personal intimacy between people and, as we said before, can be used to describe sexual intercourse. It refers to a deeply subjective form of knowledge where intellectual barriers are overcome and the immeasurable distance between knower and known is finally bridged: it approximates what the later mystics would call "union with God." Mere objective knowledge leaves the knower uncommitted, but truly *knowing* God, in the deepest biblical sense, can only be gained by a thoroughly personal, existential involvement and through a self-giving rooted in the total self-giving of the very life of God. Where the Spirit is, there will be a loving abandonment to God as well as righteous intimacy with others.

Let there be liberation and transformation

We both love the New Testament translation called "The Voice." One of the reasons is that it refers to Jesus as the Liberator. Luke 4 demonstrates that when the Holy Spirit is at work, there will be deep and profound liberation. The Spirit of the Lord anoints Jesus and the result is liberation of people from all kinds of oppression. Putting aside the unique aspects of Jesus's messianic ministry, we should still expect no less in our experience of the Spirit. Paul is right in saying, "Now the Lord is the Spirit, and where the Spirit of the Lord is, there is freedom" (2 Cor. 3:17). The presence of the Spirit frees people from all sorts of bondage: political, cultural, religious, ideological, psychological, demonic . . . whatever. The Spirit brings freedom: he is the presence of the sovereign rule of God, a lordship that displaces all that cramps the human spirit as God intended it to be.

101

In concluding this chapter, we want to say first that the above list is by no means exhaustive. But any survey of it should excite us to realize that our failure to seek the reality and presence of the Spirit really impoverishes our faith. Untamed discipleship is Spirit-filled discipleship.

Second, it is tempting to compartmentalize teaching on the Holy Spirit as part of theology and doctrine, detached from real life—which is about practical issues. Theology, properly understood, is never to be separated from life, but rather should act as a guide to life. When we compartmentalize into the false categories of "doctrine" and "life," we inevitably end up with either a tame Christianity or the toxic religion we have been describing so far in this book. This is particularly true in our understanding of God the Holy Spirit. He is the "Beyond-in-Our-Midst," and we are privileged to be bearers and recipients of his presence. Being a living temple of the Holy Spirit (1 Cor. 6:19) is not a religious thing that happens in church; rather, it takes place in every context of life. The Spirit is God, and he helps us bring our disparate worlds together so that we might experience life in all its fullness.

In our perspective and experience, the missional church movement in the West needs to seriously re-embrace the role of the Holy Spirit as part of the Christian experience. And if we really want to recover the lost ethos of authentic *missional* Christianity, we are going to have to take the risk of encountering the divine and personally experiencing God in wild and wonderful ways in order to bring the kingdom into this time and place. It's going to take untamed disciples who, as lovers and pursuers of God, have no defenses and are willing to lay bare their hearts before him to make this happen. Amen, come Holy Spirit.

The initial chapters of this book are more theological because it is vital for disciples to get a handle on the God we love and follow. As we have seen, we know God supremely in and through Jesus, but even the incarnation of the Word does not limit the greatness of God. And although we can

Callslip Request   1/3/2014 12:18:34 PM

Request date:12/30/2013 04:12 AM
Request ID: 43324
Call Number:248.4 H6691
Item Barcode:

Author: Hirsch, Alan, 1959 Oct. 24-
Title: Untamed : reactivating a missional form
Enumeration:Year:
Patron Name:Alan Totire
Patron Barcode:

5 5 2 4 4 3

Patron comment:

Request number:

4 3 3 2 4

Route to:
I-Share Library:

Library Pick Up Location:

never hope to fully comprehend God, for he is infinite and all-powerful, it is incumbent on us at least to trace the contours of the God we encounter in the Bible. We need to get the essentials right. A living and direct experience of his love, mercy, holiness, and redeeming nature are prerequisites for a healthy expression of faith.

But all this comes at a cost. It demands something from us. A disciple will need to recognize up front that God loves us way too much to leave us as we are. Knowing God and following his Son in the power of the Spirit will require that we allow ourselves to be stripped of a rebellious religion that prevents a true experience of God and restricts our capacity to truly love him. God's love is all-embracing and requires an all-exclusive relationship—he simply will not share us with other gods. Idolatry must go. So too must the lies we tell ourselves to moderate the demanding nature of the relationship. There must be a constant and dynamic movement in our lives for, as Bonhoeffer once rightly noted, to know God is to change!

Suggested Practices

- Because the work of the Spirit is not always spectacular, we have to learn to "see" the work of the Spirit in everyday life. Again, we believe the questions of the *Examen* are helpful in this regard: "Where in this last week have I worked with the Spirit, and where have I resisted the Spirit in my life?" Decide to regularly journal the responses.

- Like us, we suggest you take an inventory of your life in the Spirit. Using the list contained in the "let there be" section above, take stock of (1) your own life, and (2) your community. Where are you weak and where are you strong?

- The book of Acts has rightly been called The Acts of the Holy Spirit: reread the book of Acts and try to discern how the Holy Spirit is involved in the life of the early church. Develop your own understanding of the Holy Spirit in the church.

Discussion Starters

1. Read the Ananias and Sapphira passage (Acts 5:1–5). Discuss among yourselves how false motives, lack of accountability, and even lies can hide behind explicitly "spiritual" language.
2. The word for spirit (*pneuma*) in the original Greek text does not distinguish what spirit is being referred to—God's or ours. Try reading the word in Romans 8 first with a capital "S" (as in standard translations) and then with a lowercase "s" (which is not the standard translation). Discuss what insights come to mind.
3. Where is the Spirit to be found in middle-class life? What would happen if the Spirit entered more deeply into your urban or suburban existence?
4. How have we, corporately and individually, quenched the Spirit in recent times?

the untamed culture

4

kultcha-schmultcha

Human existence cannot derive its ultimate meaning from society because society itself is in need of meaning.

—Abraham Heschel

Because the Light is radically different from the Darkness, the manifestation of the Light always opposes the Darkness. . . . This is not to say that disciples should not agree with secular voices at certain points, but is merely to warn that simply seconding the wisdom of the world is not testimony to the Word of God.

—Gene Davenport

If everyone lives roughly the same lies about the same things, then there is no one to call them lies; they jointly establish their own sanity and call themselves normal.

—Ernest Becker

Reporting on Black Friday, an American phenomenon, the *Seattle Times* highlights a serious tragedy:

In a sign of consumer desperation amid a bleak economy, the annual rite of retailing known as Black Friday turned chaotic and deadly as shoppers scrambled for holiday bargains. A Wal-Mart worker on Long Island, New York, died after being trampled by customers who broke through the doors early Friday. Other workers were trampled as they tried to rescue the man. At least four other people, including a woman who was eight months pregnant, were taken to hospitals.

This was not an isolated incident; fights and injuries occurred elsewhere at other stores operated by Wal-Mart, America's leading discount chain. Meanwhile, two men at a crowded Toys "R" Us store in Palm Desert, California, pulled guns and shot each other to death after the women accompanying them brawled over bargains. When interviewed after the event, Joe Priester, former president of the Society for Consumer Psychology, commented, "I think it ties into a sort of fear and panic of not having enough."[1]

Something profound is being signified in these events. They are a manifestation, a parable if you will, of some of the dangerous, subterranean energies that seem to pervade our culture.

Discipleship in Reverse

Identifying the spirits of our age while living in and—to varying degrees—being immersed in the prevailing culture is one of the trickiest things disciples have to negotiate. As missionaries following the traces of God, we must affirm that which is genuinely good and present in any and every human culture, for many aspects are indeed wholesome and true and affirmed by the gospel. But the opposite is also true. There is a lot that is dehumanizing, degrading, and evil, and the disciple is called to somehow discern the difference between it and what is good. The problem is that unless we are very sensitive to God and can discern the sometimes-blurry boundaries between right and wrong, or holy and unholy, culture can have as much an effect on us as disciples as we can have on it. In our day, one is left wondering if it is us who are actually being "evangelized" by the prevailing mass culture rather than the other way around.

We do inhabit a church of what some commentators call "Christianity Lite," and, by all accounts, it is us who have been acculturated—not the other way around. We have come to believe through hard experience and lots of reflection that the church has been deeply compromised by aspects of the prevailing culture. Christians now easily reflect the characteristics and the conditions of the wider culture. But what we have gained in relevancy we lose in witness and impact, for "though popular culture holds tremendous potential for good, unfortunately, today's trend is towards a diversionary, mindless, celebrity-driven superficiality. Sadly this reflects our general societal condition, for popular culture can only rise to the spiritual, intellectual, and artistic heights of its average citizenry."[2] This is not good news for missional Christianity, for if Christianity just mirrors its culture, what is the point of its mission?

This is no excuse to withdraw ourselves from culture, but rather as disciples we must learn to live the tension between gospel and culture, to discern how to hold on to what is true and discard that which is evil (Rom. 12:9). And as agents (missionaries) of the wild Messiah, we also need to interpret and redeem the world/s in which we live. All this goes directly to the issue of discipleship formation and to the reality that the church has largely been unsuccessful at prioritizing disciple making as the primary mission of the church (Matt. 28:16–20). Only disciples formed in the ways of the radical missionary Jesus can make an impact on such a potent cultural system as the one we live and move in.

Willow Creek Association bravely admitted as much in its publication *Reveal*. The report acknowledges that what they've been doing for these many years and what they've taught millions of others to do is not producing solid disciples of Jesus Christ—numbers, yes, but disciples, no. Bill Hybels admits that "if you simply want a crowd, the 'seeker sensitive' model produces results. If you want solid, sincere, mature followers of Christ, it's a bust."[3] This should actually be of no surprise to us, as Jesus clearly lays out the conditions for following him—he calls for nothing less than death to self. This means that all personal and cultural agendas must be laid down at the foot of Jesus as a precondition to following him. If we, in a sincere attempt to reach contemporary audiences, reconfigure the processes of Christian formation, putting the challenge of discipleship off to the end, then, in our opinion, we are opening the floodgates to being "evangelized" by the culture. When we remove Jesus's preconditions to following him and use professional mass entertainment (no matter how sincere) to draw people to Christ, we should not be surprised at the results—we simply can't entertain consumers into becoming disciples, nor can people *consume* their way into following Jesus.

But the problem has even deeper roots than a consumerist church. It stems from the fact that even *before* we come to Christ, we have already been powerfully discipled by pop culture. We come to Jesus as inveterate consumers holding values that often run completely contrary to the ways of the gospel. High capitalism, the market, postmodern superficiality, and the sheer power of the mass media all conspire to ensure that we are already ardent disciples of the gods of the age. It is unlikely that there has ever been a time when the population has been so thoroughly programmed and brainwashed without even knowing it.

Dick Staub warns us of this frightening reality:

The largest companies in the world are spending billions of dollars to drive a diversionary, mindless, celebrity-fuelled popular culture down the highway of new technologies and into our lives in order to sell us stuff we don't want or need. They don't care about us, what we believe or how we want to live. The ads and products regularly reduce women to sex objects and men to voyeurs and predators. They are unconcerned with what is in our best interests spiritually or intellectually, and in fact, it is in their best interest to keep us spiritually desensitized and dumb. They play to our unhappiness, magnifying the feeling that we are missing something essential and that if we had this something they offer, we would be fulfilled. They then encourage us to shop, convincing us that shopping will do today what it failed to do yesterday—fill what French religious philosopher Pascal calls the God-shaped vacuum.[4]

This is what we are dealing with, and there is no doubt that it has deeply and indelibly shaped each and every one of us. Being conscious of this fact doesn't necessarily mean we are free from its pull. For example, when taking a break from writing this book, we found ourselves wandering around the local mall. After about twenty minutes of browsing, we looked at each other and the question occurred to us: what were we doing there? We didn't need to buy anything, but yet here we were, taking a break in a mall!

To refer to a remarkable movie that explored the totality of the system we are born into, we are born, live, and have our being in "the matrix." The matrix's appeal goes deep and reaches into our secret insecurities, our penchant for greed, our desire for status, and our need for love and freedom. If we are going to be untamed followers of the wild Lord of our lives, then we are going to have to deal with these dynamics in our culture. We have to escape from Babylon and return to Zion in order to liberate Babylon. To some of these dynamics we now turn.

The Green God

Martin Luther said three conversions are necessary when a person decides to follow Christ: the conversion of the heart, the conversion of the mind, and the conversion of the purse. And John Wesley wryly remarked that the last thing to convert was a person's wallet.

Money plays an overpowering, all-encompassing role in history and in our lives. Let's face it: the love of it, and all it represents, reaches into each and every heart. Who can honestly claim to be utterly free from its almost magical appeal? Money is big, powerful, alluring, and very demanding. So we should not be surprised that Jesus would have something to say about it.

And he does. Richard Foster notes that Jesus actually speaks more about money and wealth than any other topic except the kingdom of God! And he goes on to document the evidence.[6] Jesus devoted time and energy to the issue because he knew the power it wields over our imaginations and lives. In fact, there is no other single thing he describes as being in such direct competition to God as money. Jesus clearly states, "No one can serve two masters. Either he will hate the one and love the other, or he will be devoted to the one and despise the other. You cannot serve both God and Money" (Matt. 6:24).

There is no prevarication here, no ambiguity, no getting around it. According to our Master, money exists in opposition to the claims God makes over our lives. And if we are

The Baptism[5]

not careful, mammon and materialism can hinder the work of mission and limit spiritual effectiveness.

Susan Hope, a British missiologist, raises a good question:

> Is it just co-incidence that sees lightheartedness about owner-ship of goods as a context for healing and effective evangelism in the stories of the Early Church? "No good asking me for silver and gold—haven't got any. But I will give you what I have—in the name of Jesus of Nazareth—walk!" (Acts 3:6). "No one claimed any of their possessions was their own, but they shared everything they had. With great power the apostles continued to testify to the resurrection of the Lord" (Acts 4:32–33).[7]

Paul also has the same attitude toward wealth: among other things, he says that the "love" of money is the root of all (or every) kind of evil (1 Tim. 6:10). James the brother of Jesus does not mince words either (James 5:1–5). If we read Jesus and New Testament teaching correctly, we can only understand money if we interpret it in light of the teachings of the principalities and powers against which we must do battle. Money is not a neutral force, but is animated and energized by powers. Therefore our relationship to money is filled with moral power.[8] Richard Foster is quite clear in stating that money is an idol we must be converted *from* in order to be converted *to* Jesus.

> The rejection of the god of mammon is a necessary pre-condition to becoming a disciple of Jesus. And, in point of fact, money has many of the characteristics of deity. It gives us security, can induce guilt, gives us freedom, gives us power and seems to be omnipresent. Most sinister of all, however, is its bid for omnipotence. . . . It seems that money is not willing to rest content in its proper place alongside other things we value. No, it must have supremacy. It must crowd out all else. We attach importance to it far beyond its worth. In fact we attach ultimate importance to it. It is tremendously instructive to stand back and observe the

113

frantic scramble of people for money or things related to money [what it can buy and what it can give us]. And this does not occur just among the poor and starving. Quite to the contrary—the super wealthy, who really have nothing to gain by more money, still seek it furiously. The middle class, who are really quite adequately cared for (and who are from a global perspective the wealthy), continue to buy more houses than they need, to acquire more cars than they need, to have more clothes than they need. Many of us could live on half of what we now receive without much serious sacrifice, yet we feel that we are just barely making ends meet [because the world, the media, and the devil are telling us that this is so].[9]

Foster goes on to say that money is one of the principalities and powers that must be conquered and redeemed through the blood of Jesus Christ *before* it can be usable for the greater good of the kingdom of God. To truly walk in the way of Jesus, one must be free of the love of money and the pride that often goes along with it. In the words of our friend and colleague Wes White, "[The wealthy Christians] . . . have to be rescued . . . from the hubris that is usually [associated] with mammon and [which] invariably precludes the presence and power of God."[10] Once we are rescued, we can be free to be generous, and when we are generous, we are agents of Jesus's remarkable grace. We cannot overestimate the power of generosity in human relations. Not only does it destroy the power of money, but it introduces the one who receives the gift (as well as the one who gives the gift) into the world of grace.[11] Seen this way, giving is actually a sacrament be-cause, as theologian Miroslav Volf says, "every gift breaks the barrier between the sacred and the mundane and floods the mundane with the sacred."[12]

Volf also suggests, "We're set up to buy and sell, not to give and receive."[13] This means we are trained from a young age to calculate before giving money away rather than to be truly generous. For instance, while Bill Gates's contribution

114

to charity is very laudable, it hardly constitutes a "widow's mite." It still leaves him as one of the richest men in the world. Being calculatingly generous is not the same as being radically generous. If we are going to engender an ethos of untamed generosity, we will need much healthier images of God than the two commonly held false stereotypes of God as giver, namely, the *Wheeler-Dealer god* and the *Santa Claus god*. Unlike the Wheeler-Dealer god, God generously gives without any semblance of negotiation, because he needs nothing that we have and asks more than we could ever give. God gives simply because he is gracious. On the other hand, the Santa Claus god demands nothing of us. But is it true that God demands nothing of us? No, *God gives so that we can become joyful givers ourselves* rather than self-absorbed receivers or consumers. In the right sense of the term, God's giving obliges us to respond with *faith* (Rom. 4:5), *gratitude* (2 Cor. 9:15), *availability* (2 Cor. 8:5), and *participation* (Gal. 2:19–20).[14]

Play with Maar'kit

Have you ever noticed that financial commentators tend to personify the term "market" with reverence when they use it? Statements such as "The market punished the low profit yields of X company today," or "The market did this or that" furnish us with the distinct sense that the word is meant to be used with a capital "M" and spoken of with spiritual veneration— more like "*Maar'kit*." This is a dead giveaway for the religious awe with which many regard its power. What?! Like the market has a personality? It can make choices, determine the outcome of history, provide meaning, and even make judgments over what constitutes good or bad decisions?! In other words, it sounds awfully like *Maar'kit* has actually developed an imposing persona—we are back to that darn idolatry again! And a moody and capricious god it proves to be. Beware, those who submit to it, because *Maar'kit* has a really bad temper—he (or she) gives and takes away, at will.

115

As followers of Jesus living in the world we happen to inhabit, we need to have our eyes opened to the idolatry of wealth that is the basis of Western society. For instance, Victor Lebeau, a leading post-war economist, in what must surely be a defining comment on the nature of the society we live in, said,

> Our enormously productive economy demands that we make consumption our way of life, that we convert the buying and use of goods into rituals, that we seek our spiritual satisfaction, our ego satisfaction, in consumption. . . . We need things consumed, burned up, replaced and discarded at an ever accelerating rate.[15]

Andy Warhol famously quipped that buying is much more American than thinking! Apparently Nobel-winning economist Milton Friedman thinks it is in the economy's best interest to keep it that way: "Few trends could so thoroughly undermine the very foundations of our free society as the acceptance by corporate officials of a social responsibility other than to make as much money for their stockholders as possible. This is a fundamentally subversive doctrine."[16] Talk about the justification of Gordon Gekko's famous dictum that greed is good!

We moved to California and began our research for this book at a very historic time—the 2008 election. One of the things in the lead-up to the election was of course the systemic stock market crash. People were frantic, clutching for their dollars before they disappeared. At the height of the panic, it was interesting to note that as debates about what to do about the crisis were underway, massive bailouts and all, no one mentioned even the *possibility* of actually closing down the stock markets so that market raiders wouldn't exploit the situation or shareholders couldn't sell in a panicky way. And yet that would have resolved the immediate issues involved in the crisis—panic selling resulting in a market crash. No, it seems that *Maar'kit* and his devotees would not put up with that. It just goes to show that the market plays way too important of a role in our lives. Surely there are other criteria for followers of Jesus to make serious judgments by other than money.

Directly related to the role of money and wealth in society is the increasingly powerful religion of consumerism.

Oh Lord, Won't You Buy Me a Mercedes-Benz . . .

Alan was initially trained in marketing and advertising before becoming a follower of Jesus, and both he and I (Deb) are at least "working" theologians. When we look at the power of consumerism and the market in our lives, we are thoroughly convinced that we are dealing with a very significantly *religious* phenomenon: if the role of religion is to mediate a sense of identity, purpose, meaning, and community, it can be said that consumerism fulfills *all* these criteria.[17]

For instance, some now use the term "expressive capital" to

> **Using Truth for Dollars**
>
> Contemporary practices in advertising and marketing are explicitly exploiting religious motivations in people! Alan recently had a chilling conversation with an advertising guru who stated that "best practice in marketing is taking on where the church has left off. As Christianity vacates Western society, we are stepping right in to fill the gap." In fact, this is precisely the sin of Satan—to use truth for ends other than those for which it was intended.

brand and sell products. This is the current ideology behind marketing, and it teaches that "at the center of every human soul is the intense longing to be closer to God." A brand that can empathize with that is "powerful," and "the market for something to believe in is infinite."[18] This thinking gets close to being demonic, because it exploits people at the deepest possible level: the level of meaning and existence. In order to sell products in an increasingly competitive market comprised of innumerable consumer niches, subcultures, tastes, and preferences, marketing strategies have had to reach deeper and deeper into the human soul to make a sale. Appeal to basic needs will not do in our culture. Marketing strategy now explicitly exploits the vacuum of spirituality left by the vacating of Christianity from the public imagination. Marketing has stepped in where the church has stepped out.

The new "golden calf."

Consumerism now provides a direct link between personal happiness and the purchase and consumption of material possessions. It involves basing one's identity, including one's sense of "community," in a brand, and making choices in an attempt to find meaning in shopping and consuming. For most people in Western contexts, *shopping is spirituality*. It is an attempt to find meaning and happiness in the product. And we all do it! Lets face it: for most of us, when we go to the mall, we are not simply doing it to fulfill basic survival needs. We are seeking something else! When we buy a house, a car (or a second car, for that matter), fashion items, or electronics, far more than "basic" needs are being indulged in. Seeking status, identity, fulfillment, and happiness is often our ulterior motivation, rather than meeting basic needs.

Once again we are back to idolatry: the attempt to establish meaning and purpose on our own terms outside of a relationship with God—or as theologian Paul Tillich defined it, giving ultimate value to that which is not ultimate. Because of the total pervasiveness of consumerism and the dominance of the market, this presents a far more insidious challenge to the claims of Jesus over our lives because, in so many ways, it infects each and every one of us.

As Helen Trinca and Catherine Fox note,

> For many of us, buying the goods and services we want does wonders psychologically. When we spend, we see the rewards of our hard work. Once those rewards were more abstract. We may have felt happy when we were doing our duty to God or to a community, or enjoyed the feeling that work was itself a virtuous activity, a good thing to do. Our reward for work was financial but also spiritual or religious. Materialism, hedonism, the linking of happiness with consumption were all regarded as dubious pursuits in a religious age. . . . Consumption has filled the vacuum of meaning in the 21st century and plays a powerful role in ambitions. You may not get an interesting job—after all, not everyone can—but you can moderate the anger and sadness at missing out by buying hard, by acquiring goods that describe you and how you live your life.[19]

Mark Sayers, a good friend of ours, has noted that one of the most alluring religious appeals of consumerism is that it offers us a new immediacy, a living alternative to what heaven has always stood for in the Judeo-Christian tradition—the fulfillment of all our longings. We have at our fingertips experiences and goods only available to kings in previous eras. Because we are offered "heaven now," we give up the ultimate quest in pursuit of that which can be immediately consumed, be it a service, product, or pseudo-religious experience. Consumerism has all the distinguishing traits of outright paganism—we need to see it for what it really is.[20]

Jesus said, "So do not worry, saying, 'What shall we eat?' or 'What shall we drink?' or 'What shall we wear?' For the pagans run after [desire, search for] all these things, and your heavenly Father knows that you need them. But seek first his kingdom and his righteousness, and all these things will be given to you as well" (Matt. 6:31–33). When we try to establish meaning and fulfillment in the way that advertisers would have us do, we basically act as "pagans" do. Consumerism as a religious phenomenon is as thoroughly pagan as worshiping Baal. Seen in this light, *Queer Eye for the Straight Guy*, *Extreme Makeover*, *Big Brother*, and other lifestyle shows are some of the most pagan, and *paganizing*, shows on TV. Even the perennial favorites about renovating the house paganize us because they focus us on that which so easily enslaves us. In these, the banality of consumerism reaches a climax as we are sold the lie that the thing that will complete us is a new kitchen or a house extension. In fact, these only add more stress to our mortgages and our families.[21] These shows are far more successful promoters of unbelief than even outright intellectual atheism because they hit us at that place where we must render our trust and loyalty. And most people are profoundly susceptible to the idolatrous allure of money and things. We do well to remember what our Lord said about serving two masters and desiring things (Matt. 6:24–33).

Discipleship is all about adherence to Christ. It is always articulated and experienced over and against all other competing claims for our loyalty and allegiance. When diversion and entertainment become a way of life, "we avoid the very issues to which we should be most attentive. We are diverted from the grim, unpleasant truth that our lives lack meaning without God, that consumption does not satisfy, that the differential between wealth and poverty is unjust, and that the appropriate human response to people in need is sleeves-rolled-up service, not simply watching."[22]

My Friends All Have Porsches, and I Must Make Amends . . .

Now, if you add a third factor into the equation of money and consumerism, that of a phenomenon called status anxiety, we really have quite a potent mix.

Status anxiety originates in that distinct desire of people to climb the social ladder—those certain intangible anxieties that arise from a focus on how we are perceived by others. Alain de Botton, the man who coined the phrase "status anxiety," claims that chronic anxiety about status is an inevitable side effect of any democratic, supposedly egalitarian society.[23] He says that status anxiety stems from the following combination of cultural factors in Western society:

- *Lovelessness*: Human beings will do just about anything for love (not just romantic love). We are in constant and deep-seated need of the acceptance and good opinions of others in order to survive. This is especially true of the love of those we consider to be in our peer groups. The need for this love and the loss of it create what William James calls "a kind of rage and impotent despair . . . from which the cruelest bodily torture would be a relief."[24]

- *Expectation*: We live in a culture which promises us that we can have all our needs fulfilled. This message is confirmed through exposure to countless advertisements designed to create an unholy discontent in the consumer

121

and the expectation that only the purchasing of products can fulfill. The result is, of course, anxiety.

- *Meritocracy*: This is the name for a cultural and social system based on ability. In such a society, rewards (be they wealth, position, or social status) are given to those who exhibit talent and competence, demonstrated through past actions or by competition. Of course, because not all have equal ability, a meritocracy causes as much anxiety and unhappiness as it does happiness.

- *Snobbery*: Snobs are people who adopt the worldview that some people are inherently inferior to them for any one of a variety of reasons, including real or supposed intellectual ability, wealth, education, ancestry, and the like. The problem we all face, according to de Botton, is that although we can rely on the unconditional love of our parents, lovers, and certain friends even if we are disgraced and bankrupt, "it is on a diet of the highly conditional attentions of snobs that we are generally forced to subsist."[25] Snobs set the social agenda for all of us, and they are impossible to please. Again, unhappiness is the result.

- *Dependence*: This form of anxiety comes about from the feeling that one's fortunes are dependent on things external to one's own choice. For instance, we are dependent to a large degree on fickle talent, luck, circumstance, the employer's moods, profitability, and of course the global economy. Because these are outside our control, they create a distinct form of unhappiness and anxiety.

Any—or a combination—of these can create status anxiety. For instance, when we are part of a group of peers, we are happy to be measured by the standards of the group (Figure A); however, if just one in the group should get a better home, a salary raise, a more beautiful partner, or whatever, things happen in the group (Figure B).

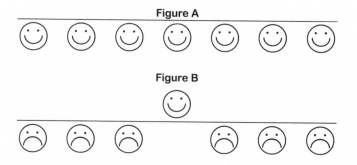

There are countless ways we might experience a combination of status-induced unhappiness. Our neighbor getting an extension on their house, a new car, or a promotion—any of these things can make us feel inadequate, and we seek to rectify the situation by getting an extension, a car, a promotion; and so it goes, on and on.

However, it is not always through the bigger, more obvious acquisitions that we seek status. It insidiously makes its way into all spheres of our lives. In *The Overspent American*, Juliet Schor documents a survey conducted on women regarding their purchase of beauty products, from cleansers to lipsticks. Her results show that women will generally spend less money on things like toners and cleansers because they are unseen by the public (usually kept hidden in bathroom cupboards). However, the amount of money women will part with increases dramatically the more conspicuous the makeup products are. The highest and most revered item in a woman's array of status beauty products is lipstick. Women will spend inordinately more for a lipstick of a known brand because it is the one piece of makeup that is used regularly in full public view: at work, at the table when out to dinner, or in the elevator. The better the brand, the higher the status inferred. It seems the lipstick makes a socially significant statement about who women *are*.[26]

Whether you are a lipstick-wearing woman or not, the fact is that all of us are plagued by a variety of status anxieties.

Consciously or not, we are constantly comparing ourselves to others; whether it is the "nicer" car parked next to us at the lights, the clothes we wear, or being in the right "clique," fraternity, or social group, we all want to be noticed, to be validated, or to climb up the social ladder.

The Great Reversal

As disciples of the "great reversal" (described in Jesus's teachings on "the first shall be last, the last first," "the least of these," "the servant-master," and so on), accumulating status should be particularly disturbing to us for a whole host of reasons, which we will get to shortly. One particularly sinister one we want to comment on is the adulation of Christian "celebrities." The impact of Hollywood and trashy gossip magazines has certainly left its mark upon us. Due to the nature of our work, which involves a lot of public speaking at conferences, we get to see this one close up, and frankly, we have been deeply disturbed by it.

We have heard many complaints of conference organizers about the demands of some keynote speakers. These range from wanting crates of bottled water waiting in their hotel rooms to charging exorbitant amounts of money just for an "appearance," not to mention all the associated special treatments such as VIP car parking, reserved seating at the front of the auditorium, and access to a well guarded "green room" so the little lord

> **Upward Equals Downward**
>
> "If people change their reference group upwards, this can seriously affect their happiness. There are many clear cases where people became objectively better off but felt subjectively worse. One is East Germany, where the living standards of those employed soared after 1990, but their levels of happiness fell; with the reunification of Germany the East Germans began to compare themselves with the West Germans, rather than the other countries in the former Soviet Bloc" (Richard Layard, *Happiness: Lessons from a New Science* [London: Penguin, 2005], 33).

need not be bothered with the masses, topped off with a personal assistant to cater to every need. We fully appreciate some of the practical realities of this and the honoring of special guests, but we need to be very careful that in providing these things we are not cultivating a culture that is more in line with Hollywood than with the kingdom. We have to ask the question of ourselves: Is this really consistent with the way of Jesus?

Part of the issue arises when we assign greater importance to more "public" gifts over and above the more "unseen" ones. This not only creates inequality within the body of Christ but a spiritually dangerous hankering after the so-called greater gifts, with all the affirmation and adulation that goes with them. This is not only very dangerous for people with brittle egos and underdeveloped characters, but when it becomes pathological and an individual resorts to seeking this from the masses in the guise of a spiritual guru, we have the very worst of human nature on show. And that, unfortunately, is often what the world tends to see.

And it shall not be so with you . . .

Money, obsessions, consumerism-as-spirituality, and status anxiety as the cultural driving force of the day make up the toxic water in which we swim. They impact all of us, no matter what our socioeconomic background. It is too easy for us to see these as issues that affect only the wealthy among us because they have greater purchasing power and therefore the means to acquire and assert influence. The fact is that issues of greed, consumption, and pecking order exist in every human community. A great challenge for disciples of Jesus is to dethrone these idols—these "gods" that promise us the world but possess our souls in the bargain. To bring an alternate message of liberation and hope requires that we ourselves first be liberated.

As Susan Hope rightly states,

The issue of freedom is a crucial one, especially for Christians involved in mission to a culture where consumerism is the dominant force. Evangelism for such a culture means an invitation to "change gods" (1 Thess. 1:9). Those who seek to minister Christian freedom must themselves be free. . . . "You cannot serve God and Mammon," says Jesus, trenchantly. Justin, in his day, remarked how pagans were turning away from violence and tyranny "because they were drawn to Christians as people whose lives were distinctive and free." I wonder if twenty-first-century Western Christians are living lives that are clearly distinctive and free as regards possessions.[27]

The Least of These

When Deb worked with the Salvation Army, her first client was a transsexual named Jennifer (not her real name; she has since passed away). Jennifer was a large, unattractive man with breasts and long hair who dressed in female clothing. She had a mild mental disability, a speech impediment, and was fairly aggressive. Needless to say she stood out in a crowd. Jennifer was what you would call a "social outcast"—not someone you naturally desired to hang out with. Yet Deb learned many valuable lessons from her. For all her social poverty she was wonderfully free from the so-called "needs" of normal people. She didn't care about status, money, or the need to accumulate possessions. Deb can remember a time when she took Jennifer to visit the local shopping mall to buy some gifts the week before Christmas. The mall was packed with people caught up in the consumer frenzy, eager to purchase their items before Christmas. Walking behind Jennifer as they made their way through the crowds, Deb recalls having somewhat of an "epiphany." Here in the midst of the consumerist frenzy, Jennifer was wonderfully free. In fact Deb was the one caught up in it! The poor can truly teach us lessons about our own "poverty."

This truly is one of the greatest challenges for the church in the twenty-first century. How we deal with these "idols of our times" both personally and communally as the people of God is of utmost importance as we seek to communicate a message of liberation to a world that is by and large enslaved to these very things. To bring an alternative message, we need to ensure that we are endeavoring to live an alternative life.

The clearest way, as far as we can see, to experience this liberation is by understanding and applying the genius of the Beatitudes to our lives. Nothing so confronts the idols of our time as Jesus's great teaching here, and in fact in the whole Sermon on the Mount. We have included both versions because we feel that together they more fully communicate the truths Jesus sought to impart to his hearers.

Matthew 5:2–13	Luke 6:20–30
And he began to teach them, saying:	Looking at his disciples, he said:
"Blessed are the poor in spirit, for theirs is the kingdom of heaven. Blessed are those who mourn, for they will be comforted. Blessed are the meek, for they will inherit the earth. Blessed are those who hunger and thirst for righteousness, for they will be filled. Blessed are the merciful, for they will be shown mercy. Blessed are the pure in heart, for they will see God. Blessed are the peacemakers, for they will be called sons of God. Blessed are those who are persecuted because of righteousness, for theirs is the kingdom of heaven.	"Blessed are you who are poor, for yours is the kingdom of God. Blessed are you who hunger now, for you will be satisfied. Blessed are you who weep now, for you will laugh.
"Blessed are you when people insult you,	Blessed are you when men hate you, when they exclude you and insult you
persecute you and falsely say all kinds of evil against you	
because of me.	and reject your name as evil, because of the Son of Man.
Rejoice and be glad, because great is your reward in heaven, for in the same way they	"Rejoice in that day and leap for joy, because great is your reward in heaven. For that is how their fathers
persecuted the prophets who were before you.	treated the prophets.
"You are the salt of the earth. But if the salt loses its saltiness, how can it be made salty again? It is no longer good for anything, except to be thrown out and trampled by men."	

Matthew 5:2–13	Luke 6:20–30
	"But woe to you who are rich, for you have already received your comfort.
Woe to you who are well fed now, for you will go hungry.
Woe to you who laugh now, for you will mourn and weep.
Woe to you when all men speak well of you, for that is how their fathers treated the false prophets.
"But I tell you who hear me: Love your enemies, do good to those who hate you, bless those who curse you, pray for those who mistreat you. If someone strikes you on one cheek, turn to him the other also. If someone takes your cloak, do not stop him from taking your tunic. Give to everyone who asks you, and if anyone takes what belongs to you, do not demand it back."

How contrary are the Beatitudes to the endemic greed and status anxiety that so easily prevail over us! How free from status anxiety is the person who lives by them! According to Jesus, it is such a person who is truly "happy" or "blessed." But these are inversions of what our society says makes a person happy. Truly the idols have deceived us yet again. Full of blather and promise, they deliver nothing but sadness and despair.

Aunt Betty and Uncle Simon

In 1999 we visited Al's former homeland, South Africa. As this was Al's first visit back in twelve years, we went to visit some of his family and old friends. We'll never forget the day we visited old, very wealthy Aunt Betty (not her real name). After driving up the long, tree-lined driveway to get to her homestead, we were welcomed at the door by her butler—in a tuxedo, no less. While the butler served us tea in beautiful china, Aunt Betty apologized for her husband not being around, for he was on their yacht off the coast of Spain! While

I (Deb) came to terms with my shock at how much money this woman had, Al began to share with his aunt how he had come to know Jesus while living in Australia. She said she sensed there was something different about him and that he looked really happy and content. We chatted throughout the afternoon; then, much to our surprise, not long before we left she commented on how envious she was of Al's peace. She also said that throughout her whole life she had had everything a person could ever want but, despite that, she had never found real happiness. What a confession! Here was a woman, despite her mansion with its many servants and marble floors, confessing to being profoundly unhappy and even depressed. She recalled that the only time she had ever felt happy was when she was a student with very little and living a simple life.

The tragedy of the Aunt Betty story was highlighted further when we went to visit a wonderful black man named Simon later in that same week. Simon was one of the servants who had worked for many years in Alan's parents' hotel, and Al, as a young guy, was particularly close to him. To get to Simon's house we had to drive down miles of dirt roads filled with potholes. Along the way children were out laughing and playing, and as we pulled up outside Simon's house, his whole family was there waiting to greet us. They welcomed us into their very modest brick home, which had basic furniture sitting on a mud floor. We were served coffee in cracked mugs while chickens and children with very worn clothes ran in and out of the house, having the time of their lives. We had never felt so welcomed or embraced. Sharing with his family that afternoon, we came to the profoundly unnerving conclusion that he was one of the happiest, most content people we had ever met. Our minds could not but think of Aunt Betty as we drove home that day.

In the West we often confuse "being poor" with "poverty." Now let us be clear, we do not believe there is anything good about poverty and wouldn't want to be seen as idealizing it. Poverty not only results in the loss of significant choices; it also involves the loss of all human dreams and hopes. But being "poor" economically speaking doesn't necessarily equal being in "poverty." What we saw that day with Aunt Betty was something akin to a poverty of the soul, despite all her material wealth. We observed the opposite in Simon: his soul was rich, yet he had nothing in terms of material wealth. This is often the reverse of what our culture assumes. We are conditioned to think money brings happiness, and though we agree that it certainly may open up doors and bring a degree of comfort and security, these things are temporal and ultimately not of eternal value. Of course, not all wealthy people are unhappy as Aunt Betty was. It depends on what you invest in to find security, identity, and purpose.

In the wonderful, feel-good movie *The Pursuit of Happyness*, starring Will Smith, we find the classic portrayal of an individual triumphing over all obstacles in the pursuit of the American dream. It is a stirring story line, particularly given the fact that it is based on a true story. However, when reflecting a little deeper on the movie, we found that the message undeniably communicated was again that happiness is to be found in financial gain, respectability, and success. We don't want to diminish the wonderful story told in the movie, but rather want to point out some of our cultural presuppositions that seem to permeate our understanding of where true happiness is found. In *The Pursuit of Happyness*, money mattered—more so than in many films of a similar genre that set their sights on the poor—largely because Chris's (Will Smith's character) pursuit of happiness eventually becomes interchangeable with his pursuit of money.[28]

In C. S. Lewis's *The Screwtape Letters*, we get to listen in on the upside-down, and therefore profoundly demonic, advice that Screwtape gives to Wormwood about the evil possibilities of wealth, prestige, and power over human lives.

> Prosperity knits people to the world. We feel that we are "finding our place in it," while really it is finding its place in

us. Our increasing reputation, our widening circle of acquain-
tances, our sense of importance, and the growing pressure
of absorbing and agreeable work build up in us a sense of
really being at home on Earth, which is just as we want. You
will notice that the young are generally less unwilling to die
than the middle-aged and the old.[29]

This should alert us to the dangers of giving our hearts
to lesser things. Money, things, and status, despite what our
culture might say, are clearly not the answers to a life of
peace and contentment—in fact, they are very much part of
the problem. The Beatitudes portray another type of truth
to us. Many people live out the meaning of the Beatitudes
daily and are genuinely happy as a result. People living in
today's Western society—thought to have everything—are
over-indulged, over-entertained, and yet are too often the most
depressed, bored, anxious generation of all time. A. W. Tozer
says, "The blessed ones who possess the Kingdom are they
who have repudiated every external thing and have rooted
from their hearts all sense of possessing. . . . This is what the
word 'poor' as Christ used it actually means. These blessed
poor are no longer slaves to the tyranny of things."[30]

When we put the Beatitudes into the context of the radical
Sermon on the Mount (Matthew 5–7), the truly revolutionary character of the untamed Messiah's way comes to the
forefront. If we simply lived this little section of New Testament Scripture out, we would literally change the world. Ap-
proximately 30 percent of the world's population identifies
itself as Christian. Think about it—what if 30 percent of
the world's people simply took the Sermon on the Mount
seriously and applied it to life? What do you think would
happen? Or if that seems too far-fetched, know that over
50 percent of Americans claim to believe in Jesus. What if
50 percent of America took Jesus with utmost seriousness
and sought to live out his message faithfully? What do you
think would happen? If Jesus could turn the world upside

down (the right way up) through the Twelve and the Seventy, what could we do with one hundred fifty million madcap Americans?!

Authentic missional Christianity not only reclaims and redeems culture through incarnational engagement as Jesus did, but also imperils the culture in which it manifests itself, in exactly the same way the early disciples did to the Roman Empire. When we experience deep liberation from idols by the King, we become aware that we do not have to squander and dissipate our lives on things that don't matter. Following Jesus in the power of the Spirit, we are freed to be the good news to a world around us captive to sin. We can live with no regrets knowing that in seeking first the rule of God, all things are ours.

We'll let U2's Bono have the last word here: "In order to serve our world, we must betray it."

Suggested Practices

- *Watch* The Matrix *series again*: Movies, especially sci-fi, tend to contain powerful critiques of culture and act as warnings to us by suggesting a future that is all too possible. In many ways, this is the function of biblical eschatology (doctrine of the end times).
- *Be generous until it hurts*: Generosity is one of the most powerful ways to break the power of money in our lives and (re)introduce grace into the equation.
- *Humble yourselves*: The incarnation of God in Jesus is a powerful demonstration of the truth that *God is humble*. Also, we learn from this that we too are called to a life that is "downwardly mobile"—instead of the so-called "upwardly mobile" way of the world. Status anxiety arises from the constant comparisons we make between ourselves and others. To overcome this toxic aspect of culture, practice the Beatitudes.

- *Simplify your life*: We can honestly live with a lot less "stuff" in our lives. Actually, there is a worldwide movement to downgrade our lifestyles called "The Manifesto for Wellbeing." Aspects of it include doing meaningful work (not just money-related), limiting work hours to thirty-five-hour weeks, spending more quality time with the children, discouraging materialism, promoting responsible advertising, building communities and relationships, and more. Check it out on http://www.wellbeingmanifesto.net/. Another one to look at is the Advent Conspiracy: http://www.adventconspiracy.org/hope/.
- *No advertising*: Cut back on exposure to desire-producing advertising. Limit the TV or, even more radically, practice a "TV fast" for some period of time. If it doesn't kill you, it's going to make you a whole lot better.

Discussion Starters

1. "If everyone lives roughly the same lies about the same things, then there is no one to call them lies; they jointly establish their own sanity and call themselves normal" (Ernest Becker). Is this true? If so, how can we avoid collective deception, especially as it relates to middle-class values?
2. What can the story of Jennifer (and people like her) in the text box found on page 126 teach us about ourselves?
3. How has consumerism damaged you, your church, and your Christian witness in the world?
4. Is money a neutral force in your life? Discuss how much of your life revolves around acquiring it and what effects it has on you, your family, your church, and your church's mission.

5. What would a perfect human existence look like? What can you do now to try to make this happen?

6. Read Dave Andrews's *Plan Be: Be the Change You Want to See in the World*. This is a wonderful book on the Beatitudes about changing ourselves and our worlds. See his great website for more information and study guide/resources: http://wecan.be/.

5

the church that jesus built

We argue that the political task of Christians is to be the Church rather than to transform the world. . . . The Church doesn't *have* a social strategy; the Church *is* a social strategy.

—Stanley Hauerwas

It is easy to think that we love an abstract, spiritualized, de-historicized Church just as it is easy to love abstract, spiritualized, de-historicized people. In truth to love abstractions is not to love at all; it is but a sentimental attachment to our own whimsies.

—Richard J. Neuhaus

The Church is nothing but a section of humanity in which Christ has truly taken form.

—Dietrich Bonhoeffer

Every believer a church planter, every church a church-planting church" is one of the most powerful mantras to come out of the Chinese Underground Church in recent history. It's a great slogan, not simply because it is the key to unlocking a people movement, but because it faithfully captures and communicates the incredible potential that is contained in every individual disciple—it legitimizes the fact that every believer is an agent of the King and therefore has the potential for world transformation in him or her. Dig deep into these few words and you will find that the full potencies of the church that Jesus built are actually coded into it. As a seed contains the full potential of the tree, so the tree contains the full potential of the forest. But it's all there in the seed in the first place. Likewise, as a spark contains the full potential of the flame, so the flame contains the potential of the forest fire. But it's all contained in the spark. Recognizing the world-transforming power of the people of God is essential to becoming a missional church again in the West.

If you lived in China and came to know Jesus through this particular movement, you would be told before you committed your life to Christ that it is expected that *little ol' you* will one day have the privilege of starting and leading a community of faith (usually not big or complex), and that this will be one of the joys and privileges that come with following Jesus. It is also expected that the church will itself plant many other churches in its lifetime—however long that might be. In other words, it is expected that there is actually a potential movement in every believer. Disciples are designed to change their world—that's why Jesus could entrust the gospel to the first disciples, knowing the inevitability of the message itself.

This all sounds pretty radical to those of us whose idea of church is captivated by an institutionally stylized way of seeing ourselves. In fact, we believe that this "scripting" actually inhibits us from becoming the untamed Jesus revolution we are made to be.[1] Implicit in the slogan above is the core belief that everyone, young and old, male and female, spiritually mature and immature, rich and poor—*everyone*—gets to play a role in the unfolding drama of the church as Jesus designed it to be. This of course raises many serious questions about how we in the West have become a domesticated (and domesticating) institution, even though we live by the same gospel under the rule of the same Lord as our Chinese brothers and sisters. Surely we carry the same potential in ourselves and in our communities as our Chinese counterparts. What are the obstacles that stop us from becoming a dynamic movement? What's the difference?

In this chapter we want to address a number of issues related to our understanding of the church. Now, we fully recognize that countless books have been written on ecclesiology (the doctrine of the church) and we don't want to claim too much in one single chapter. It is not our intention to say all that there is to say about the one true church (if there is one), nor do we wish to idealize it. The church *is* what it is. What we want to do is perhaps expose a few glitches in our understanding that hold us back from becoming the collection of untamed disciples that Jesus calls us to be.

The Community for Me

Of all the ways culture influences the church, nothing has had more of an impact on us than that of a consumerist vision of society. As we stated in the previous chapter, in some way or another we have all been impacted by the powerful experience of a society that is preoccupied with the acquisition of consumer goods. From good old Santa Claus (a religious symbol co-opted to disciple children in thoroughgoing materialism from early childhood on) to the complete ubiquity of niche marketing, we are daily being nurtured in the worldview generated by late capitalism of the twenty-first century—*consumerism*. It's a genuine *-ism* because it implies that more than just basic needs are being met. Twenty-first-century consumerism is much more a generator of *wants* than it is a fulfiller of basic human *needs*. And it must do this to keep the massive engines of the global economy running—if they stop, the whole thing will come collapsing down on our heads.

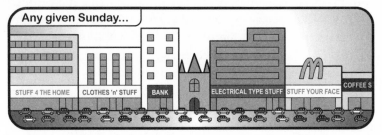

Any given Sunday...

STUFF 4 THE HOME   CLOTHES 'n' STUFF   BANK   ELECTRICAL TYPE STUFF   STUFF YOUR FACE   COFFEE S

. . . there are plenty of places where you can go and worship.

It is a religious scripting born of a powerful economic system. As we have already seen, consumerism exhibits the hallmarks of a very virile meta-spirituality offering meaning, identity, purpose, and belonging to its various devotees. Make no mistake, we are all being discipled into "the faith" many times a day and throughout our lives by a combination of trillion-dollar advertising budgets with the delivery of immediate reward for good behavior (read "purchases"). It is, for all intents and purposes, a disciple-making system of its own—and a powerful one at that.

The church, far from being immune, has drunk deeply from its wells. In fact, we have pretty much designed contemporary expressions of church around consumer values. It's not all bad. In many ways this is a legitimate expression of the contextualization of the church. But when attempts at contextualization concede too much to the culture and distort the fundamental beliefs and practices that shape us, then we must challenge it.

This radically affects discipleship. The implicit message church members get from a church that adopts a consumer-driven model (with marketing and all) is that they are essentially discerning consumers and that the local church is

138

a vendor of religious goods and services. No longer is the church a disciple-making medium operating under the Great Commission; rather, the church is viewed as existing to serve my spiritual needs, and if it doesn't fulfill them according to my particular tastes, then I simply find one that does. In this case, the community exists for me, not me for the community.

Viewed from the perspective of untamed discipleship, something is seriously wrong with that equation. This is very personal for us: in *The Forgotten Ways*, Alan tells the story of how at one point in our life together at South it dawned upon us that in focusing on creating cool, experimental worship and cultivating an embracing community with a party-like atmosphere, we had all but missed the point of making disciples. We had just created more fussy consumers.[2] As previously mentioned, the Willow Creek Association came up with a similar conclusion in their findings based on massive research across the system. In *Reveal*, the courageous book that documents their findings, they confess that for all the sexiness of seeker worship and its effectiveness in evangelism, it basically has failed to make mature disciples of Jesus.[3] This is no small confession from the leading church in the seeker-sensitive movement—we *must* take notice.

It's as though the church-as-vendor has become a giant feeding trough where largely capable, middle-class people come to eat their fill. Actually, many don't even eat for themselves; they come to "get fed"! The very language of "getting fed" at church betrays the fact that many attendees are not disciples at all, but rather passive (and somewhat dependent) consumers. Want to test this? Simply stop preaching every Sunday for six weeks, or close down the children's ministry, or stop some other "service" or another, even temporarily, and see what happens. Attendance and tithing will drop immediately. Disciples tithe to the Lord; consumers are merely paying for services. There is a world of difference between the two. Thinking of the church as some sort of feeder is an obstacle to discipleship that must be overcome if we want to be untamed Christians.

We remember many years ago hearing prominent discipleship-proponent Bill Hull compare the process of discipleship with that of being a child and growing up. It's a great metaphor. For instance, when we are babies, it is appropriate to get fed, as one clearly cannot feed oneself. But as we mature, we learn to feed ourselves, and eventually we learn to cook and feed others. But this is not what we find happening in many churches. In fact, if we had to be honest with ourselves, the systems we have developed actually create dependencies. We are not helping people grow up into the type of disciples that will change the world in which they live, and the clergy and religious professionals who maintain this are entirely complicit. The word in social psychology is *co-dependent*! Imagine this: if a mother was still breast feeding her ten-year-old child, we would think something was wrong (mainly with mom in this case), but if the child was twenty years old, then the two of them would probably be jailed or committed to the psych ward!

We think this is nothing less than a faulty (and perhaps an overly *pastoral*) view of the church that is being perpetuated here, and it needs some serious correction. We don't say this to be mean or disparaging of the sincere ministries of many wonderful people, but it is wrong to create and foster dependent consumers when we should be about disciple making. It has to be said, or else we will simply perpetuate the situation. And we believe part of the problem stems from the dangerous (and profoundly false) division between the clergy and "laity," which creates a professional and amateur Christian class.

We need to stop thinking of the church as service provider, as a consumable product, as something that exists for my (and by extension, my family's) personal benefit. Rather, we must move from the-community-for-me to me-for-the-community.

Jesus is clear about this; it is in loving that we are loved, and in giving that we will receive.

MORE!

Conversion Is Commission

At South we took the "priesthood of all believers" (that every person is a minister and needs to be released as such) seriously.[4] This didn't mean that our community always lived this out, but it was a value we tried to live by (and at times used humor to reinforce). In order to drive this point home, one Sunday morning, as our community arrived for our gathering, we greeted each person at the door and handed them a two-inch-wide strip of white flexible card and a fastener. Many looked puzzled but decided to play along, wondering just what we were up to. A short time after the service began, Al asked everybody to stand up and fasten the white strip around their necks. He then proceeded to lead the whole church through an ordination ceremony. It wasn't quite what people were expecting, but that morning each and every person gathered at South was officially ordained into the ministry of Jesus. Once they were all ordained, they could dispose of the symbolic (and very unnecessary) dog collars and just live out their commission.

When we look at the early church, the Chinese Underground Church, and *every* other Jesus movement that has had significant impact in its time and place, we are confronted

141

with the reality of a people movement where everyone is regarded as a significant agent of the King and is encouraged to find their place in the unfolding of the movement. In other words, in the church that Jesus built, *everyone* gets to play! For these movements, a person's conversion *is* their commission into ministry, and this is exactly the way Jesus designed his church to be. Disciples simply *are* ministers—they are created that way.

Contrast this notion that everyone is engaged in ministry with a recent, somewhat generic experience when we visited a relatively new church plant where the whole service was basically a one-man show. The pastor opened the service with announcements and prayer, then handed it over to the worship leader to sing the few ever-present Hillsong hits. Then it was handed back to the pastor for the sermon, offering, and closing prayer. Now, sadly, this picture isn't an unfamiliar one, but the tragedy here was that it was a new church plant! These guys had an opportunity to do things differently, to be more inclusive, to break away from what we all surely recognize as an outdated model of church. We don't want to sound harsh here, and perhaps our response is more about style and cultural differences. But we fear it at least has something to do with theological deficiencies in the common understanding of church, worship, and discipleship.

Recently when speaking at a conference engaging the issue of becoming a missional church, Alan was politely dancing around the idea of the priesthood of all believers, its significance for movements, and how ordination might be problematic. The denominational leader, being a good, forthright Canadian, sprang up and loudly invited Alan to take the gloves off and just say it as it is. To which Alan said, slightly tongue in cheek, "OK then, I really think that ordination is a doctrine of devils!" Once the laughter subsided, Alan delved into why this actually had some real truth to it. The idea that ordination as we commonly practice it is demonic in source was not simply suggested for dramatic effect. If one wanted to destroy the sheer transformative power of the body of Christ as a people movement, then the creation of the clergy-laity divide is nothing less than a stroke of demonic genius. One of the most catastrophic—heinous is not too strong a word—barriers to being a truly untamed church full of authentic disciples lies in the suppression of one of the most potent of Christian truths about the church—the priesthood of all believers.

It is interesting that although Martin Luther rediscovered this potent aspect of the New Testament teaching—the priesthood of all believers—as soon as the truth of it began to leak out to the peasants, he quickly hid it again because he feared losing control of "his reformation."[5] Instead of backing the people, he opted for the age-old Christendom embrace with the state and called in the prince and his troops to quash the peasants' uprising. This was his lowest moment. And by and large, for Protestants and Catholics, it has remained a mere doctrine ever since. Every now and again it pops up—we would argue that it is an aspect of every revival and renewal of the church—only to be suppressed again by the rise of religious professionalism (clericalism). If we are going to answer the challenge of our time, we are simply going to have to recover this untamed piece of New Testament truth again.

We suggest that there have to be several shifts for this to take place in the local church.

From "minister" to ministry team

In movements it is important to distribute power and function to the outermost level. As described above, one of the biggest shifts needed is to de-professionalize the ministry/clergy class and give ministry back to the people of God. This does not mean that we do not have leaders: any movement that makes any impact has definite leadership. They simply don't confuse leadership with ministry. Not all are leaders, but all are ministers. Leadership is a calling within a calling.[6]

From pastoral team to APEST team

We believe it is absolutely critical to broaden our concept of ministry from the traditional pastor-teacher models to at least the fivefold understanding of ministry giftings described in Ephesians 4:1–16 (apostles, prophets, evangelists, pastors/shepherds, and teachers, hence the acronym APEST). This does not diminish the irreplaceable roles shepherds and teachers play in the life of the church,

> We highly recommend that you and your community look into doing the APEST test, which will help people understand their multi-layered ministry styles and get needed feedback and accountability from the group. Go to www.apest.org.

but indicates that if we want an untamed, missional Christianity, we simply have to embrace a more missional form of ministry as well. The shepherd and teacher are basically maintenance ministers—they maintain health in an existing community. What is needed for missional impact beyond the congregation are the more generative ministries associated with the apostolic, prophetic, and evangelistic giftings. When we restructured our ministry at South along these lines, it unleashed elemental spiritual energies in our church.[7]

One of the most revolutionary aspects of the Ephesians 4 text is that it is not a leadership text—it is a text about the ministry of the church! This is another dimension of the

priesthood of all believers. Look at it—it is a circular let-
ter written to the entire church. Leadership is implicit, not
explicit, in the text. One of the most potent things any community can do is to re-legitimize the Ephesians 4 ministries
and help develop people in their various ministries, in other
words, grow them from undeveloped ministers into mature,
Christlike leaders.

From men of God to people of God

One of the biggest hindrances to the untamed discipleship
of all of God's people is the binding of ministry and leadership to the role of men. Not only are many of our problems
directly created by the false and profoundly unbiblical category of ordination as described above, but we have effectively cauterized more than half the ministry of the body of
Christ. Felicity Dale, one of the global leaders of the house
church movement, speaks of the American church as being
hemiplegic—a condition where one half of a person's body
is paralyzed. In other words, we work with only one arm,
one leg, one eye, and so on. She
rightfully says that the church
in America will never reach its
fullest potential unless it takes
seriously the women's issue.[8]
The whole body needs to be released in order to fulfill God's
purposes.

It's interesting to note that
in just about every outbreak of
a missional church movement
in history, women have played
a critical and up-front role.
Around 65 percent of the leaders of the church in China are
women! It is similar in the exploding people movements of
India at the moment. The early (pre-Constantinian) church
was free from the issue we so struggle with, as were the

> **The Greater Sin**
>
> We remember exceptional church leader and friend Mike Breen once saying something like this: "How-ever one might understand the controversial texts in Paul's writings regarding the place of women in ministry, the greater sin by far is to relegate women to the role of being secondary agents in the kingdom." We couldn't agree more.

Wesleyan revivals, the Salvation Army, the Azusa Street phenomenon that launched Pentecostalism, the Jesus People, and so it goes. Interestingly, God doesn't appear to have the same hang-ups certain sections of our church currently have regarding women's involvement in official church ministry. It's time to find our way beyond the current impasse and recognize that God gives women equal status and agency in his kingdom.

As mentioned in the introduction, ministry for us has always been a partnership. Both of us felt a clear call to serve God with our lives; for us it was never about one of us being called into the ministry and the other one "supporting" them in it. We represent God far better together than we ever could apart.

Undercover Discipling!

Another strong paradigm we need to break down is that discipling is limited to Christians within the context of the church, and performed by a select few. The Great Commission tells us that each and every one of us is to engage in the role of discipling the nations—it is our biblical mandate.

> And Jesus came to them and said, "All authority in heaven and on earth has been given to me. Therefore go and make disciples of all nations, baptizing them in the name of the Father and of the Son and of the Holy Spirit, and teaching them to obey everything I have commanded you. And surely I am with you always, to the very end of the age." (Matt. 28:18–20)

This means first that all of us are called to disciple others—discipling is the task of *every* Christian. Second, it means discipleship is not just for those who have accepted Jesus as their Lord and Savior—it's for everyone! We believe it a great mistake to restrict discipling to just Christians and keep it within the confines of the Christian community. We as believers are called to disciple everyone who comes into our orbit of influence—it's that simple.

If each believer understood discipleship in this way and then took their biblical mandate seriously, we would have lots of people growing and becoming more and more like Jesus—and hopefully at some point coming under his lordship. It's not our role to convert them, but to disciple them. Conversion is God's business. How much better would the world be? And the fun thing is that in many cases those who haven't yet accepted Jesus as Lord may have no idea that they are being discipled!

We so easily forget that the role of the church is to form what we call "little Jesuses." C. S. Lewis rightly reminds us of this fact.

> It is easy to think that the Church has a lot of different objects—education, buildings, missions, holding services. . . . [But] the Church exists for nothing else but to draw men into Christ, to make them into little Christs. If they are not doing that, all the cathedrals, clergy, missions, sermons, even the Bible itself, are simply a waste of time. God became man for no other purpose. It is even doubtful, you know, whether the whole universe was created for any other purpose. It says in the Bible that the whole universe was made for Christ and that everything is to be gathered together in Him.[9]

If Lewis is right that the whole universe was made for Christ and everything is to be gathered together in him, then the Great Commission is not about "evangelism" as we have come to understand it—that is, simply telling people what Jesus has done for them and leaving it at that. It is not just about the transfer of vital information, a data download, but rather the transfer of the very life of Christ through the medium and message of our own discipleship. It is about bringing people closer to Jesus and teaching them his ways. It is about loving people and exposing them to the grace and wonder of God's heart, helping them see and experience the values of the kingdom and calling forth those values that may lie dormant in their own hearts and lives. It is about letting the beauty of Jesus and his kingdom come through. Let's tease this out with a couple of examples.

"Stitch 'n' Bitch"

The women in our community house decided to gather together a number of non-Christian colleagues in order to build relationships, love on them, and ultimately, over time, help them become more like Jesus (undercover discipling). So we set up what we called a "Stitch 'n' Bitch" night. This was simply a time when women came together to knit and connect with each other. Well, it was a great hit, with heaps of women joining in. One of the first things we established with the group was that the night wasn't going to just be about us, that we needed to also somehow serve our community. As our home was located in the red-light district and it was the middle of winter, we decided to start by knitting scarves, one for ourselves and one for the working girls who were freezing out on the streets. Of course, we had to make sure they were more sexy than what our own grandmas would knit! Over time, our projects included cooking for people in a trailer park, doing up Christmas packs for the homeless, and becoming involved in the Make Poverty History campaign.

Our intention with these women was ultimately for them to know Jesus. So we began to disciple them. Did they know we were doing that? Absolutely not—I doubt they would have come at all if they did. Rather, our discipling of them was to expose them to the values of the kingdom and the heart of Jesus for the outcast. These women knew that we were believers, but we never abused our relationship with them by imposing our views or inappropriately "evangelizing" them in the narrow understanding of this term. We exposed their

148

hearts to the issues of injustice and serving others, and helped put the poor on their radar. Most of these women started as professional women concerned with becoming affluent, getting bigger and better homes, and living more comfortable lifestyles. Discipling for them meant that over time they began to look more like Jesus by embracing values that were more in line with the kingdom, and as this transformation began questions about God and Jesus started taking place.

"Mentoring" Jack

Imagine this: you know your neighbor Jack, at least enough to be chummy with him. Taking this discipleship approach, you might begin the journey by saying, "You know, Jack, we get along just fine, but I have been thinking. I believe part of the reason for my life is to make yours a whole lot better. I have some skills in developing people. How about I invest some time into helping you achieve your greatest dreams?" If Jack says, "Sure, lets give it a go" (people like Jack pay up to a thousand dollars an hour for good life-coaching), what will happen is that we will start sharing the events, people, stories, and dreams that have come together to make Jack what he is today. Eventually, the dreaming gets beyond the red Ferrari, meaning will be shared at a deeper level, and Jack will begin to communicate his deepest longings, hurts, fears, and hopes. If all goes well, God does "his thing" on Jack, and he becomes a believer. We suggest that we just continue the process of discipleship: the process does not change even though the content will.

We want to propose that this be taken with the utmost seriousness: put aside your prevailing understandings of evangelism and simply (re)adopt the Great Commission as your guide. We suggest that we should all simply disciple people everywhere. And we should see discipleship as a process, illustrated above—including pre-conversion discipleship and, if God does his thing, post-conversion discipleship. The person's salvation is God's business; our part in it is to be a "little Jesus" that devotes significant time and commitment to making disciples of whoever wants to go on the journey with us. Of course it's about Jesus, and we will get to share the saving message of Jesus along the way, but we need to reframe evangelism within the context of discipleship. That's where it belongs in the Bible (read the Great Commission again)! If we fail to take this seriously, then discipleship just drops off the agenda, we become preachy Bible pushers, and the church actually forgets its own mandate.

Now, before you dismiss this as a tad weird for your liking, we suggest that in fact this was precisely the case with Jesus and his followers. The question scholars argue over is when the disciples were actually "born again." Some say John 20:22, where Jesus breathes the Spirit on them, and others say that it was actually at Pentecost (Acts 2). None would say before that! So, even "the Twelve" (and "the Seventy") were all what we would call "pre-conversion disciples." What is more, the standard practice in the church in its first three centuries was that people had to prove their adherence to Jesus in discipleship before they were allowed to become part of the church! This was the original purpose of the catechisms.[10] In other words, discipleship started long before a person became a convert. In movements that change the world, discipleship is an ethos—a way of life—not just an optional extra for the more dedicated Christians. That we have somehow managed to build a church without discipleship is anathema to authentic Christian faith.

Actually, this squares pretty nicely with what evangelism gurus call the Engels Scale, which acknowledges that there is a definite process people undergo in coming to faith and growing in discipleship. It will look something like the following continuum, ranging from −6 to +6:

- −6   Awareness of supreme being
- −5   Initial awareness of gospel
- −4   Positive attitude toward gospel
- −3   Personal problem recognition
- −2   Decision to act
- −1   Repentance and faith in Christ
- **New birth in Christ**
- +1   Post-decision evaluation
- +2   Incorporation into Body
- +3   Growth in Jesus
- +4   Communion with God
- +5   Stewardship
- +6   Reproduction

Reframing mission and evangelism around discipleship makes space for long-term, authentically loving relationships with the various people in our lives. This in turn will give credibility to our message and space for real and meaningful friendships—something we are not always known for. And hey, if everyone did this with just two or three people in a lifetime (in a "pay-it-forward"-style movement), we would actually get the job done in one generation!

Wells and Fences

Another way we can become a disciple-making community is by reframing church to include pre-conversion disciples on the journey. In *The Shaping of Things to Come*, Alan and Michael Frost discuss the idea of social set theory (the theory of social dynamics, or how and why people gather together as they do) by illustrating it with a practice in farming.[11] In some farming communities, the farmers might build fences around their properties to keep their livestock in and the livestock of neighboring farms out. But in rural communities, where farms or ranches cover an enormous geographic area, fencing the property is out of the question. In our home of Australia, ranches (called stations) are so vast that fences are simply not a viable way of keeping the animals together. Under these conditions, a farmer has to sink a bore and create a well, a precious water supply in the outback. It is assumed that livestock, though they will stray, will never roam too far from the well, lest they die. As long as there is a supply of clean water, the livestock will remain close by.

In social set theory, the two main reasons people organize and/or gather are the following: the closed, or bounded, set, and the open, or centered, set.

The bounded set

The closed, or bounded, set describes a social system that has clearly delineated boundaries but no strong ideological center. It is therefore hard at the edges and soft at the center. In this type of church, it is clear who is "in" and who is "out" based primarily on a well-defined boundary—usually moral and cultural (for example, dress and language) as well

Closed (or Bounded) Set

as theological. Viewed in this light, most established institutions, including denominational systems, are clearly bounded sets.

The centered set

Then there are open, or centered, sets. In many ways, these are the exact opposite of the bounded ones. They have a very clear ideology and vision at the center, but have no real boundaries that people have to cross in order to join. This organization is therefore hard at the center and soft at the edges. It is more of an open invitation to join on the basis of vision and values. We propose that it offers us a far more missional, and in many ways a far more biblical, way of being the church that Jesus built. To use the ranch example above, churches that see themselves as a centered set recognize that Jesus is Lord at the heart of the community and that the gospel is so refreshing that, like a well in the Australian outback, people who are thirsty will not stray too far from it.

Conceiving church as an open set engenders a truly Christ-centered approach to holding together, unlike the more standard religious organizations with their theological and cultural boundaries and formulas developed to keep certain people in and others out. Rather than seeing people as Christian or non-Christian, as "in" or "out,"

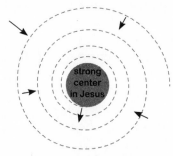

Open (or Centered) Set

153

we would see people by the degree of distance they are from the center. In this way, we see people as Christian, not-yet-Christian, and somewhere on the path toward (or away from) Jesus in discipleship. It allows us to see anyone who identifies with the movement as being somewhere on the journey of discipleship. And because of this, we can acknowledge the contribution of not-yet-Christians to the Christian community.

Clearly Jesus's faith community was a centered set, with himself at the center and all sorts of weird and wonderful people in his orbit—some far, some close, others edging closer, still others moving away. Clearly some disciples are closer to the center than others (Peter, James, and John), and at least one disciple drew away from the center (Judas). The Gospels speak of faith communities varying from twelve to one hundred twenty, and make explicit reference to a number of women who traveled with Jesus. It seems that the community of Christ was not as simple as thirteen guys roaming the countryside. There was a rich intersection of relationships, with some nearer the center and others farther away, but all were openly invited to join in the kingdom-building enterprise. In many ways, this kind of movement allows for a sense of belonging before believing.

Belonging before believing

At South, adopting a more centered-set approach to being the people of God meant we took seriously the whole concept of *belonging before believing*: people didn't need to agree with us on the finer points of theology in order to belong. They were invited into a journey that led to Jesus. The closer people would get to Jesus, the more they were pulled into his orbit, and eventually into conversion. The closer people get to Jesus, the more likely they are to be formed into disciples. Viewed from "the side," a centered-set church, operating as a community of disciples, calls people into greater commitment to Jesus (see diagram below).

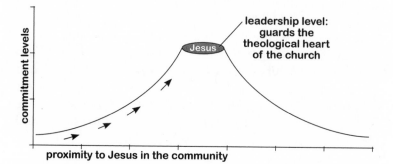

Divergent ideology or behavior didn't necessarily exclude people from the family (although in some rare cases, church discipline was necessary, mainly because of some sort of predatory behavior—sexual, theological, or otherwise). We operated from the simple basis that if people wanted to hang around a bunch of Christians, then in most cases it was because they found something attractive about the Jesus factor in us. We overcame our anxieties about the stranger by living out the belief that "greater is he that is in you, than he that is in the world" (1 John 4:4 KJV), and that we were like yeast in the dough.

A case in point was when an openly gay man named Adam, a practicing wiccan, became part of our community. While he was resistant to Christianity, he was a deeply spiritual man and would show up at our church gatherings every now and again. One Sunday morning Deb was asking for volunteers to help with the church newsletter and, much to her surprise, he volunteered. Conflicted over what to do, Deb tried to stay true to the "centered set" approach and accepted his offer. This meant he came in to use the church computer every Tuesday, where he compiled the community news as well as other bits of creative writing. He saw himself as a writer-poet and really did develop the newsletter significantly. Over time, through hanging out and working with us, Adam came to see the great beauty of Jesus and wrote the most amazing poem about how he identified with the sufferings of Christ.

Adopting a "centered set" approach and allowing people like Adam to belong before they believe is certainly risky, but if we lock them out of our lives because of their lifestyles then they may never come to know Jesus. It is us who are meant to shine the light of Christ to this dark and lost world. We have allowed fear to dominate and our need for safety and security to keep the world at a safe distance.

Letting go of control

We found that one trick of being an open-set missional church is getting over our need to control people and processes, and to instead open the way for people to meet with Jesus in the community. One way to do this is simply to see ourselves as priests (1 Peter 2:9). Consistent with what priests ought to do, our role is to mediate the true knowledge of God and maintain the God relationship. Practically, it means that our function is to introduce others to a right understanding of God. This does not mean that we legislate morality in the name of Jesus—our job is to free people, not to bind them up with religious complexities.

We ourselves experienced freedom from control-freakery by renovating our idea of priesthood. We needed to, because much of our early ministry involved working with street prostitutes and the drug-addicted—people whose lives were normally out of control. Most of these people were working the streets not because they thought it was a good career, but because of horrific life circumstances exacerbated by drug addiction. This meant that their lives were utterly broken and chaotic.

In the beginning of our ministry, we mistakenly saw it as our role to take control of their lives—to make right choices on their behalf—hoping that it would turn their lives around. In almost every case this failed. Deliverance came to us when it dawned on us that it was not our role to control people, but rather to bring them into an authentic relationship with God. He would do all the changing that was needed. When we played the role of the Holy Spirit, we inevitably bungled it. It was liberating indeed to realize he was a whole lot better at it than we could possibly be. The disciple is a servant-priest, and our role is to introduce people to Jesus and Jesus to the people, and then, as quickly as possible, move out of the way.

Open-set communion

One of the ways we symbolized the idea of the centered set was by having an openness about the way we did communion. For us an "open" table was extremely important: if people wanted access to God through partaking in the breaking of the bread, then who were we to stop them? Our communion table became a table of healing where the broken could come, sit, and commune with God and others. For many years our big, square, purple table was set up in the middle of our gathering, symbolizing Jesus as our center rather than the band or the pulpit. On it sat several large loaves of bread, bottled wine, and grape juice. The community members were encouraged to come alone in their own time, or with someone else, and meet with God.

We have some deeply moving memories of times around the communion table. One such memory for Deb is a mental snapshot of the incredible diversity present around the table. On one particular day, sitting at the table breaking bread was a lady who had known Jesus her whole life. She was our oldest member, then in her eighties, and dressed in her lawn bowling outfit. Right next to her sat a naughty, very gay Jewish man with HIV-AIDS who was curious about Jesus. There were three others present—one married woman with four children currently going through a divorce, a speech pathologist who worked at a local hospital, and a former exotic dancer who had found Jesus in a bar. What a symbol of the broken, diverse body of Christ.

157

Diverse-city

One final point we wish to make about faulty views of church is one many of us entertain: that the church is meant to be a high-conformity community. While none of us would consciously believe this, the way the majority of our communities are configured show this to be the case. It seems to us that the more religious we get, the more exclusive we tend to become. But the gospel undermines religion; it is for the world, and it won't be narrowed down for our own private concerns. God wants to be all inclusive.

We have recently reread the book of Acts and noticed that it didn't take long for the church to close in on itself, to lose its heart for mission beyond its cultural boundaries—boundaries which, left to their own devices, would get narrower and narrower. The church in Jerusalem quickly forgot the Great Commission to include the nations and needed a kick in the pants to get them out of their self-enclosed concerns (Acts 15). Peter had to have a direct vision from heaven for him to be able to grasp the fact implicit in the death of Christ: table fellowship can take place between the "clean" and the "unclean" (Acts 10:1–23). And Paul had a pretty direct confrontation with the religious "heavies" to ensure that the Gentiles were equal members of God's household and didn't need to submit to Jewish ritual to be included. It seems that the great ingathering of the nations is constantly being hindered by people with a sinful tendency to close ranks, thus marginalizing "outsiders" and people different from ourselves.

But when it does this, the church cannot resist becoming a high-conformity, culturally closed, and ultimately oppressive clique. The church (both local and universal) is meant to be a motley collection of imperfect people included in the family of God by means of God's sheer grace (1 Cor. 1:26–31; 6:9–11; Ephesians 2). Dr. Seuss captures the hilarious variety that should make up God's church when he says in *One Fish,*

Two Fish, Red Fish, Blue Fish, "From there to here, from here to there, funny things are everywhere."

What we see in the event of the incarnation, that is, in the earthly life and ministry of Jesus, is a remarkable and unsettling cultural freedom. The incarnational character of the church's mission means that the expanding church will also be wonderfully diverse. Our unity must be centered in Jesus Christ, our Lord and Savior. But the unity of Christian witness must never be defined as organizational or cultural uniformity.

Sadly, it wasn't.

The church that Jesus built was filled with spiritual desperados. And no church genuinely following the untamed way of Jesus could be a neat and tidy experience. Desperate people are rude, frantic, reckless, focused, and uncompromising in their desire to get what they want (Matt. 11:12). Someone who is desperate will crash through the veil of niceness. Mike Yaconelli reminds us, "The New Testament is filled with desperate people, people who barged into private dinners, screamed at Jesus until they had his attention, or destroyed the roof of someone's house to get to him. People who are desperate for spirituality very seldom worry about the mess they make on their way to be with Jesus."[12] The church is meant to be one, holy, and, we would add, *messy.*

The untamed, love-revolution movement Jesus started was never meant to be a "nice," high-conformity, culturally uniform collective like "The Borg," that all-assimilating being in the *Star Trek* series. (Remember their slogan? "Resistance is futile; you *will* be assimilated.") If we are to be genuinely untamed followers of Jesus, we will be holy nonconformists, captured by a vision of the world that will be when the kingdom of God is finally fulfilled.

If we truly follow Jesus, we will reject any status quo that has not fully adopted the vision of the kingdom of God—and which human situation has? Here is a vision of the church worth striving for! Christianity at its best has always been the major agent of change by rejecting the existing state of affairs in pursuit of something much holier. Theologian Richard Neuhaus is right to make the necessary connection with the church and the kingdom of God when he suggests that "our restless discontent should not [necessarily] be over the distance between ourselves and the first century Church but over the distance between ourselves and the Kingdom of God to which the Church then and now is the witness."[13] The kingdom of God "maddens" us with a vision of what God's agenda is for his world—and it is therefore the driving agenda of the church.

We end this chapter with a powerful quote from missiologist Darrel Guder:

> In all of his relationships, Jesus broke through the boundaries of likes and dislikes, social proprietary and religious acceptability, that characterized Palestinian society in the first century. Incarnational witness, as it was practiced by Jesus, challenged the accepted patterns of interpersonal relationships and community formation. It began with Jesus' own roots in Galilee, which marked him as a man from the margins. He was not identified with the religiously prominent and respected circles of his day. He came "from the wrong side of the tracks". . . . His choice of disciples continued the pattern of incarnational reversion of the acceptable structures of society. He called people to follow him who were ritually unclean (fishermen), nationally suspect (publicans), and politically dubious (zealots). He demonstrated the revolutionary char-

acter of the in-breaking reign of God by reaching out and touching lepers, by conversing publicly with women, healing the children of Gentiles, allowing prostitutes to touch him, and going to parties with acknowledged con men. The church he founded continued this revolutionary pattern of incarnational witness, although it struggled with the challenges it represented. The Jerusalem church had to be convinced that Samaritans could really become followers of Jesus. Philip was led to evangelize a eunuch, who could never have joined in the ritual worship of the Temple community in Jerusalem. . . . From very early on, however, it was clear that the church was to challenge the world as a community in which there was "no longer Jew or Greek, slave or free, male and female; for all of you are one in Christ Jesus" (Galatians 3:28).[14]

Suggested Practices

- *Adopt a freak*: Often, those seen as social misfits can give real insight to our own cultural narrowness and help us see God in a bigger way. One of the simple ways we can reach beyond our own cultural cliques and grow in awareness of the other is to begin to really encounter people we normally would not engage with.
- *Think about this statement*: "Every disciple carries within themselves the potential for world transformation." Try and see yourself and the people around you in light of the stories of the "ordinary people" who make up the kind of movements that change the world.
- *Disciple not-yet-believers*: Try the approach suggested in this chapter of simply beginning to invest in the lives of your neighbors and workmates. Try to see them as disciples of Jesus who have not yet encountered Jesus, and see your task as to disciple them to become more like Jesus.
- *Ponder in what ways you exercise your God-given function as a priest*: This relates to the fact that you are com-

161

missioned at conversion and also that priests mediate the knowledge of God in Jesus. How can you step into that role more consistently?

Discussion Starters

1. "In every apple there is an orchard" (Donald McGavran). Do you think that every believer is a potential church-in-the-making?
2. Do the APEST test together (www.apest.org) and discuss the implications for your ministries.
3. Do you use the phrase "I feel fed" when attending a great worship service? And what do you say when you weren't? Critique the church-as-feeding-trough for middle-class Christians.
4. Watch the movie *Pay It Forward* together and discuss the implications for discipleship, church planting, and mission.
5. To what degree is your community based on a bounded or centered set? How would you open things up a little?

6

refocusing the family

The problem for someone like me who desires that his children lead successful, competent lives, is knowing that the cost of this may at times be insensitivity to others, that in urging them to do well I may well be urging them to be inconsiderate, lacking in thoughtfulness about others. In other words, the Christian values of community and equality are not the easiest standards to hold up when you're also interested in perpetuating your privileged situation in society through your children and your own behavior.

—Robert Coles

The only home which is safe for anyone to be born into is the home that is ready to welcome someone who does not belong there by right of kinship, but belongs there in virtue of hospitality.

—James T. Burtchaell

We'll never forget, years ago, the confused and distressed look on one of our friend's faces. Cath had just returned from speaking at a fairly large, middle-class church in the Bible belt of our city. She had been invited to speak about the work she did with the possibility of generating some type of support, and not simply the checkbook variety.

The youth organization Cath worked with had developed a fairly effective ministry to young teenage girls who, for various reasons, found themselves homeless. One aspect of the ministry was to provide accommodations, so they had set up a number of community homes in which our friend worked both as a lead tenant and director. The problem was that they had a huge waiting list of young homeless girls who couldn't be accommodated because they had run out of rooms.

During her message that morning, Cath appealed to the congregation and asked them if anyone among them was willing to house some of these girls over the short-to-medium term. She emphasized that it wouldn't be a permanent thing, and that she wasn't asking for them to provide for the girls' emotional and psychological needs, as the ministry would look after them. All she was asking for was just a roof over their heads, without which they may remain on the streets.

After the service, Cath said she was inundated with people wishing her well and congratulating her on the good work she was doing, and some promised to pray regularly for her. Some who were deeply touched gave money, but no one, *not one* person, offered to take in one of the many girls they had on their books.

Cath came back from church that morning pretty deflated. She said she didn't really need the money, or even the well wishes; what she really needed was accommodation. What disturbed her more than anything was that she knew that many of those families did indeed have spare rooms in their homes, and had ample resources to make a difference. But for reasons probably related to a sense of safety and security for their family, and perhaps fear of the stranger, these Christians chose not to open their homes.

164

Contrast the story above with that of the folks of Urban Neighbors of Hope, friends of ours who are part of a missional order among the poor. When they are confronted with a homeless person, they have the policy of asking themselves, "Are there any reasons why we should *not* take this person in?" If they can't come up with any good reason, and if they have place, they take them in.

What's going on here? Why would so many followers of Jesus close their hearts to people in desperate need? In the Bible, hospitality is just assumed to be part of life. Living in a culture that valued extended relationships, people inherited a heightened sense of obligation and felt a personal responsibility to give hospitality to both friends and strangers. The Gospels portray Jesus entertaining and being entertained in many different situations (some of these took place around the table of people who were actually hostile to what Jesus was all about). And we are directly encouraged to entertain strangers with the possibility that they might just be angels (Heb. 13:2). Surely our lack of hospitality points to something deficient in our culture, our sense of missional obligation, and therefore also our discipleship.

Refocusing the Family

We think that one of the major reasons for our current lack of hospitality to the stranger lies in the modern redefinition of what it means to be *family*. The writing in this area is extensive and complex and outside of the scope of this book, but it seems many would agree that the "nuclear family unit" as we now experience it has a very recent history—some say as little as fifty years![1] Certainly it has its early roots in the breakdown of extended families that started in the nineteenth century with the industrialization of Western culture, as people moved from the country to work in factories located in the newly formed cities. In this situation, usually the father went to work long hours away from the family, leaving the raising of children to the mother and other nonworking members of the family. Prior to the Industrial Revolution, spouses, children, and servants would simply work together to produce goods, and the family would include relatives and friends within the social unit. But under the pressures of mass marketing in the twenteith century, the process of narrowing the family, now seen primarily as a unit of consumption, was accelerated. Over time, the family has been reduced to a unit consisting of parents (single or mixed) and 2.2 kids. The net result is the narrowing of the vision and purpose of the family from that of a supportive and productive unit to one of conspicuous consumption, whose aim is to climb the social ladder.

Now, in the single family home, both parents pursue careers, often in order to pursue the idealized vision of the middle-class home created by late capitalism. Responsibilities beyond that of the direct nuclear family have been relinquished, and have narrowed even more as child rearing was eventually outsourced to professionals and schools. People now work all day in pursuit of a materialistic vision of the good life generated by marketing, only to come home exhausted to a house full of appliances and alienated relationships. Family relations are stretched to a maximum: witness the skyrocketing divorce rates and increasing alienation of children from their parents and from each other. The so-called "screenagers" are now raised and mentored by screens, be they TV, computers, video-games, or movie theaters—and all this in the name of keeping our means of production operating at peak capacity (*The Matrix* again?).[2]

Under such enormous cultural pressure and stress, families have become highly protective. They have become fortresses from the world around us—defensive units designed to keep the cultural onslaughts at bay. Sociologist Christopher Lasch calls it our "haven in a heartless world" in a book on the family by that name. This is "our" space, and those we may "invite" into that space are carefully chosen based on whether they will upset the delicate status quo, inconvenience us, or pose a threat to our perceived safety. In other words, visitors, especially strange ones, stress us out. And while this is in some sense culturally understandable, the negative result in terms of our spirituality is that the family has effectively become a pernicious idol—a sphere where the commands of the Shema are no longer applied to the whole of life. Culture has once again trumped our social responsibility. In such a situation, missional hospitality is seen as a threat, not as an opportunity to extend the kingdom; so an idol (a sphere of life dissociated from the claims of God) is born. None of us intended this; we simply inherited it. We never stopped to seriously question it. But we can, and must, do something about it.

Soft centers.

Part of the problem is that the church, a bastion of conservative values, has now taken the family to be the frontier in its stand against the eroding forces of secularizing culture. In many ways this is right—the family is eroding—but the problem is that we find ourselves defending a non-biblical idea of the family! It's not hard to see how this is absolutely disastrous from a missional perspective. Our families and our homes should be places where people can experience a foretaste of heaven, where the church is rightly viewed as a community of the redeemed from all walks of life (Revelation 21). Instead, our fears restrict us from letting go of the control and safety we have spent years cultivating. But

167

as Scott Bader-Saye notes, an ethic based on personal security produces a skewed moral vision.[3] Any sense of personal obligation is tapered down to exclude anything beyond "me and my family." This culture of fear is totally inconsistent with Jesus's redemptive vision of the kingdom of God.

The problem is that, by and large, our churches and church leaders are not challenging us to get beyond this captivity. In fact, they end up catering to it by justifying it on biblical grounds. The so-called "family church" usually assumes the very narrow understanding of the nuclear family and gives it theological legitimacy. But the way the Bible conceives the term *family* and the way we see it are worlds apart. The concerns of the "idol" take precedence over other "social" concerns. As Janet Fishburne points out, a church that focuses its concerns around the needs of the "nuclear" family inevitably tends to become conservative, class-conscious, sexist, and ineffectual in the society at large.

She goes on to say,

> Family idolatry is a tragically misdirected form of religious devotion. It involves a preference for the familiar over the unknown, the local over the universal, and treats the familiar and local as if they were absolute. When Christians direct reverence toward love of family without acknowledging the source of that love, they may imagine they are expressing reverence for Christ when they are, in fact, engaging in idolatry.[4]

Who is my mother, my father . . . ?

Our foster child Jacob's biological mother was a heroin user and prostitute, and the identity of his father was unknown. He was removed from his mother not long after he was born because she was unable to care for him. Jacob was then placed into a foster home. His main foster parents were a lesbian couple. Our household, consisting of us (a married couple without children), two single women (who just so happened to be sisters), a gay-oriented man, and a dog called Ruby all became Jacob's other foster parents. We provided respite care for Jacob when his main foster moms needed a break. In Jacob's little three-year-old world, "family" in the traditional or nuclear sense simply didn't exist, or even make sense. Who, or what, was family for Jacob? Real stories like Jacob's force us to reconsider just what family is.

Janet Fishburn, mentioned above, in her book *Confronting the Idolatry of Family: A New Vision for the Household of God*, rightly asserts,

> Where a domesticated piety dominates, or where the concerns of the nuclear family become the focus of a church, the conservation of middle-class ideals can blind both leaders and people to the prominent concern for social justice found in the Bible. And even when leaders are committed to seeking social justice, they have not been able to sustain a legitimate critique of poverty and injustice in America because the family ideals of the American Dream continue to be linked to democratic values and economic stability. . . . Uncritical loyalty to "the family pew" makes it very difficult to see or comprehend the plight of the poor and the homeless and the oppression of minority persons, as anything but their own fault.[5]

She then goes on to say that it requires courage for any pastor of a mainstream congregation to preach prophetically. "To ask middle-class Americans to see American culture as Jesus would see it is to ask them to vote against their own privileged position in society."[6]

Now, please understand us: we say all of this not to further attack the family and erode its still-positive influence on society, but rather to reclaim it by giving it a broader definition. We want to refocus it by putting it in its proper context—the family of God.

As Rodney Clapp states it, "The family as a narrow social unit is not God's most important institution on earth—rather the church *is* the First Family. The family is not the social agent that most significantly shapes and forms the character

169

of Christians. The family is not the primary vehicle of God's grace and salvation for a waiting, desperate world."[7] Rather, the church is God's agent commissioned to fulfill these functions. Even a brief reading of Ephesians makes this abundantly clear. "Restoring and redeeming the family, then, does not begin with the nation or with the family itself. It begins with the Church."[8]

The perfect family, if there is such a thing, is not an idealized nuclear unit of consumption, but an inclusive, warm, inviting environment where people can get a glimpse of true community, and therefore of heaven. In contrast to the narrower perspective of the nuclear family, the Bible has a much larger vision that incorporates the nuclear unit but goes well beyond it to include grandparents, cousins, friends, servants, and the stranger.

This is no *family first* approach as we now conceive it. Rather, for disciples, it must be *Jesus first* and all things in relation to him. "Only by seeing Jesus and all that he means can we begin to build . . . families that serve the one and final reality which we call the Kingdom of God."[9] Jesus, following the logic of Shema spirituality, radically redefines all our loyalties, including those of family relations, around himself; our love for parents may even appear to be hostility in comparison with our love for him.

> Do not suppose that I have come to bring peace to the earth. I did not come to bring peace, but a sword. For I have come to turn a man against his father, a daughter against her mother, a daughter-in-law against her mother-in-law—a man's enemies will be the members of his own household. Anyone who loves his father or mother more than me is not worthy of me; anyone who loves his son or daughter more than me is not worthy of me. (Matt. 10:34–37)

Jesus is once again challenging our natural loyalties and claiming right of rule. And he totally redefines family around the community of disciples.

He replied to him, "Who is my mother, and who are my brothers?" Pointing to his disciples, he said, "Here are my mother and my brothers. For whoever does the will of my Father in heaven is my brother and sister and mother." (Matt. 12:48–50)

Fishburn is absolutely right when she says, "If love of family is stronger and deeper than love for Jesus Christ, this is family idolatry."[10]

The Church as the Family of God

Nelson Mandela, in his autobiography *Long Walk to Freedom*, exposes the reader to a concept of family much closer to that of the biblical world. He says that when he visits another village or city, he need not call ahead to let them know that he is coming because when he arrives everyone is his mother, uncle, sister. It is this wider understanding that we must apply to the church as the household or family of God in order to understand it correctly. The nuclear family idea simply will not do. Think about it: if God's family were a nuclear family as we define it, none of us would be included! Only the "insider members" would be included. It probably wouldn't go much further than the inner relations of the Trinity. If it did manage to include humans, then perhaps the nation of Israel would be included, leaving everyone else as outsiders. But we know that is not the case in the New Testament. All the redeemed are together, co-heirs with Christ, adopted into the family with full membership privileges (Rom. 8:13–18; Gal. 4:4–6; Eph. 2:11–22), thus making God's family a massive, culturally diverse collection of plain, beautiful, dumb, brilliant, weird, and wonderful people—God's own redeemed freak collection! While *missionally* we need to live incarnationally among a distinctive group of people, *theologically* we need to see the church as a very big, massively extended family. The two aspects ought to be held in creative tension.

171

The big household of God can only be realized if we deal with our fear of the other and truly value diversity. But, frankly, most churches are anything but diverse! We do tend to look the same, think the same, and behave in the same way. As we say in the preceding chapter on the church, we tend to be fearful of the other, and yet this encounter with people unlike us is exactly what we need, for we learn more through differences than we do by similarities.

The Home Is an Extension of the Heart

Again we ask, Why is it that so many Christian households remain firmly shut to the outsider? Why is it that we find it so hard to open up our homes? Most of us will serve at the church, give some money to the poor, and perhaps even go out on mission trips, but when it comes down to bringing that mission "home," we flatly refuse. More than that, we see it as our personal space that ought not be intruded upon. After all, isn't the home the domain of the family? And isn't my family the safe haven for those I am responsible for?

Perhaps we can alter the equation: perhaps we need to see the church as modeling a "home." For us, church was always meant to be an extension of the home. So when we first started at South, one of the first things we did with the chapel area was totally refurnish it. We put in carpets, couches, beanbags, pop art, lamps, and the types of things one may normally have in their living room. The chapel, previously somewhat uninviting, was converted from a "religious space" to a place where people could feel as comfortable as they might in their family rooms at home. Too many churches create artificial, neat, "nice" environments, almost like a perfect display home. The same applies even more to high church architecture. They are not particularly *human* environments—try sitting on the pews! People can never feel at home or naturally free in cold and impersonal environments. Architecture certainly does

172

communicate! Compare a cozy local restaurant with a not-so-cozy local McDonald's—the one communicates "eat and stay," the other, "eat and get out." We believe that how we design and decorate our church buildings often gives insight into how we want our congregation members to appear—neat and tidy, and definitely with no messy behavior!

Interestingly, the home (*oikos*) was in fact the primary model and place of meeting for the church of the New Testament (see diagram on the next page). They had no dedicated "religious" church buildings. Homes then functioned very differently, operating as they did under a different idea of the family. For one, they included extended family, friends, guests, and servants. Most would therefore house around twenty-plus people. But we must also remember that (since they had no TV) after work everyone would hang out in the courtyard or dining area, which was obviously very large. They would eat, chat, drink, and generally be together until late at night before going to sleep.

As you can see in the diagram on the next page, these houses were situated along a street. Various houses in the neighborhood would take turns offering hospitality to others along the street. It was a dynamic social system. Viewed this way, a house in the Greco-Roman world operated more like a local café or pub would in ours—it was what we would call a classic *third place*, not a first place as we define it.[11] It was into this complex and rich relational environment that the gospel was introduced, and in which the church took root in the ancient world.

Now, we are *not* saying the church should be limited to our houses! Given the prevailingly narrow understanding of family, this could prove missionally disastrous because the church in a nuclear-family house can (and often does) become even more closed than the more institutional forms! So please don't misunderstand us here. What we *are* saying is that we certainly can become more "homely" in our churches, and we can certainly learn from the complex and open relational

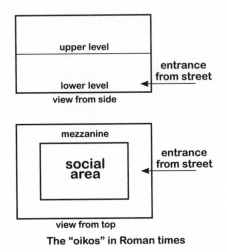

view from top
The "oikos" in Roman times

structure that was created through bringing the church home, so to speak. Actually, we think that the third place, and not necessarily the home, provides us with the richest social context for engaging in mission in the West.

Eating our way into the kingdom

One of the most significant ways in which we can start changing our world is by practicing simple kindness and hospitality. We remember clearly when our friend Nick Wight (a missionary and former pastor of Matthew's Party, our first church plant) suggested that if every Christian household regularly invited a stranger, or a poor person, or a work colleague into their home for a meal with the family once a week, we would literally change the world by eating! At first we thought that this was an overstatement, but upon reflection we actually believe it is true.

For instance, we have experienced missional generosity with our friends, the Graf family. Phil, Laina, and the kids are missionaries in Europe and totally *get* the power and grace of hospitality. They believe part of the reason people don't open up their homes is because they have yet to understand the kingdom value of hospitality—we agree and believe we all need to learn from people like them. Following her belief in the power of hospitality, Laina actually tattooed a large Celtic cross, facing outward, on the inside of both her arms. When we queried her about the unusual placement of these beautiful tattoos, she said that it reminds her that when she is serving a dish (the tattoos are presented to the person she is serving) it shows them that Jesus is serving them through her. For the whole Graf family, their home is not *their* haven but rather a sort of welcoming inn, gracing all who come through their door. The home and family are without question a reflection of what a real kingdom family can look like. They do not have a locked-door mentality but rather an open-door policy which, to our thinking, correlates to an open-heart mentality. Closed door, closed heart; open door, open heart—the home is an extension of the heart. Isn't this what communion is all about?

Implications for housing

The call to be hospitable people, to welcome strangers (and even perhaps angels), must reach beyond table fellowship and impact how and where we live.

Sharing a home allows the community in that house to share common life around Jesus. Not only does it mean exposing one's life to the accountability of other disciples (something essential to authentic discipleship), but it also allows all to develop common disciplines and rhythms, such as community meals, corporate prayer and reading of Scripture, hospitality, service, and so on. There is a great synergy in simple community and it provides a real-life opportunity to learn how to love. It many ways, it gives us an opportunity to experience what the Bible means by *oikos*, or the household—the basic unit of "church" in the New Testament.

175

We have always believed in both the power and necessity of community for discipleship, ministry, and mission. Except for two months when we first got married, we have never had a time when we did not have people living with us! Our church was a community, and was made up of many different community houses stuffed full of Jesus freaks. We have also questioned our personal right to private ownership in the way that is assumed by Westerners. As a result, we decided to buy a house with a five-party ownership. Actually, it is a great, one-hundred-year-old house, but because of its location (in our red-light district), we got it for a bargain. And besides, with our rather financially deprived community, most of us could never afford to buy a house like that on our own—it made much more economic sense to buy together. Living there has been a wonderful, missional, fun-loving experience of extended family—church as we describe it above.

A Message Tribe

In this chapter, we have focused primarily on the way in which we reconfigure and live out what it means to be the family of God. This is by no means the last word on what it means to be a missional church. A thorough rethinking here is likely to open us up to significant new missional possibilities and new ways in which to live out what it means to walk in the untamed way of Jesus. If how we think of God and self profoundly affects the nature of discipleship and mission, then the same is true for the church. Distorted perspectives of the church damage our witness and our capacity to live out its message. The church is, in the end, a "message-tribe," a community with a mission that only it can fulfill. If we limit our view of the church to that of the one-dimensional, attenuated nuclear family, we will violate something fundamental to a genuinely missional understanding of the church and damage our witness.

176

We agree with Rodney Clapp when he says that witnessing means incarnating the church in peculiar shapes and through rich practices that can only be explained by resorting to the story of Israel and Jesus Christ.[12] When we see ourselves in the light of the biblical narrative, forsaking false cultural definitions of ourselves, we can see the redemptive impulse of God reaching out through his people into a lost and broken world. We cannot but open up our hearts, our lives, *and our homes*, and so actively participate in what God is doing in the world.

> Through followers of Jesus like yourselves gathered in churches, this extraordinary plan of God is becoming known and talked about even among the angels! (Eph. 3:10 Message)

Suggested Practices

- *Mi casa es tu casa* (my home is your home): Take the risk of opening up your lives to others. Do so with open hearts, but also with wisdom. Start slowly: perhaps a day per week, perhaps extending as the family adjusts. Or you can take in an overseas student as a renter. The task is to allow the home to become a haven for more than just the nuclear family. Think seriously about fostering a child or doing some relief work for those who do foster care.

- *Practice regular hospitality*: Try this—commit to table fellowship beyond the nuclear family three times a week: one time with people inside the community of faith, one time with people outside the church, and one spare.

- *Do a social audit of your relationships*: How many of the people in your circle are of the same socio-political and economic profile as you? To open yourselves up to the diversity of God's family, you might need to "adopt a few freaks"—people unlike you and your current social circle.

Discussion Starters

1. How has the narrowing of the idea of the family changed our view of the church?
2. Conversely, how would broadening our understanding of the family change how you see yourselves and what you do?
3. The renewal of the family will not start with focusing on the family as a unit of society; it will start with the church as God's redeemed family. Do you agree?
4. Discuss what Jesus had to say about family and what constitutes a family.

the untamed self

7

the lying mirror

From the lying mirror to the movement of stars, everybody's looking for who they are.

—Bruce Cockburn

We do not see things as *they* are, but as *we* are.

—Jewish proverb

Be sure that the ins and outs of your individuality are no mystery to him [God]; and one day they will no longer be a mystery to you. Blessed and fortunate creature, your eyes shall behold Him and not another's. All that you are, sins apart, is destined, if you will let God have his good way, to utter satisfaction. . . . Your place in heaven will seem to be made for you and you alone, because you were made for it.

—C. S. Lewis

Numerous stories and movies explore the concept of identity and finding oneself. Movies like *Memento*, *The Lion*

181

King, *The Matrix* trilogy, and *The Chronicles of Narnia* are all structured around this theme. The children's fantasy *Hook* (starring Dustin Hoffman, Julia Roberts, and Robin Williams) explores how Peter Banning, who is actually Peter Pan but has forgotten his real identity, is placed in a situation where he simply has to recover his lost self in order to save his children who have been whisked off by the pirate (and Peter Pan's arch enemy) Captain Hook. Having been unwillingly transported by Tinker Bell to Neverland, at first Banning refuses to believe in Tinker Bell's perception of him—that he is indeed Peter Pan and that he can fly—and so cannot seem to find the lost powers needed to overcome Hook and save the kids (and Neverland) from the marauding pirates. But eventually, through sheer desperation, and helped along with a kiss from Tinker Bell, he remembers his lost identity, thus activating his powers and winning the day.

This story, and others like it, provides a clue to any search for identity: the idea that when one discovers one's true identity, not only does it bring authenticity, but it delivers real authority. In *The Matrix*, Neo fulfills his destiny as he embraces his identity. The same is true for the children in Narnia—in that land they are royalty, and only by embracing their regal calling can they play their role in delivering the captive creatures of Narnia.

Nothing could be truer for the disciple—our authenticity, as well as our power, is unleashed when we live out our true identity and calling in Christ. We believe that part of the gracing process inherent in becoming more like Jesus is the increasing discovery of the identity God gives to us in him. So much of the New Testament is dedicated to helping us find ourselves again "in Christ." Why is so much attention given to this end? Because, quite simply, we were created to. And if we do not find our identity in Jesus, then we will surely find it in something else.

You Are, Now Be

The Scriptures are full of statements about our identity—who we are in Christ. Scholars call these more descriptive statements of the New Testament *indicatives* because they express our deepest identity and form the basis of the *imperatives* (commands) of Scripture, that is, the calling of living out discipleship in the world. For instance, it doesn't take the reader of Paul very long to note that the first half of his letters are generally more theological-descriptive (describing who we *are* in Christ) and the last sections ethical-prescriptive (directing us how to live *based on who we are*)—for example, compare Romans 1–11 to 12–15, or Ephesians 1–3 to 4–6.

This is very important for us to understand because any attempt to live as a disciple that is not properly founded on a true identity in Jesus will result in deviant religion. But any attempt to simply be a Christian without doing anything beyond will be equally aberrant. Throughout the Bible, a person who is redeemed by God must live a life consistent with the God he or she worships. In simplest terms, *being* and *acting* belong together—our identity and our sense of purpose are inextricably linked.

This chapter will focus on the importance of getting the indicatives right: of finding and grounding our identity in Jesus.

Loving God, Loving Others

According to the best thinking in theology, philosophy, and psychology (at least as far as we can discern), developing a true sense of identity requires two essential directions in relationships: one with God and the other with people. Of the two, the God relationship is absolutely foundational. However, this will require that we activate the deepest and

183

most elusive aspect of our humanity—the *spiritual*. Our relationships with people, while sometimes also tricky, are generally easier because they tend to be more concrete. We come to know who we are through our relationships with both God and others. We are relational beings by our very nature. Or, as the social sciences would say, we are constituted by our relationships.

As we have pointed out on numerous occasions, how we think about and relate to God determines *everything*. That of course includes what it means to be a person, and in particular what it means to be a disciple of Jesus. We think Søren Kierkegaard was absolutely right when he claimed that without God there is no possibility of a self, because "we are constituted by the relationship to that which brought us into being." In the words of a philosopher, he is saying that it is only when we ground ourselves in God that we will be able to form a self. If we avoid this most basic of all relationships, we will be doomed to an existential restlessness that will inevitably lead to deep despair.[1] Augustine said our hearts are restless until they find their rest in God. If this is true for every human being, it is even more so for those being transformed into the image of God in Christ (Rom. 8:29; 2 Cor. 3:18; Col. 3:9–11). Without this most elemental relationship, we simply cannot develop into the people God intends us to be.

But our relationship to other people is also essential; we need people to be a "person" ourselves. We cannot find or form our identity nor our personality in isolation from one another. Our social interactions play a critical role in identity formation. In other words, we can only really know ourselves in relation to the "other." Play with us here: we are suggesting that even if you had all the genetics of a human being but were raised by pigs, nurtured by pigs, and lived all your life in the company of pigs, you would not be able to form a human personality in the strictest sense of the word. Language, human contact, symbolic gestures, love (or the lack of it)—all go together to make us who we are. Our *person*-ality, therefore, can only be formed in relation to other persons. As the poet Rainer Maria Rilke said, we come of age "haphazardly assembled from voices, and fears, and little pleasures." Those irritating siblings, the sacrificial love of parents, the painful socialization of school, the spiritual community of church, and so forth, are all essential to the formation of a healthy identity.

Broken Image

In a broken world full of less-than-perfect relationships, is it any wonder that most of us struggle with our sense of self? A healthy identity and a basic security in who we are as individuals seems to be hard to come by. In our pastoral experience, journeying with people from all walks of life has helped us conclude that it is quite a feat for any individual to become secure in who they are. From the property developer to the bricklayer, it seems nobody can claim to have a whole, healthy sense of self. Insecurity in who we are, in our capacity to achieve, in our contribution to society, and invariably in our relationships plagues all of us to varying degrees, making us wonder whether we are worthy, capable, lovable, and the like.

M. Scott Peck talks about the fact that the world is full of what he calls "half adults"—people who, for whatever reason, have never really grown up. We would link this directly to an inability to arrive at a healthy sense of self. The sad tragedy is that who we perceive ourselves to be directly relates to how we behave. That's why the Scriptural "indicatives" are so important. Paul is at pains to create in us a new identity, knowing that when we embrace who God says we are, it will dramatically alter the way we live our lives. We have seen the truth of this in our own lives as well as in the lives of those in our faith community.

The connection between identity and behavior can't be denied. If you think of yourself as worthless or ugly or incompetent then, in all likelihood, it will work itself out in your behavior. Deb saw this time and time again, especially when she worked with prisoners. One of her "clients" in particular really believed herself to be unlovable and a bad person. This terrible scripting had been reinforced throughout her whole life until she ended up in prison after committing a number of misdemeanors. As Deb grew in her relationship with this woman, she realized that deep down this woman thought she was a "bad apple" and that was just her lot in life. She had been told this from a very young age by her mother, as well as others around her. As simple as it might sound, in this woman's mind, bad people did bad things, so she would constantly reoffend and end up back in jail. It was a self-fulfilling prophecy. To break this cycle between identity and behavior is no easy feat. But eventually, over a long period of time, through constant encouragement and positive reinforcement and loving relationships, this woman began to realize that she was indeed lovable. She wasn't a bad person after all, and even if she did do the occasional bad thing (like all of us do!), this didn't define who she was. Today this woman is no longer in prison; she continues to work on her identity, but she no longer defines herself as "bad," which has profoundly impacted her behavior. She is quite simply a different person.

> Through the laughter, dancing, dining, supping of people,
> Inside of dresses and ornaments, inside of those wash'd and trimm'd faces,
> Behold a secret silent loathing and despair.
>
> —Walt Whitman, "Song of the Open Road"

In a broken world, without a proper connection to God or wholesome relationships with others, one is bound to get things messed up. The extreme of this can be seen in both the psychopaths and sociopaths within our society. The twin aspects of knowing ourselves before God and knowing ourselves through relationships with other people are precisely what are missing in these types of antisocial personality disorders. A failure in essential relationships can ultimately result in terrible human evil. The lack of being properly loved and nurtured can wreak havoc on one's own sense of worth, let alone one's value of other people. You only need to study some of these extreme cases in our society—those individuals who have done incredibly evil things—to know that the lack of these life-giving relationships caused them to have a severely corrupted sense of self and others.

Author Shirley Lynn Scott, in her article "What Makes Serial Killers Tick?" documents some chilling words from some of history's most famous psychopaths.

> "I'm the most cold-blooded sonofabitch you'll ever meet," said Ted Bundy. "I just liked to kill, I wanted to kill." The hallmark of the psychopath is the inability to recognize others as worthy of compassion. Victims are dehumanized, flattened into worthless objects in the murderer's mind. John Gacey, never showing an ounce of remorse, called his victims "worthless little queers and punks," while the "Yorkshire Ripper" Peter Sutcliffe brashly declared that he was "cleaning up the streets" of the human trash.[2]

If identity and self-perception constitute the foundational base we operate from, then we can clearly say these men had a very distorted and twisted view of themselves and others. These more extreme cases only highlight the absolute need for ongoing love and affirming relationships in the formation of a healthy human being.

The Shema

Consider again the remarkable ecology of biblical spirituality when we look at the dynamics of the Shema. We see just how important the two greatest commandments are. If acknowledged and lived out in our lives, they will bring the much needed corrective for a world full of broken images. Just listen to Jesus again:

> "The most important one," answered Jesus, "is this: 'Hear, O Israel, the Lord our God, the Lord is one. Love the Lord your God with all your heart and with all your soul and with all your mind and with all your strength.' The second is this: 'Love your neighbor as yourself.' There is no commandment greater than these." (Mark 12:29–31)

Who Am I?

Consider the following conversation: Author: "I am writing a booklet, to be called, Why Am I Afraid to Tell You Who I Am?" Other: "Do you want an answer to your question?" Author: "That is the purpose of the booklet, to answer the question." Other: "But do you want my answer?" Author: "Yes, of course I do." Other: "'I am afraid to tell you who I am, because, if I tell you who I am, you may not like who I am, and it's all that I have."

—John Powell

As we have seen, the self is formed primarily in relation to God and completed in the act of loving others. These truths are found here in the Shema, and they square with the best current thinking on the healthy formation of the self. Here the God relationship is presented in terms of an absolute commitment to the love (and as we have seen in chapter two, this also implies knowledge) of God. This is the grounding relationship Kierkegaard and others speak of. But we are also called by Jesus to move on to loving other people. This is no small task, as learning to love the way Jesus meant requires sacrifice, service, and commitment—real heart. Only

188

in doing precisely these things will we come into contact with our true selves. In other words, if we simply live the Shema, the greatest of all instructions, we are well on the way to becoming more mature in our identity.

Again, our relationship with Jesus is central to everything. If we fail to conform to him, we must suffer the anxieties inflicted on us from other sources, be they cultural forces, idols, or whatever. It is worth asking here: If God-in-Jesus is not at the defining center of our self-awareness, then who or what is? Pop culture? Our work or professions? The brand or the amount of "stuff" we own? Perhaps it's the expectations of peers and/or parents? Maybe our sexuality? But these are not sure foundations for healthy formation of identity! At best they are secondary. Human beings learn to live behind many masks and mistakenly think this gives them security. But once it is recognized that the mask is no more than a finite construct, and that underneath the "happy and secure" exterior is only emptiness, then the individual *might* begin—and it is only a possibility—to take God seriously.[3]

Loving Love

We recognize that loving God and others is foundational to the formation of our identity, but knowing we are *loved by God and others* is perhaps even more important for us to arrive at healthy selfhood. In our ministry experience, not many of us start from this solid foundational base.

An image that has continued to burn in Deb's mind is a confession made by one of her clients she worked with at the Salvation Army. Caroline (not her real name) had been hospitalized over a dozen times in thirty days because of self-mutilation, among other things. By this time, Deb had reached a place of physical and emotional exhaustion. Feeling overwhelmed and that she was making little progress with her, Deb arrived once again at the hospital to be by her side. While sitting by her bed, Deb began once again to gently question her and to listen to her heart. It was then, in the midst of great vulnerability, that they shared a special and intimate moment. Caroline confessed to Deb that she regularly hurt herself so that she could go to the hospital, because the nurses "touched" her and were nice to her. In the hospital, she never had to be alone; there was someone around all the time. The sad tragedy is that there are many people like Caroline—unloved, untouched, and needing the affirmation from God and humanity that they are indeed loved and lovable. Tragically, this story is not uncommon; many of Deb's other clients would reoffend just to go back to prison because life on the outside proved to be too lonely or unstructured. In prison, life was predictable and they got attention. Even if it wasn't always positive, some attention was better than none.

> A secret unrest lies at the roots of our being.
>
> —Carl Jung

Endless psychological conditions, including behavioral and personality disorders as mentioned above, are the direct result of a failure of loving. John Powell, a priest and author, simply and powerfully stated this many years ago when he said that we all are a product of those who have loved us and those who have failed to love us. For if to love and to be loved is part of what defines our humanity, then to not be loved certainly must have a damaging effect on our sense of self.

With You I Am Well Pleased

Susan Hope, in her book *Mission-Shaped Spirituality*, comments that the story of Jesus's baptism, and the Father's proclamation of love for him at that moment ("You are my Son, whom I love; with you I am well pleased" [Luke 3:22]), provides an insight into the importance of the disciple being grounded in the knowledge and assurance of God's love.

This is the start of the public ministry, the kick-start to all that follows. And it is kick-started with a word, not about the mission, but about being a son, and being greatly beloved.

190

And not only greatly beloved, but greatly delighted in—"with you I am well pleased"—carrying not so much the meaning, "I'm pleased with you (because you've done a good job/obeyed me/you've met my demands)" as, "You delight me; I enjoy you; I like what I see."[4]

We all need that same assurance. It is important that we remember that God loves us unconditionally. The Bible tells us that while we were still sinners, Jesus died for us. He didn't wait until we cleaned up our lives or stopped sinning, but died for us right in the middle of our mess. We are loved ones, the bride of Christ, the beloved of the Lord. We are Christ's ones, not because of what we do, but because we are in relationship with him—and nothing can change that. Nothing can separate us from the love of God in Christ Jesus (Rom. 8:35).

God loves us, but his love is not static. It is active and at times demanding because he requires our all. This compelling love of his pushes us forward into becoming whole persons. Through our very selves, where his image shines forth and where his love can be felt, we experience the humanizing love of God.

But make no mistake, his love is not always comfortable; it is also a fierce, sanctifying love, and it will change us. We come to him with many false selves, and we are in great need of redefinition. Because of this, God has to strip, or "undragon," us.

Being Undragoned

There is a powerful scene in C. S. Lewis's *Voyage of the Dawn Treader* (part of *The Chronicles of Narnia* series) where Eustace, a somewhat selfish and greedy boy, is sleeping on a dragon's hoard. He is thinking greedy, "dragon-ish" thoughts in his heart and suddenly turns into a dragon himself. Now, in this story a dragon is not only a selfish monster that hoards treasures, but also a profoundly lonely creature because it likes

191

nothing better than to eat anything that comes into its world. After a while, Eustace-turned-dragon begins to experience how lonely it is to be a monster, and finds that because of his dragon-like, antisocial ways he can't even enjoy his treasure. It all turns sour on him, and he begins to see what kind of person he has been. As the full realization of his nature settles upon him, he begins to weep inconsolably.

Through his tears he sees a huge and awesome lion coming toward him, beckoning him to follow. So great is Eustace's remorse by this time that he will do anything the great beast asks. The lion leads him to a huge, round well and directs him to undress. Eustace has no clothes, so he realizes that he is being asked to remove his snakelike, scaly skin. He thinks he can easily shed his awful dragon hide. He starts scratching away at his scaly self and soon manages to step out of his dragon skin. But just as he steps into the water, he notices he has yet another dragon skin on underneath. He scratches away at this hide and, stepping out of it, starts again into the water. But again he sees he is still a dragon. He thinks to himself, "Oh dear, how ever many other skins do I have to take off?" He then scratches away for the third time and is horrified to find he has yet another dragon skin on. It is then that the lion says, "You will have to let me undress you." Eustace is afraid of the lion's claws, but he's so desperate that he surrenders his ugly dragon self and lets the lion "undress" him. The very first tear the lion's claws make goes so deep that Eustace thinks it has gone right through his heart. It hurts worse than anything he's ever felt. Then the lion catches hold of him and throws him into the crystal clear pool. Hurting terribly at first, Eustace the Dragon sinks deep into the delicious waters until, surfacing, he finds himself turned back into a boy.

Few if any write better of our need to be undragoned than Lewis. In the case of Eustace, Lewis saw with terrible clarity that conversion from loving self to loving God and our neighbors is a radical one indeed.[5] According to Christian doctrine, the sinful and false self must be destroyed by a force beyond itself because it does not have the power to lift itself out of its own narrow interests. Yet when the sinful self is broken and the real self is brought to the surface, the consequence is a new life of transformation and discipleship.

At the very beginning of following Jesus, we are all called to be undragoned by repenting, dying to our fallen selves, and surrendering our identities and purposes to the lordship of Jesus. When we forget this need for repentance, it always comes back to haunt us. We've experienced this personally and witnessed it in those we minister to. If people, when coming to Christ, are not discipled in such a way as to challenge the false views they bring to faith (1 Thess. 1:9), this goes on to seriously undermine their faith. Christian life and mission then become seriously distorted by the unredeemed ego and/or the culture of the convert. There was a stage at South when we forgot this most basic of truths, and as a result, we indulged the false self. We never challenged the sinful motives and ideas that coalesce around selves formed outside of a relationship with God. The formation of a true self has everything to do with discipleship, mission, and evangelism. For instance, if we never challenged the identity, self-understanding, and lifestyle of the would-be convert (be they homosexual, straight, or otherwise), the result was an ill-born disciple, and he or she would either struggle in the faith or eventually give up following Jesus altogether. Of course, this death to the old self is required throughout the believer's life, but it must begin at the start of the life of faith.

Start Here: *Imago Dei*

Early in our ministry, we remember being deeply impacted by Rowland Croucher, a church consultant in Australia, when he led a workshop for ministers. He began by asking the question, "What is the *first* thing you can say about Adolf Hitler?"

Answers to the question ranged from "horrifically evil" to "fallen," and just about everything in between. At the end of the feedback, he simply said, "No, the most fundamental thing you can say about Hitler is that he is 'like God'! Yes, he is fallen, evil, and degraded, but he too is made in the image of God. Even though it is very marred in him, it nonetheless is there." He went on to say that no matter who we are or what we have done, this is the most fundamental truth about us all—we in some way reflect God.

Rowland was right, and our paradigms had been rocked! We had been scripted to give the first and obvious answer, that Hitler was indeed a sinner. But this was to get first and second truths the wrong way around. Sure, he—like us—is fallen and in need of redemption, but this is a secondary truth that only builds on the primary truth, which is that all humans carry the *imago Dei*. On this liberating truth rests a more genuinely biblical understanding of human beings. This truth also provides the disciple with a more compassionate (and humane) basis for mission and ministry. Let's see how this works out in two takes.

Take one: If we operate assuming the primary truth is that every person is first and foremost a sinner, and that the image of God is all but obliterated, then the way we engage in our own personal discipleship and our missional endeavors will be radically altered. Historically, five-point Calvinism has tended to have a very negative, "worm-theology" view of humanity that has at times communicated a sense of self-hatred in its adherents and in the wider culture shaped by its teachings. In this view, our sense of sinfulness will tend to outweigh our sense of redemption: even though I will see myself as saved by Jesus, my primary identity as "sinner" will remain predominant and assert itself into my sense of who I am.

This negative view of the human reveals itself fully in the way we see, and subsequently treat, non-Christian people. Because the grace that covers the Christian person is not applied to the unsaved, the image of God within them will be obscured by their sinfulness and we will tend to view them in a dark and cynical light. But we miss the gift that lies under the mess of sin. Our focus will be on the external (behaviors and the like), rather than on the heart.

Take two: If we operate assuming the primary truth is that every person is first and foremost created in the image of God but is also fallen and capable of great evil, then we will still see ourselves as something very special that went badly wrong. In this viewpoint, there is something essential in our humanity that is fundamentally God-like, no matter how fallen we may perceive ourselves or others to be. Not only does this change us, but it should also profoundly modify the way we see people and therefore engage in mission. We can see beyond the sin and brokenness to a being that was made to reflect God. And even though something went badly wrong, this can—and must—be restored through Jesus's saving work on our behalf. We will then have much more respect for the unbeliever and the sheer dignity of being human. Think again of the way Jesus treated people, and see which perspective fits better.

This paradigm shift has been incredibly significant in our ministry. While seeing the holy in the other has come more easily to Deb, Alan can recall having to choose to "see" the image of God in people. Al can remember an encounter with Howard, who was one of those people everyone would do everything to avoid. He was very needy, lacked social skills, cornered his victims, rubbed himself up against people when he hugged them, talked too much—you get the idea! One time Al was simply not able to dodge him and was effectively sequestered in a corner with him. He knew he was going to be there for a while. And then about halfway through their time together, the *meaning* of Howard, so to speak, came through. Al saw him as a marvelous, God-like creature. He can honestly say that it felt like an encounter with God in and through Howard.

Another humorous example: about fifteen years ago, Diana came into our lives. She was a transsexual-without-

195

the-operation. Another profoundly unloved individual, she'd had a traumatic upbringing. Like many "trannies," Diana was an over-the-top type of person people tended to reject and avoid. However, Deb lovingly pastored her and soon became the point of relational stability in her very topsy-turvy life. As a result, Diana decided to "adopt" us as parents. (Not a legal adoption, rather a relational one.) At first we tried to resist this, but eventually we gave in. In the beginning, in the midst of all the drama, we had to constantly remind ourselves that Diana bore the God-image, and in fact, in his/her rather strange kind of way, did it very well. She is an incredibly kind, generous, and forgiving person who will sacrificially serve others whenever a situation requires it. We can honestly say that we really do love her and have learned so much about God from her. We are proud to be her "adopted" parents.

Seeing the image of God in people generates compassion. Henri Nouwen makes the point that if we have true compassion for people, then we will not focus primarily on their outward behavior.[6] And he is exactly right! We would add that if we start with the presupposition that the person is created in the image of God rather than simply being a sinner, we will be compelled to look to their heart and attempt to call forth the image of God we know is there, no matter how hidden. We are wise to remember the words of C. S. Lewis:

> There are no ordinary people. You have never talked to a mere mortal. Nations, cultures, arts, and civilizations—these are

mortal, and their life is to ours as the life of a gnat. But it is immortals whom we joke with, work with, marry, snub, and exploit—immortal horrors or everlasting splendors. This does not mean that we are to be perpetually solemn. We must play. But our merriment must be of the kind (and it is, in fact, the merriest kind) which exists between people who have, from the outset, taken each other seriously—no flippancy, no superiority, no presumption. And our charity must be real and costly love, with deep feeling for the sins in spite of which we love the sinners—no mere tolerance, or indulgence, which parodies love as flippancy parodies merriment. Next to the Blessed Sacrament itself, your neighbor is the holiest object presented to your senses.[7]

Ich und du

Following from this is the poetic Jewish philosophy of Martin Buber. Once again, if taken seriously, this can greatly impact our discipleship and missional endeavors.[8] Buber talked about the two primary ways of relating. The first primary relationship is called "I-It." This type of relationship is characterized by the objectification and control of nature and people. The "I" in this relationship seeks to acquire and possess as much as it can and perceives itself as being an individual set over against the objects in its orbit. When we treat people as a thing (as an *it*), we depersonalize them and see them as objects. First, this is to misunderstand their true nature, but it also changes the sense of self. The "I" in this relationship pays a price for such selfishness; it too becomes depersonalized because it is isolated and alienated from the source of life.

Alternatively, there is a more authentic and deeper way of relating to the world, which Buber calls the "I-Thou" relationship. This is the sphere where people come together and encounter one another on the deepest level possible. To relate to someone as a *thou* is to offer them the dignity and honor of being a holy other, another free being . . . a *person*. We can see from this observation that Buber was not just talking about a casual conversation at the local pub or a heated negotiation to resolve a labor dispute, although these can indeed be occasions for such an encounter to take place. Rather, he is describing a meeting not only of minds but of souls, of wills, of that which resides at the core of one's being. When you say "Thou" to another person, you are sharing the mystery of your being, you are responding with the totality of self to the Thou who is addressing you, you are meeting one another on the level of spirit.

Again, relating to people in this way changes the nature of the "I" as well as giving dignity to the "Thou." Wonderfully, Buber says that when we do this we perceive reality from a new and higher vantage point. From this perspective I am able to extricate myself from the more closed world of I-It. I see that I am a free person, and this permits me to discern my destiny, the "grand will" guiding my life. Through my relationships, in which I give of myself, I will become real, more alive. When I am able to turn my being toward the center of reality I approach the face of God. By relating to our world in I-Thou terms, I am introduced into the world of God—the Eternal Thou.

Now, don't let all the poetic philosophy and tricky language obscure the essentially biblical message about the meaning of people, relationships, and the way we relate to and find God in our world. Buber's framework has been extremely influential in shaping our best thinking ever since he wrote on the topic (including C. S. Lewis, Karl Barth, Carl Rogers, and Dietrich Bonhoeffer, to name a few). To see people as objects of almost impossible worth is to see them as God sees them. Just look deeply into the eyes of any person, recognize them as objects of God's redeeming love in Jesus, act toward them in the way our Jesus acted, and you will change both yourself and your world. If God is love, as John so profoundly states, then Buber's approach gets us much closer to seeing the world through the eyes of the love that is God. Hear these words again:

Dear friends, let us love one another, for love comes from God. Everyone who loves has been born of God and knows God. Whoever does not love does not know God, because God is love. This is how God showed his love among us: He sent his one and only Son into the world that we might live through him. This is love: not that we loved God, but that he loved us and sent his Son as an atoning sacrifice for our sins. . . .

And we have seen and testify that the Father has sent his Son to be the Savior of the world. If anyone acknowledges that Jesus is the Son of God, God lives in him and he in God. And so we know and rely on the love God has for us.

God is love. Whoever lives in love lives in God, and God in him. In this way, love is made complete among us so that we will have confidence on the day of judgment, because in this world we are like him. There is no fear in love. But perfect love drives out fear, because fear has to do with punishment. The one who fears is not made perfect in love. (1 John 4:7–18)

Own it!

The (real) shining

Finally, we have found it helpful to be reminded to "keep the end in mind" when it comes to understanding identity formation in both discipleship and mission.[9] Theologian James Payton reminds us to look at salvation as *theosis*, the process of increasingly becoming "partakers of the divine nature" (2 Peter 1:4), rather than as a once off "get out of hell free card." He turns to the Eastern Orthodox who emphasize this by starting with God's words at creation: "Let us make human beings in our image, make them reflecting our nature" (Gen. 1:26 Message).

In Eastern Orthodox teaching, "image" and "likeness" are not the same: the first is gift, the second a goal. With these words, God distinguished what human beings were from what they were to become. Adam and Eve bore the image of God, but they were to grow into the divine likeness. They were to live in communion with God, walk in his ways, serve him, tend his creation, and love him and each other and the children they were to produce. If they did, they would grow in holiness, righteousness, and love—becoming ever more like God, who would bless them with the eternal life that belongs only to him.[10]

Payton goes on to show that the idea of salvation as *theosis*, though not fully understood in evangelical circles, was something that strongly influenced John Wesley's view of sanctification, as well as that of C. S. Lewis, who wrote, "God said that we were 'gods' and he is going to make good his words."

Payton goes on to show some of the differences:

> In evangelicalism's polished doctrinal teaching on salvation, we distinguish phases in the reception of salvation: conversion, justification, sanctification, and glorification. In the last step, we are completely conformed to the image of Christ (Rom. 8:29) and made like him (1 John 3:2). We are resurrected as glorified human beings, fully in communion with God, though remaining distinct from him.
>
> However, the way we typically speak about salvation emphasizes only the beginning of the process: conversion, justification, and to some degree, sanctification. Eastern Orthodoxy emphasizes the final result, the glorification by which we are made entirely like Christ: holy, righteous, perfect in godliness, and enjoying the fullness of eternal life. And in this, I believe Orthodox believers have something

that can help better balance how we preach and teach about salvation.[11]

This idea of being glorified through Christ seems to suggest that we are somehow incorporated, without loss of our individual, human uniqueness, into the Godhead through Jesus. Lewis coined the term "transposition" to describe this same phenomenon. "We are told in one of the creeds that the Incarnation worked 'not by conversion of the Godhead into flesh, but by taking of the Manhood into God.' And it seems to me . . . that humanity, still remaining itself, is not merely counted as, but veritably drawn into, Deity."[12]

To embrace this understanding is to always keep in mind the development of others and ourselves in becoming more like God. Salvation isn't simply about changing behavior; it is about growing more and more into God himself and bringing that reality to bear on all humanity. We are changing, we are becoming more like God, and this changes everything!

Many things intrude on our sense of identity: vocations, culture, sexuality, idols, and other people, to name but a few. The formation of correct identity is crucial to both our discipleship and our mission into the world, because how we image ourselves is what we become. And how we view others determines the way we relate to them. As followers of Jesus, we must embrace our God-given identity, for it is as we embrace the *imago Dei* and live out of this image that we come alive to ourselves, to others, and to the world around us.

Kierkegaard was right in saying that how we relate to God determines everything, including our identity and, in fact, our very personhood; without God there is no possibility of a self. It is only when we ground ourselves in God and turn to him that we will be able to form our identity. Without this most fundamental relationship, we simply cannot develop into the people that God intends us to be. It is into his face that we must look, for without him we are nothing.

We finish with Meilaender's description of a scene from *The Last Battle* (in *The Chronicles of Narnia* series), which powerfully illustrates this very thing.

> In the great scene of eschatological judgment at the conclusion of *The Last Battle*, a division is made between those who look on Aslan with love and those who do not. More accurately, the creatures of Narnia themselves make the division. As they come streaming up to the door of the stable at which Aslan stands, all must look on his face. Some look and find with delight the face for which they have always been searching. Others look and see only fear and terror. They veer off to the left into the nothingness created by Aslan's shadow, and significantly, they cease at that moment to be Talking Beasts. In turning from Aslan they turn from their true selves; for loyalty to self in opposition to Aslan has turned out to be self-destructive loyalty.[13]

Suggested Practices

- *Read the Bible as identity statements*: This relates to the descriptive elements of the Bible, especially the New Testament. For instance, when it says that we are "holy ones" (saints), then accept that as a fact. We are not holy because of our behavior, but because we have been "sanctified in Christ." These kinds of statements (such as "seated together with Christ," "adopted into God's family," and "justified before God") are essential markers of who we are in God.

- *Seek the face*: There is no Hebrew word for relationship, but the idea of relationship is fully contained in the notion of God's face—the face is the essence of relationship. It follows that to know ourselves truly we must seek the face of God. This is not as easy as it sounds, because there are aspects of our humanity that resist a relationship to the holy. It is uncomfortable at times. But resting in God is absolutely essential to a healthy soul, and therefore to being a disciple. Loving God involves prayer and trust. Make sure you spend time alone with God.

- *Find yourself in relationships*: The other aspect of knowing ourselves is the social dimension. If we withdraw ourselves from the drive to know and be known by others, we damage our capacity to be authentic and healthy humans, let alone disciples. Practice friendships. Get to really know people. They provide an irreplaceable clue to knowing yourself.
- *See the image of God in others*: Look at people the way that God sees them, not as they present themselves to your immediate senses.
- *Take an audit of things that make up your identity*: This will involve relentless questioning, such as to what degree career, being a parent, being a respected member of the community, and so on plays in defining who you really are. These are important parts of our lives, but must be secondary to our identity in God.
- It can be helpful in your quest for greater understanding of the self and others to use the many wonderful personality profiles that are available.

Discussion Starters

1. "Who am I?" "Where am I going?" and "Who will go with me?" Alan and Deb use these questions in marriage counseling with wannabe marrieds. Getting the order right when answering these questions is absolutely essential to maintaining the covenant of marriage; failure in the more basic questions creates real trouble later on. Discuss this in relation to discipleship, marriage, and community.
2. Discuss how the Bible views the role of the ego in discipleship. Why does Jesus say that we must first die to self in order to follow him?

203

3. Discuss the paradigm shift Debra and Alan experienced in relation to the *imago Dei*. How can this change the way you see people in your life?
4. How can Buber's teaching on "I and Thou" change your perspectives on life and people?

8

too sexy for the church?

Yes, sex without love is an empty experience, but as empty experiences go, it's one of the best.

—Woody Allen

Sex and religion are intricately interwoven because they are dealing with the basic elements of intimacy and the stuff of ecstasy.

—Eugene Peterson

Ultimately, becoming one is not limited to the lovers, for there is a divine nature in sexual intimacy.

—Miguel A. De La Torre

A number of years ago, Alan conducted a wedding cere- mony during which he mentioned the connection between God and orgasms. He invited people to think about getting to know the amazing Person who can invent things like the orgasm—appropriate, we thought, given the context of a

205

marriage. As expected, it created quite a buzz among some of the listeners. Strangely enough, it was the Christians who had more trouble with it than the non-Christians. It seems they had never made the connection, let alone mentioned the words "God" and "orgasms" in the same sentence. For the non-Christians present, it was quite a hit; as a result we were engaged in very interesting conversations about spirituality for the rest of the night. We are not being flippant here. Think about it: if God didn't create the orgasm, then who did? The devil? Surely not! And if we can't even seem to bring the two words together, then what does that say about our view of God, creation, redemption, and, in the end, our witness in a sexually broken world?

That many of us continue to struggle with even talking about sexuality should be of concern. Historically, this issue perhaps more than most has both intrigued and confounded us; given the surging and insistent nature of sexuality, this is no surprise. But not talking about it hasn't helped our case at all—many Christian young people still rely predominantly on sources other than the church to learn about their sexuality.[1]

Much needs to be said about human sexuality—far more than can be expressed in one simple chapter—and, in fact, this will be the subject of Deb's next book. What we hope to do here is to raise issues as they relate to both our discipleship and our mission. With these qualifications, let's proceed.

The Sexy God

We find it amusing that while some of God's people tend to be ignorant, anxious, and even embarrassed about all things sexual, God clearly is not. Not only is he the creator and designer of sexuality, but he also doesn't mind documenting some pretty risqué stories in Scripture.

For instance, Jonathan Kirsch starts his book *Harlot by the Side of the Road* by noting,

> The stories you are about to read are some of the most violent and sexually explicit in all of Western literature. They are tales of human passion in all of its infinite variety: adultery, seduction, incest, rape, mutilation, assassination, torture, sacrifice, and murder. And yet every one of these stories is drawn directly from the pages of the Holy Bible.[2]

Kirsch then proceeds to give a commentary on seven stories from the Old Testament chosen for their particularly scandalous content. These narratives have, over time, been deliberately passed over, toned down, or even outright banned by a church incapable of integrating them into its worldview. Why, he rightly asks, if they are part of our Bible, do we tend to dodge them so? Good question.

While Kirsch does not profess to be a disciple of Jesus, he has raised the profile of the Bible in a way that many Christians fail to do, for he is not afraid to make public all the "naughty" bits we prefer to avoid. The reality is that those same naughty bits can offer great hope to those who have walked similar roads. By describing the failings of the biblical saints, it serves to normalize sexual brokenness as part of the yet-to-be-redeemed human condition. For instance, when the great King David not only commits adultery but also lies and murders in order to soothe his desire, then no matter what we might have done, God's forgiveness, love, and grace can be experienced by all.

Little bits of creation we don't like to talk about

207

I'm Too Sexy for the Church

The church has had a hard time reconciling sexuality as an aspect of Christian experience. Some very spiritual people have seriously misread the creational purposes of God in this regard and, as a result, have produced a harmful legacy for those who inherited their defective theology.

God created humans as sexual beings; in Scripture and in human experience, spirituality and sexuality are linked at a very deep level. To embrace one significant aspect of our humanity at the expense of the other *must* inevitably cause problems. Like it or not, we are very much spiritual and very much sexual. Failure to integrate these can cause us to live a fragmented life that operates at two irreconcilable levels: a disembodied spirituality that floats at least two inches above the earth *and* a suppressed bodily sexuality that will inevitably seek to express itself in dark ways.

It's as though we believe our sexuality directly opposes our spirituality and that the more sexual we are, the less spiritual we must be. Or the reverse can also be true: the more spiritual we become, the less sexual we are. While neither of these is true, one can certainly overcome sexual problems by deepening one's spirituality. Our experience working with sexual addicts provides adequate testimony to this reality. We have observed many times dramatic decreases in sexually "acting out" when an individual grew in the ways of the Shema—in loving God and others. Relationships were the key; loving and being loved is what they really needed. As with most addictions, the presenting issue is just a symptom; the real issues are of the heart.

One does not have to be a driven sex addict to live the dualistic, segmented existence described above. Most people struggle to integrate the two. But because of Christianity's historic suspicion that pleasure (especially sexual) is somehow "of the devil," Christians generally tend to get this aspect of their lives, at least to some degree or another, wrong.

208

Take a cold shower, Origen!

Most of our problems related to sexuality and spirituality come from the incursion of a false, unbiblical dualism into our sense of what it means to be a human and disciples of Jesus. Essentially, dualism stems from the mistaken belief that humans have two basic natures, the physical and the spiritual, or the body and the mind, and that these two are in irreconcilable conflict with each other. All pleasures (*especially* sexual ones) originate from the body and are therefore viewed as fundamentally evil because they take us away from God. As a result, the disciple has to suppress all sexual urges to be a truly spiritual person.

This form of bodily dualism was introduced in Christianity very early on as Christianity moved out of the more holistic (non-dualistic) worldview of the Hebrews to the essentially dualistic worldview of the Greeks—we need look no further than some of the early church fathers to see this. A good example is the brilliant philosopher-theologian Origen. He was famous for helping guide the church theologically, but one of his more renowned actions was that he castrated himself because he believed his sexuality contradicted his love for God. In Origen's mind, something had to go! Thankfully he chose the sexual part, because he was needed by the church of his day. But you would agree that it was a pretty extreme measure. In his hilarious book *The Year of Living Biblically*, A. J. Jacobs comments, "Origen is said to have interpreted literally Matthew 9:12 . . . and castrated himself. Origen later became a preeminent theologian of his age—and an advocate of *figurative* interpretation" (italics ours).[3]

A bit late for his offending organs, perhaps, and no doubt brought about by the realization that sexuality could not be taken out by the removal of his testicles, Origen and others like him tragically found that castration fails to eradicate the issue of sexuality; sex is more than simply what we do with our genitals. It has deep connections with our psyche as well as our spirituality.

Then there was Augustine, a fifth-century theologian whose thinking has profoundly influenced Christianity. He was a great man, but because he struggled with dualism and a strong sex drive he also became well known for his highly conflicted views about sexuality. He stated (rightly) that the act of sex was acceptable only within the context of marriage and (wrongly) for the *sole* purpose of procreation. He also taught that any pleasure associated with the act of intercourse was to be rejected as evil. In fact, he went on to teach that original sin was actually passed on to the child in the physical act of sex itself. So, folks, you can have sex if your purpose is *purely* to have babies. But you had better focus on the cross while you are doing it, because if you happen to enjoy it at all, you are sinning and damaging your child! It took us a good fifteen hundred years to get over the bad guilt trip Augustine introduced into Western culture.[4] Theology has consequences.

It gets far more bizarre than that! Enter the so-called desert fathers. These guys were without doubt the spiritual heroes of their day. What they did to their bodies would be absolutely hilarious if they weren't so sincere and the effects so tragic. They sought to resolve their issues with sexual temptation by taking seriously extreme measures. One guy, suffering sexual temptation, went out naked into the desert to be bitten by mosquitoes. It was his way of dealing with the temptations and evils of the flesh. He didn't come back that night. When some of the brothers went to find him, they discovered a blubbering blob of humanity nearly bitten to death by the bugs. He barely survived. Others like Simon Stylites resorted to living on top of a pole for forty years—far from the reach of women. Fired by dualism, the desert fathers reviled and mistreated their bodies, loathed their all-too-human lives, and saw salvation as a final relief from the passions associated with the body. While these people were utterly sincere, spiritual people, they rejected the sexual and other bodily dimensions, thus severing humanity from its source of meaning in relation to God (see Figure 1 below). From these examples, we can see that the church's theological conflict in relation to sex has to do with the splitting in two of the spiritual and the physical.[5]

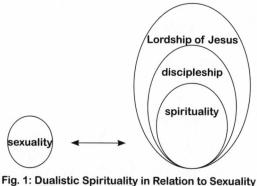

Fig. 1: Dualistic Spirituality in Relation to Sexuality
(Sexuality Ejected from Spirituality)

It's high time we got over dualism! This unbiblical concept not only distorts our understanding of humanity, but also creates a false distinction between sacred and secular, work and play, religious experiences and ordinary social experiences, spirituality and sexuality. It is profoundly suppressing and antihuman. And it still informs much of the church's thinking, as, for instance, in the Catholic doctrine of the celibacy of the clergy.

But how can this be? Clearly our bodies are a gift of creation (Genesis 1–3), and their associated passions are elemental forces out of which arise many great human works, the holy included. Martin Buber is absolutely right when he says, "Of all the works of creation, it is passion which is the very good, without which man cannot serve God, or truly live."[6]

To which Heschel adds,

God is not only the creator of earth and heaven. He is also the One who created delight and joy. . . . Even lowly merriment originates in holiness. The fire of evil can better be fought with flames of holy ecstasy than through fasting and mortification.[7]

Suppressing our basic humanity is the counsel of despair. The answer lies rather in redeeming and directing our passions. For disciples, the answer must be found in rejecting dualism and attempting to integrate our lives by bringing the whole of life, sex included, under the sovereignty of God.

There is no doubt in our minds that the link between sexuality and spirituality is a sacred one. As Paul Jewett says, "Our sexuality is a quality of being that penetrates the deepest ground of our humanity."[8] Karl Barth maintained that the way we reflect our Creator, the way we are like God most precisely, is in our sexuality.[9] Theologian Stanley Grenz, among others, also hints at this when he talks about human sexuality being the basis for the human drive toward bonding, as it relates to the defined goal of establishing community among humans and between humans and God.[10] Like the *imago Dei*, no matter how damaged it is, our sexuality is still a primary part of us. The poet Rainer Maria Rilke says,

> Human experience lies so incredibly close to that of sex, to its pain and its ecstasy, that the two manifestations are indeed but different forms of one and the same yearning and delight.[11]

Kissin' cousins

Before we more fully explore the connections between our spirituality and sexuality, it might be helpful at this point to suggest a working definition for both.

Sexuality is the deep desire that drives us beyond ourselves in an attempt to connect with, to understand, that which is other than ourselves. Essentially, it is a *longing to know and be known by other people (on physical, emotional, psychological, and spiritual levels)*.

Spirituality is a vast longing that drives us beyond ourselves in an attempt to connect with, to probe, and to understand our world. Beyond that, it is the inner compulsion to connect with the Eternal Other that is God. Essentially, it is a *longing to know and be known by God (on physical, emotional, psychological, and spiritual levels)*.

God understands we are both spiritual and sexual, for he made us that way. To deny one or the other is to deny integral parts of our humanity. And to keep them compartmentalized within us is to remain fragmented. In this light, spirituality can be seen as a vertical longing and sexuality as a horizontal longing.

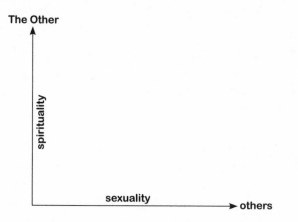

Viewed this way, we see that spirituality and sexuality are indeed very similar: both involve searching for connection, one for the Divine, one for the human. Our deepest longings as humans are to be in relationship with both God and our neighbor—this really and simply *is* the human condition. We can see why some have called these two dimensions "kissing cousins."[12] And remember that the Hebrew word *yada* (to know) is used for both our relationship with God as well as for sexual intercourse. In the Bible, intimacy (time, belonging, and commitment) is required for both of these relationships to function as they are meant to. Weird, but true!

Clearly, then, sex isn't just about sex. Writer Christopher West is right when he says, "The way we understand and express our sexuality points to our deepest held convictions about who we are, who God is, the meaning of love, the ordering of society, and even the ordering of the universe."[13] Therefore, the more integrated we become in these, the more whole we will become. Wholeness will not come through a suppression of one's sexuality; that would be to deny a vital aspect of our humanity.

Heavenly Orgasms

A few years ago we decided to set up a stall at *SEXPO*, the massive, annual sexuality exhibition in our city put on by the porn industry. The purpose in doing this was to be a living presence of Jesus in dark places and to generate discussion around sexuality and spirituality. The name of the stall we set up was called "Heavenly Orgasms"—not the best name, but provocative enough to attract attention. Well, it worked! Most people that passed by commented on the name and asked what it meant. As you can imagine, conversations ranged far and wide, and we were able to share the gospel with a number of people.

Is there anywhere God is not? And if he is there, can't we join him? For us this has meant that we've joined God in some pretty strange, dark, and even dangerous places.

Rather, our sexuality must always be seen as not only integral to who we are as humans, but as part of the intended created order. It is a gift from God—not some seedy idea of the devil that came after the fall, as some, such as the church fathers mentioned above, have been tempted to think.

Something is still missing. To our two definitions above, we need to add one more to make sense of it. We need to see how this all relates to discipleship. Lets see what happens when we add this definition to the equation.

Discipleship *involves knowing and being known by God through Jesus and living our lives in the kingdom of God.* As followers of Jesus, we are not called to a vague and undefined spirituality but to a spirituality that exists within the context of discipleship.

Discipleship, the lifelong process of becoming more and more like Jesus, will therefore require offering all that we are to our Lord. This involves striving in the power of the Holy Spirit to gather our drives and passions and directing them toward God in worship. Sex is sacred, but not to be used for idolatry. Remember, biblical spirituality involves the extension of Jesus's kingship over all spheres of life. The body is a temple, not an amusement park. When we bring all these together, it looks something like Figure 2 (compare with Figure 1 on page 211).

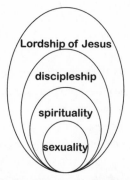

Fig. 2: Holistic Discipleship in Relation to Sexuality
(Sexuality Integrated with Spirituality and Discipleship)

Integrating sexuality requires moving beyond an undefined notion of spirituality to that of following Jesus in the task of discipleship. Once again, we touch on the spirituality of the Shema, where we are instructed to love God with all our heart, soul, mind, and strength (spirituality) and to love others as we love ourselves (which must involve all loves, including our sexuality).[14]

The loathsome toy

In *The Great Divorce*, C. S. Lewis tells a great allegorical story about a ghost of a man afflicted by lust. Lust is represented by a red lizard that sits on the shoulder of the man and whispers convincingly into his ear. The man eventually begins to despair about the lizard, at which point an angel offers to kill it for him. But the man is torn about what to do. He fears the death of lust will kill him; he makes excuse after excuse to the angel to keep the lizard. But finally the man allows the angel to seize and kill the lizard. The angel grasps the reptile, breaks its neck, and throws it to the ground. This ghostly man is gloriously transformed into a real and solid being while the lizard, rather than dying, is turned into a powerful white stallion. Weeping with tears of joy, the man jumps onto the horse and they fly to the heavens. What Lewis is saying here is that *eros* (and in this case, lust), redeemed and directed, becomes holy passion and will take us to God.

When we fail to integrate our lives under God, sexuality becomes a dangerously isolated part of our nature—unsanctified, yet potent. And when so strong a force as sexuality is left to itself, it invites the darkness. Unredeemed, it becomes a major problem for followers of Jesus in a world dominated by sexual imagery and impulses. Listen to the universal male struggle as expressed by novelist Frederick Buechner:

> Lust is the ape that gibbers in our loins
> Tame him as we will by day
> He rages all the wilder by night
> And there is no river in the world that flows cold and
>   strong enough to strike him down
> Almighty God, Why dost Thou deck men out with
>   such a loathsome toy?[15]

216

A loathsome toy indeed! Author Robert Hicks says that without a proper understanding of their sexuality, "men will carry around in their psyches a spiritual God-hunger so mysterious and powerful that when it is driven underground, it will seek spiritual fulfillment only in the secrecy of hotel rooms, nightclubs, and endless secret affairs."[16]

So what about women? Without wanting to generalize or point out the obvious, men and women will express their sexuality in similar but also different ways. Male sexuality, as evidenced above, will tend to express itself in more "genital" ways, and female sexuality in more "social" ways, including insecurity, emotional over-attachments, inappropriate interest in other people's affairs, and promiscuity, among other things.[17] We recognize not all men or women fit neatly into these obvious stereotypes, but stereotypes exist for a reason.

A good example that highlights the differences between men and women is the magazines we purchase. The top-selling men's magazines are listed in the category of "soft porn"—*Playboy*, *Ralph*, *Maxim*, and the like. The highest selling women's magazines are *Who Weekly*, *Woman's Day*, and so on. One is more about *genital* sexual interest and the other *social* sexual interest. We would include all these magazines in the pornographic category. If male porn has to do with looking at people's private parts, the female version has to do with looking at people's private lives. We call this "social pornography." It fills women's gossip magazines and does enormous damage to the women addicted to them.

We can't count the number of young women we have ministered to over the years who were damaged by the "beauty myth" promoted through these magazines (nevermind the gossip, unhealthy interest in people's lives, and addiction to the celebrity cult). When we set up certain people as the "beautiful people," and their lifestyles as the glamorous way to live, we set up an unattainable standard. The problem with standards of beauty is that they imply standards of ugliness.

217

And let's be honest, how many of us really look like that? Moreover, the gossip these magazines engender is seriously disturbing. We ought not be poking around in people's lives without being invited. By doing so, we assume a certain false intimacy that shortcuts real friendships, just like male pornography shortcuts a healthy sexual expression.

As far as the Bible is concerned, prurient interest in both is out of bounds for the disciple. If women insist on men not looking at *Penthouse*, we suggest that women might want to give up on *People* magazine as well. Either way, unredeemed male and female sexuality is a major cause of human brokenness and a major reason why many walk away from following Jesus.

The spiritual power in sexuality is extremely strong. It is interesting that all sexual compulsions seem to have a religious air about them. They are profoundly ritualized, and ritual is the mark of worship. Sexual addictions and aberrations can easily become our expressions of worship—to a false god. Our sexual problems only reveal how desperate we are to express, even in some perverted form, the deep compulsion to worship God.

When agony meets ecstasy

When people fail to redeem and redirect their sexuality toward the holy, when it is isolated from the Shema's challenge to love God with body, soul, will, and spirit, then it *will* take us where we don't really want to go, and it will become a "loathsome toy." Left unredeemed, and without the moral and spiritual restraints that come with following Jesus, the full-blown spiritual power of sexuality becomes an enslaving idol and will almost definitely become extremely harmful to both men and women.

In Shema spirituality, as we have seen, the task is not to suppress our humanity with its pleasures and drives. On the contrary, we are to direct our passions in such a way that, without losing their force, they cease to be evil. The way to do this is to reorient them toward God in holiness. This reorienting of life, or "hallowing"—making holy—transforms the urges by confronting them with holiness and making them responsible to what is holy. "Transforming the evil passion into good," Buber writes, cannot take place inside oneself, but only in relation [to God and others].[18] What Buber is saying here is that salvation is not simply a private affair of the soul; it involves responsibly relating to God and people—hence, the Shema. If C. S. Lewis was right in saying that all our sins are virtues gone wrong, our task is to redirect them to God in the power of the Holy Spirit.

If we really believe God is Creator *and* Lord of all, there can be no realm of life that cannot be redeemed if we are to be authentic lovers of God. There is no sacred and secular if God claims all. And redemption is not simply a private affair of the soul but must include our involvement in the world through active engagement with God and others in every arena of life. God demands that we offer *all* to him as an act of love and worship. Holiness in the Scriptures has less to do with opposing or denying daily human experiences than actively redeeming them by *directing* them toward God. C. S. Lewis rightly taught, "There is but one good; that is God. Everything else is good when it looks to Him and bad when it turns from Him."[19] Besides, we have found the only way to overcome an enslaving passion for bad things is to have a greater passion for that which is good. For instance, we suggest lust is essentially the love of beauty divorced from the love of goodness.

What, then, do we do with those passions—especially our sexuality—that have terrible power to enslave us, ruin relationships, and damage society? As disciples, we must, as an act of worship, learn how to direct them toward God. Our passions are part of our humanity, and passion is only evil when it remains directionless, when it will not accept the way that leads us toward God.

219

You're Too Sexy for *My* Church

We have a friend who refers to himself as "the harlot by the side of the road." He is a gay man who has been HIV-positive for almost twenty years. He deeply loves Jesus and because of that has struggled with his sexuality for as long as he can remember. The path of discipleship has never been an easy one for him, partly because of his struggle but also because the church has not really known what to do with him. Much of his journey is walked alone, and much of his struggle is known only to him and God. Our friend is not alone; there are many people out there who feel like harlots by the side of the road and who would never dare to become part of a living community of faith because of the guilt, shame, or even stigma they carry.

Although the sad reality is that our friend is "too sexy" for many of our churches, some communities of faith are becoming much more intentional about breaking down the stigma that so often attaches to people who struggle with their sexuality. We recently saw the movie *Milk*, in which Sean Penn portrays Harvey Milk, a gay political activist. The movie is based on the true story of Milk's life and eventual assassination. It is set in San Francisco in the politically tumultuous seventies and portrays a very ugly side of the church, with Anita Bryant leading the charge against gay people—all in the name of God! We thank God that we as a church have come a long way since those days, but are conscious that we still have a long way to go.

The reality of this is seen in the research, mentioned in an earlier chapter, by David Kinnaman and Gabe Lyons in their book *unChristian*. They looked into what "outsiders" thought of people in the church, and reveal that 91 percent of the people surveyed, people aged between sixteen and twenty-nine, stated that their prime perception of the church was that it was "anti-homosexual" and attacked gay people incessantly.[20] These are staggering statistics. How did we find ourselves in a place where the primary thing "outsiders" can say of us is that we are anti-gay? Not that we are amazingly graceful, loving, or compassionate people, but that we hate homosexuals! This is truly remarkable when you consider that the One we follow doesn't mention homosexuality, not even once! The second and third most prominent descriptions of Christians made by outsiders were that they are judgmental (87 percent) and hypocritical (85 percent).[21]

...and make all sorts of terrible assumptions about me.

Our dear friend Mark, a psychologist who specializes in AIDS and sex education, has a mantra: "Ignorance breeds fear, and fear breeds judgment." This dictum, that we fear what we do not understand and judge that which we fear, certainly seems to be the case with a lot of Christians regarding the issue of homosexuality. In fact, Christians tend to fear all things sexual, which can cause us to be judgmental toward others in issues relating to sex and sexuality—even though we ourselves have not generally lived up to the biblical standard. Hence, Kinnaman's statistics ring true!

Mirror, mirror, on the wall . . .

It is glaringly obvious to us that what is at work here is the biblical principle "judge not, or you will be judged, and at least in the same measure by which you judge" (Matt. 7:1–2). If we were to be really honest with ourselves, most of

221

us have, for years, feared, judged, and actively persecuted this particular community. Remember, for many non-Christians the first thing that comes to mind when thinking of Christians is "anti-homosexual." This has enormous implications for the church as we seek to do mission, particularly among those between the ages of sixteen and twenty-nine, let alone among the gay community itself.

Our judgments have boomeranged back on us—it was bound to happen, for we were explicitly warned by Jesus about this. Now, whether we want it or not, an issue that perhaps wasn't even on our radar has foisted itself upon us, because we are all painted with the same brush—we are all seen as unChristian! Our very reputations as Christians are now tied in with a people group most of us at best tolerate and at worst have outright contempt for.

Key missiologist Ed Stetzer rightly notes that based on the church's treatment of homosexuals alone, there will be increasingly more people that will simply not give you and your church a hearing.[22] If we are perceived to be ungracious in our attitudes and responses to gay people, we will effectively be foreclosing on meaningful conversations with many. The issue is not what we ourselves believe about human sexuality, but rather how we *treat* those with differing perspectives on sexuality. The issue is our flagrant lack of mercy and compassion—the very things we so gratefully claim for ourselves. This bears false witness to what we stand for—that we are all sinners who have freely received grace and forgiveness. Why can we not offer it in return? We should pay attention to Jesus's warning about lack of grace (for instance, in Matt. 18:23–35).

Jesus explicitly warns his followers to be very careful of the "yeast of the Pharisees, which is hypocrisy" (Luke 12:1). Pharisees (ancient and modern) live inauthentically: their lives do not match their beliefs. As a result, they are dishonest and hide behind religion. The "pharisization" of Christian discipleship is a profoundly treacherous process—it works its way into the believer like yeast through dough. This is partly because of the lure of moralism and the desire to control. We suggest that if one has been a Christian for even a few years, it is absolutely necessary that we read the Gospels with the viewpoint that it is *us* who are the Pharisees! At the very least, we should admit some real sense of empathy toward them as they are not all that different from us. As Bruxy Cavey says, "Jesus critiques the Jewish religious leaders because they are *religious*, not because they are *Jewish*. And if we grab hold of that, we can see how his rebukes are transferable for all religions at all times."[23]

For instance, they were sincere, loved their Scriptures, believed in the supernatural, were waiting for the Messiah, were decent and morally upright, were zealous, tithed beyond duty, were "missional," and maintained Israel's identity and tradition in a time of occupation. In many ways, they were *exemplary* religious people. It's not hard to see how they are very much like us! We believe that if we do not read them as ourselves, we miss much of the truth of what Jesus has to say to us, and we will likely commit precisely the same sins that are associated with them. It is a problem every religious person encounters in life. Religious people get very fussy about "things" and then become coercive about it. If we are not careful, we can end up defending truths and at the same time miss Truth—just like the Pharisees. It's all about how we *inhabit* our beliefs and how we allow the power of our beliefs to inhabit or mold us.

For some reason, religious people have always picked on sexual sinners. To be honest, it's hard to know *why* exactly this is the case. Why single them out for special attention? Perhaps it has to do with the difference between what some have called *sins of the spirit* and *sins of the body*. It is much easier to hide the more respectable *spiritual* sins like greed, hypocrisy, self-righteousness, pride, envy, and so on. The "sexual sinner" is much more vulnerable to the graceless judgments of others because what they do is more obvious.

Alternative punchline: Once I lay my gavel down, I'll have a life.

Darn it—a covetous, self-righteous so-and-so can get into the ministry of the church and never be challenged about his or her sins, but we won't let those "filthy fags" or "unrighteous fornicators" even come to worship! Yet Jesus dealt very harshly with the former and compassionately with the latter (Matt. 11:19; Luke 7:36–48; John 8:1–11). How can we claim to follow Jesus when we are so unlike him in this regard?

Who's the greatest sinner of them all?

Over the years of journeying with people who have struggled with their sexuality, we still continue to be amazed at the way the church tends to focus on sexual sins, which are narrowed down to what we do with our genitals. We neglect other, more "acceptable" sins—for instance, the sin of greed and what we do with our money. How did we get it so backward? To be perfectly honest with you, we've come to believe that Jesus cares more about what we do with our money than what we do with our genitals! That doesn't mean he doesn't care what we do sexually, as of course he does, but he seems to care a whole lot more about what we do with our money.

Why is it that we have created a sort of hierarchy of sins the way we have, somehow putting sexual sins above most others? Perhaps part of the answer lies in Paul's teaching about sexual sins in 1 Corinthians 6. What Paul is talking about in this passage is that when we sin sexually, the consequences of our sin will be different to others because we will feel the effects within ourselves. However, Paul never says these sins are worse than others. In fact, he takes great pains to list a whole host of sins in the very same passage (1 Cor. 6:9–10), implying they are all at least equally sinful, lest any of us think we can assume higher ground. Sin is sin is sin.

What is true of course is that different sins will have different consequences. Let's return again to the comparison between sexual sins and sins of greed. In our estimation, if you were to weigh the consequences of, say, adultery, we would all agree it is a pretty bad sin because its ramifications include betrayal, relational breakdown, impact on families and friends, and loss of personal integrity. Recovery from adultery, including learning to trust again and to forgive, is difficult and may take a long time to work through, perhaps even a lifetime. All in all, pretty serious consequences.

But let's compare this to the consequences of the sin of greed. Greed, the excessive desire to acquire more (especially material wealth) than one needs or deserves, can play itself out in a host of ways, and not all financial. For instance, greed is one of the major reasons for murder, violence, and all sorts of other crime. But let's focus on the financial aspect just to prove a point. If avarice involves an excessive desire to acquire or possess more than one needs or deserves, it will not only impact our character and relationships; it will have more far-reaching, even global, implications, including issues of world poverty, abuse of poor people for cheap labor, environmental exploitation, and war. A study by the World Institute for Development Economics Research at United Nations University reports that the richest 1 percent of adults alone owned 40 percent of global assets in the year 2000, and that the richest 10 percent of adults accounted for 85 percent of the world total. The bottom half of the world adult population owned barely 1 percent of global wealth.[24] Now, we may think that one individual being greedy won't have an impact, but we need to face the reality that if every Christian repented of greed and lived much closer to the simpler ways of Jesus, we alone could probably solve the world's hunger problem!

Please don't misunderstand us here. We don't want to be seen as creating a hierarchy of our own, nor do we want to excuse any sin, but we do want to make the point that as disciples we need to look to Jesus as our reference. Committing to becoming more like Jesus means we must act like he does and do as he says. His priorities must become ours.

Acceptance must precede repentance

The best example we can find of Jesus's approach toward someone broken in their sexuality is found in John 8, the story of the woman caught in the act of adultery.

> While He [Jesus] was teaching, the scribes and Pharisees brought in a woman who was caught in the act of adultery, and stood her before Jesus. "This woman was caught in the act of adultery. Moses says in the law that we are to kill such women by stoning. What do you say about it?" This was all set up as a test for Jesus; His answers would give them grounds to accuse Him of crimes against Moses' law. Jesus bent over and wrote something in the dirt with His finger. They persisted in badgering Jesus, so He stood up straight. "Let the first stone be thrown by the one among you who has not sinned." Once again Jesus bent down to the ground and resumed writing with His finger. The Pharisees knew they had sinned, so there would be no stones thrown this day. Eventually only Jesus and the woman remained, and Jesus looked up. "Dear woman, where is everyone? Are we alone? Did no one step forward to condemn you?" "Lord, no one has condemned me." "Well I do not condemn you either; all I ask is that you go and from now on avoid the sins that plague you." (vv. 3–11 Voice)

This story is a beautiful example of grace and acceptance. Here is a woman caught in the very act of adultery; she was most likely naked in front of a leering crowd, totally humiliated and terrified, knowing her fate lay in the outcome of this encounter between Jesus and the religious leaders. The first thing Jesus does is restore something of her dignity by taking the focus off her and placing it on the crowd. Then, by exposing the hypocrisy of judgmentalism, he effectively levels everybody. In fact, this is a total reversal of what the crowds were expecting—religious people were put in the same category as adulterers! No doubt the woman herself was just as shocked. Jesus does not condone sin, but he knows grace is the answer, not judgment. It turns out that they (and we) are all simply human beings trying to work life out—some doing a better job of it than others.

We believe this story is important, not just because of how Jesus responded to the woman, but because of the order of the components of his response. He restores dignity to her, offers her his grace, and *then* calls her to repentance. Why? Knowing human need, he knows that the right context for real and lasting repentance is God's forgiveness, acceptance, and grace. He knows it is God's kindness that leads us to repentance. But we know that too. Isn't that exactly how we ourselves have been saved by Jesus? Of course! But if that is the case, why do we seem to get it the other way around? Why do we seem to send the message of acceptance based on repentance and socially suitable behavior? Jesus deliberately changed the order of things in his day, instituting the kingdom values of mercy, grace, and forgiveness over the rules and regulations of the Pharisees. We must do likewise.

Summing Up

Sexuality and spirituality are sacred and go to the heart of who we are as relational beings created in the image of God. Neither can be denied or neglected at the expense of the other without damaging the ecology of discipleship. Sex and worship are part of the way we fulfill the two greatest commandments of loving God and loving others.

As people who have received God's radical gift of grace, we are called to embody grace and extend it to others, particularly as we live in a broken world. Being called unChristian by non-Christian people has revealed that our treatment of the so-called "sexual sinners" has the character of bearing false witness to the radical nature of God's grace in Jesus. Disciples must leave the judgment of sins to God, but take seriously our call to model an alternative life that testifies to the gospel by which we ourselves are saved.

Suggested Practices

- *Connecting the dots*: As we have seen, the God of the Bible is the inventor of the orgasm, and he doesn't shy away from using sexual metaphor to describe the relationship he has with his people. He even describes idolatry as whoring after false gods (Jer. 3:2; Ezek. 23:27; the book of Hosea). Learn to say "God" and "orgasm" in the same sentence!

- *Getting over dualism*: This again is a difficult issue that relates largely to the intangible aspects of worldview. But to become integrated disciples, we simply have to get over the dualism that pervades our thinking and actions. We must constantly exercise the belief that this is all God's world and pleasure is his design.

- *Develop a theology of beauty*: Start by reading C. S. Lewis's *Cosmic Trilogy*, particularly the second volume, *Perelandra*. Get a feel for how Lewis can integrate almost inconceivable beauty and pleasure into the love of God. Let him help you redefine your understanding of heaven as a disembodied state. Read this book with friends and discuss it together.

- *Stop the sin of judging*: There is clearly a place for discernment of good and evil in the life of discipleship, but we are forbidden the type of judgment that places us in a false superiority to other people (Matt. 7:1–5). Let's take Jesus's advice here with utmost seriousness, because failure to do so poisons the life of faith. Focus on your own issues; do not try to solve other peoples' without first understanding the role of grace in your own life. Remember always that the measure by which we judge will be the measure by which we are judged, so be very careful. We are all beggars telling other beggars where to get bread.

- *Engage people on the "other side"*: If you know a homosexual person, why don't you try to have a conversation where you are the main listener seeking to understand their situation? Try not to pass judgment; just listen.

Discussion Starters

1. Do you have problems with relating sexuality to spirituality? Why?
2. How does discipleship redeem sexuality?
3. Discuss the definition of lust as the love of beauty divorced from the love of goodness.
4. Why do you think religious people reserve their harshest judgments for sexual sinners and not for other forms of sin?
5. How is it possible for a generation to think of Christians as essentially unChristian?
6. Would you run a stall at SEXPO, and if not, why not?

the untamed mission

9

going out, going deep

The reality of the Son of God, true God entering our humanity, is astounding, humbling, and mysterious.

—Dan Russ

To be a follower of Christ does not mean to imitate literally
but to express him through the medium of one's own life.
A Christian is no unnatural reproduction of Christ. . . . The
task of the Christian consists of transposing Christ into the
stuff of his own daily existence.

—Romano Guardini

The one thing that we can't bear for Jesus to be is *ordinary*,
for his ordinariness invites us to follow him by providing us
with a template of how to be Godlike even as an ordinary
human being.

—Michael Frost

We have already confessed to being captivated by the incarnation. The fact that the almighty God, Creator of

233

all that is, hung out in a regular neighborhood doing regular things for thirty years without anyone noticing is simply staggering. So hidden was God in Jesus that even his disciples didn't quite get who they were dealing with until after the resurrection! How is this possible? How can the omnipotent God be so hidden that no one noticed he was in the neighborhood?

The incarnation provided believers with a wonderful and completely definitive understanding of God. N. T. Wright suggests that we must again and again look "into the human face of Jesus of Nazareth, until the awesome knowledge comes over us, wave upon terrifying wave, that we are looking into the human face of the living God."[1]

This gazing into the human face of the God-Man Jesus is absolutely critical for us to get a true understanding of what it means to be an untamed disciple in the way of Jesus. The incarnation therefore shapes our discipleship (the Christian life bases itself on the Master) as well as how we engage our world in Jesus's name (the method of mission takes its cue from the incarnation).

We are really excited about the fact that so many Christians are now engaged in aspects of the missional conversation; the church in our day is increasingly adopting a missiological understanding of itself, and individual Christians are also beginning to realize that every one of us is sent by Jesus into the world—in other words, that we are all missionaries. Mission is no longer merely relegated to a minority subcommittee with a view to overseas mission alone. All this is good, but in our opinion there is one more step required if we are going to become a truly untamed movement—we must embrace the full missional implications of the incarnation. If incarnation is the most profound way that God engaged the world, then we, his people, must follow in his footsteps—we must become incarnation-*al*. If *missional* defines our being sent out into the world, then *incarnational* must define the way in which we engage the world.

The incarnation of God in Jesus causes us to see the world in a different light—it changes our perspectives on God, discipleship, culture, and mission. Call it a missional mode, stance, posture, or whatever; the *way* in which we actually incarnate the gospel among the people we are seeking to reach will implicitly communicate the meaning of Jesus's incarnation . . . or it won't. If a church displays a sign out front saying "God loves you" but has no active engagement in the community around them, their message will fall on deaf ears. Words, or signs in this case, can be cheap; actions communicate everything.

In our ministry with Forge Missional Training Network, one of our core emphases is on developing leaders in incarnational ways of doing mission. We use six incarnational discipleship practices called "the six P's" to help embed incarnational mission into the life of the intern: *presence, proximity, powerlessness, prevenience, proclamation,* and *passion.*[2] What we want to do in this chapter is simply suggest these as practices we should adopt if we are to engage the world in ways that are more consistent with our Lord.

1. The Practice of Presence

This missional stance draws inspiration from the fact that God was fully present in the incarnation of Jesus. Jesus was not merely some representative of God, a prophet, or an angel. He was God, 100 percent, fully present, in human flesh (John 1:1–16; Col. 1:15–20; Heb. 1:1–4; 1 John 1:1–3). If God is one of us, he knows our situation, our struggles, our yearnings, our temptations, our bodily functions and limitations (such as aging), and so on from *direct* experience (Heb. 4:14–16). It's hard to comprehend the meaning of this profound act of identification with us. At the very least it means he knows us, loves us, and has our very best interests at heart. We can trust him.

235

We believe that an incarnational stance is an extremely important aspect of missional lifestyle. As God identified with us, so ought we identify with others. This will mean taking a given culture or people group seriously and deeply investing in them. We will need to take significant time to understand their history, their stories, their heroes, their books, and so on, in order to get *their* take on things. It is about immersing ourselves into their lives. When we identify with a people, we take their culture and concerns to heart.

Lawrence and Louise Hirsch and family (Al's brother and sister-in-law) give us a great example of what it means to identify with a given culture. Following Paul's exhortation to reach the Jew first and then the Gentiles, they started a ministry in Melbourne, Australia, called Celebrate Messiah. It is an outreach to Jewish people and has had an incredible impact on the Jewish community in Melbourne. They have planted two churches so far and have seen hundreds of Jewish people come to know their Messiah. Beyond this, there is now evidence that Messianic Judaism is actually being considered to be a living part of the local Jewish life.

These Jewish believers see themselves as fulfilled Jews and continue on with many of their traditions. Of course, there are Gentiles present, but in order to identify with the Jewish people they have adopted many of the outward forms of the Jewish culture. This means that most congregants have *Shabbat* meals every Friday evening and celebrate Passover and all of the other feasts. Following Jewish customs, forms, and rituals, they meet for worship on Saturdays rather than Sunday. In spite of the fact that the wider Jewish community struggles to integrate them because of the historical anti-Semitism of the church, the members of Celebrate Messiah see themselves as part of the broader Jewish community in the city, and their impact is felt throughout.

This incarnational approach to mission is evident among many missionaries to Muslim contexts. For instance, we know of a group called Frontier Servants who, in order to identify with Muslim people, have for all intents and purposes actually become Muslims. Following Jesus (*Isa* in Arabic), they moved into the community and adopted the culture, customs, dress codes, and aspects of the religion where these did not conflict with explicit teaching of the Bible. One of them is now the official prison chaplain for Muslims in Melbourne prisons. This type of identification was particularly costly for the women, as they had to give up some of the basic freedoms Western women take for granted.

Paul tells us in 1 Corinthians 9:19–23 that he sought to become all things to all people in order to save some. Now, this might beg the question of how far we go in our attempt to identify and present the gospel in terms that people can understand. No doubt there are some limits. But if we are serious about identifying with a given people group, there is going to be a cost, whether that be in adopting a culture not our own or giving up personal freedoms. So be it.

But incarnational living need not necessarily be with another racial group. It can and must include the myriad subcultures in any Western city. It should also include various suburban settings, such as businesses, sports clubs, and so on.

2. The Practice of Proximity

This practice is largely focused around issues of what we do about geographic setting and relational closeness. Once again it draws its inspiration from God's action in Jesus. God became a man not only in order to identify with us (presence), but also to live with and among us! He was no recluse, keeping a safe distance; he literally immersed himself in people. Much of his time was spent just hanging out and getting to know the people around him. Jesus didn't expect people to come to where he was, as we so often do, but rather went to them. He hung out in their social spaces, markets, and synagogues, and visited their homes. In other words, he came into direct proximity; he was *near* to them.

Likewise, we need to reflect this in our own lives. Too many Christians "hang out" only with other Christians and in environments frequented by other Christians. If we are to follow Jesus, we need to make intentional choices to move out of our religious zones and be where the people are. It will require that we come into direct social contact with others and become a regular part of the natural rhythms of their community. Mike Frost makes this point in his excellent book *Exiles*.

> Close Your eyes.
> For into their guileless gaze the world will pour its pain,
> Forever heaping its anger on Your heart,
> And You must bear the outrage of its wounds,
> And You must bear the blame.
> Is it for this that You are here?
>
> —J. V. Taylor

> So, if we take the Incarnation seriously, we must take seriously the call to live incarnationally—right up close, near to those whom God desires to redeem. We cannot demonstrate Christlikeness at a distance from those whom we feel called to serve. We need to get close enough to people that our lives rub up against their lives, and that they see the incarnated Christ in our values, beliefs, and practices as expressed in cultural forms that make sense and convey impact.[3]

Where you stand determines what you see and do. A great example of this is set amidst the luxurious California beach city of Santa Barbara and involves the ministry of a friend of ours named Jeff Schaffer. We have lovingly nicknamed Jeff "the Jesus Man" because of the way he goes about his life and mission. Jeff was a pastor in a local church until a few years ago. Through much prayer, reading, and reflection, Jeff felt called to resign from his pastoral position at the church and spend the time and energy that was given to ministry within the church to those outside of the church. Having seen what Jeff does firsthand, we are truly amazed what a shift in proximity can accomplish. In a few short years, Jeff has built relationships with people who would never have darkened the doorsteps of a church. He leads several groups of not-yet-Christians in cool bohemian pubs and housing developments, and the homeless in parks. One group has recently identified itself as a church and adopted the name Holy Chaos, which is appropriate given the wild lives of some of the people. Jeff followed Jesus out into the streets, parks, and cafés; he went to be *near* the people and is now bringing the light of the kingdom to the dark, lost, and broken places of his city.[4]

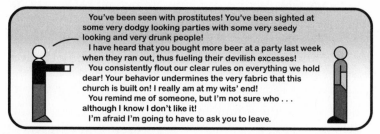

Pastor Roger misses the obvious.

For our primary calling to more marginal groups, a commitment to proximity meant that we relocated to the local red-light and gay area of our city. On the one side of our house is a heroin rehab facility, and on the other the "working stroll" of some of the local street prostitutes. Across the road are boarding houses for semi-homeless people, many struggling with mental health issues, and a famous "drag queen" bar on the corner. Being located in this environment meant that we could not but see the world differently. Every time we went out our front door, we were reminded of a broken and lost humanity and the issues that confront the mission of the church.

Obviously this view is utterly different from that of a middle-class suburb. There are real needs in a middle-class suburb, but for many cultural reasons those needs are much more hidden and enclosed in privacy. People are very busy, so they don't tend to socialize much outside of a very narrow group of friends. The practice of proximity in the suburbs will mean that the disciple will need to be far more creative in getting beneath the surface, in actively building meaningful relationships and developing a context of trust in order to touch base with the needs of the people. We know of missional disciples who variously host regular street parties, train people in the art of recycling, run mother's groups outside of Christian circles, organize backyard blitzes (cleaning, painting, gardening), adopt and maintain local parks, provide chaplaincy wherever needed, and use myriad other ways to engage people in the burbs.

Whatever the context, followers of Jesus will need to make very intentional choices about where we position ourselves so that we can see and respond to the need around us. Being incarnational is about how we live out what it means to be little Jesuses in the community we are in. For each of us this will look and feel very different, as there are many aspects to being the hands, heart, and feet of Christ in a given context. The places we find ourselves, whether through circumstance (for example, Paul in prison) or through the choices we make about where we decide to set up home (be it in the suburbs, urban settings, or the slums of India), will to some degree determine our perspectives and actions. And how we live out the incarnation will look very different depending on the context God has called us to.

3. The Practice of Powerlessness

While we can probably find many images in our culture of powerlessness, perhaps none is more obvious than that of a baby whose survival is totally dependent on others. Therefore, to think of Jesus as a dependent, vulnerable, and even needy baby is perhaps one of the most difficult things to grasp in God becoming man. Dan Russ rightly notes that when we reflect on the humanity of Jesus, our minds most easily leap to Jesus as a mature man.[5] But Jesus didn't come to us as a grown man. In order to fully identify with us, he literally came into the world as we do, born as a dependent, vulnerable child.

The great challenge for us is to recognize that to be weak, needy, and even powerless is part of the human condition, not something to be abhorred. When we give up our sense of power and control, we can truly become human in a way that conforms to the image of Christ.

One of the most amazing things we can say about Jesus (and therefore God) is that he is actually humble! The creator of all things is humble! We know this through what theologians call "his humiliation," powerfully described in Philippians 2. In Jesus, God does not come as an invading tyrant, but in the humblest of forms: the servant. This was not very "cool" in the Roman empire, as the slave was the lowest in the pecking order. This says a lot about God. But it ought to say a lot about us as well. "Every true follower of Christ must, through his own existence, try to express the same fact, that humility and self-denial are inseparable from the Christian life."[6]

So many of the sins of the historical church could have been avoided if we had simply understood this fact. There have been times when the last thing people would have called Christians is humble. We have been highly coercive, often unkind, and repeatedly judgmental. And yet Paul tells us to have the same attitude as Jesus (Phil. 2:5–8), to be *like* Jesus, who "emptied himself of all but love" (Charles Wesley).

When one applies this to our missionary calling in the world, it means that we come very humbly among a group of people. Like Jesus, we don't come into town wielding a sword (or a stick, for that matter) or riding in like the cavalry. Nor do we come legislating people's morals or flouting celebrity, money, and ego. Rather, we come to subvert evil and brokenness through Christlike service. Following our humble Lord, we can never approach incarnational mission from an arrogant perspective. Missional disciples must not expect to conquer by power or by force; they must use the same means as Jesus: steadfastness in the truth, acceptance of being misunderstood and rejected, and a willingness to achieve victory through redemptive suffering. This is a dreadfully difficult lesson for us to learn. We want to have it the way of the world.

4. The Practice of Prevenience

If you reflect back on our personal stories in the introduction, you might notice that both of us were involved in lifestyles that were removed from the influence of the church. Both of us had some sort of sensitivity to God and, strangely enough, both of us can testify to direct God experiences in and through drugs that eventually led us to Jesus! Many people might balk at this, but for us it is simply a fact. And it is not really all that strange; insofar as taking drugs is a search for ecstasy, for *otherness*, they are part of a person's spiritual quest. Many can get totally lost in this, and we believe most do, but we cannot exclude the spiritual factor in the equation. Both of us found that God (the true God—is there any other?) did speak to us even in the strangest moments and the weirdest drug-induced conversations.

The truth is that God doesn't limit his presence to baptized Christians—he is an unrelenting evangelist. He is always at work in his world—right in the thick of things—in sinful people's lives, including our own. Not all respond appropriately, but that doesn't seem to put our God off very much—he's persistent, he's insistent, and he's got a lot of mercy. John Wesley called this reality "prevenient grace" (preparatory grace), and he built his entire ministry squarely on it! He really believed that God was always preparing the way

242

for the preaching of the gospel, that he was *at work in every person, wooing them into relationship in and through Jesus.* It is sound biblical doctrine. We don't "bring God" with us into any situation—he's there long before you or I arrive on the scene. We simply need to discern God's prevenient work in people's lives and join with him. All of us are living testaments to this truth.

We have since come to understand that many people have God-moments, or what are sometimes called "theophanies," in their lives. A theophany is some form of religious experience, a manifestation of God, that could be prompted, for instance, by watching a sunset: suddenly the wonder of it all dawns on a person—time seems to stand still and eternity fills the moment. On other occasions, it could be in conversations—in a moment of in-breaking revelation, a significant truth dawns upon a person. This is what poet Gerard Manley Hopkins called an "inscape," and many people experience these at some time or another. As agents of Jesus, we can draw upon these experiences and give them their true meaning by directing people to the One who is the fulfillment of all human longing.

A funny story illustrates this idea of prevenient grace: in 2001 we bought a café-nightclub in order to set up a "proximity space" in one of the entertainment districts of our city. We both worked there in various capacities: bartender, waiter, manager, cook. One night, after Deb was closing up, she bumped into an anxious guy named Jason who asked her if she was "working." Deb immediately checked to see what she was wearing, thinking he had mistaken her for a prostitute. When she realized that wasn't what he was after, she asked him what he wanted. He replied that he needed help rolling a joint and held up his hand to show two fingers missing. Sensing his distress, she agreed and followed him to his car, which happened to be located around a dark, back corner. As she was following him, several things were running through her brain, including ethical questions about what she was about to do, whether the guy was going to kill her, and if she would even remember how to roll a joint—it had been a long time, after all!

Deb ended up rolling four joints for Jason, and as he began to smoke one, they began talking. In the course of probably an hour, he shared how he had struggled with homosexuality his whole life, had never told anybody, and how alone and isolated he felt as a result. Of all the people for him to share with, he meets Deb, who specializes in ministry to (and who genuinely loves) homosexual people! As they talked about the love and grace of Jesus, Jason began to weep. He was so thankful for Deb's time and heart that he tried to give Deb a thick wad of cash—which was graciously declined. God brought Jason and Deb together in that strange situation. In some weird way, Deb met with God as much as Jason did.

All disciples, regardless of our stories, are called in some way to practice prevenience—to somehow discern the traces and activity of God in people's lives and so join in the *missio Dei* (the mission of God), God's grand redemptive activity in his world. God is already doing this, and we can join him in the strange places of our cities. If we are not willing to follow our missionary God into such places, people on the edges of the church will likely never get to hear the gospel. The kingdom of God (God's active rule and activity) is not limited just to the church, but extends over the entire cosmos; we, being commissioned agents of the King, can join with God in the redemption of the world, anywhere, anytime.

5. The Practice of Passion

The great symbol of the Protestant church is the cross, and rightly so, as it is a representation and reminder of where and how our Lord died on behalf of a lost humanity. But, in case you hadn't noticed, the cross is empty. This symbolizes for Protestants the reality of the resurrection of Jesus, without which, as Paul says, we may as well all pack up and go home! (1 Cor. 15:1–32).

The truth of the resurrection and all that it signifies in the life of the believer is not to be taken lightly in any sense. We want to affirm not only that Jesus did indeed rise from the dead, but also the significance of his resurrection in the life and liberation of the individual believer and the church as a whole.

We also suggest, however, in line with our Catholic brothers and sisters, that the empty cross fails to represent the full story—we also need to embrace the image of the crucified God. In the crucifix, we are confronted with an image of the suffering Christ in all its forcefulness and brutality. While the act of the crucifixion was a one-time historical event summed up in Jesus's very own words ("It is finished"), Jesus still continues to suffer every day for you, for me, and for a lost humanity.[7] To overemphasize the resurrection without the balance of the crucifixion is to fail to comprehend the full picture of the death of Christ. This very thing caused Mel Gibson to portray the death of Jesus so vividly in his disturbingly graphic film *The Passion of the Christ*.

How can one make sense of Paul's words in Colossians without an understanding of the sufferings of Christ for the life and mission of the individual Christian? Paul is very clear in saying that not only is it a privilege to suffer on behalf of the gospel, but that he makes up in his own body what was lacking in the sufferings of Christ (2 Cor. 1:4, 6, 8; 2:4; 6:4; 7:4; 8:2; Phil. 1:7). He says, "Now I rejoice in what was suffered for you, and I fill up in my flesh what is still lacking in regard to Christ's afflictions, for the sake of his body, which is the church" (Col. 1:24).

While most commentators are not really certain what Paul is saying, we do know he's not suggesting in any way that what happened on the cross was incomplete or lacking. But in light of Paul's constant references in other passages to the church's "mystical union" with Christ (Rom. 6:3–11; 2 Cor. 4:10–14;

Phil. 3:10), perhaps what he *is* suggesting here is that suffering will continue to be borne by God's people. The church, *his body*, will in some way participate in the sufferings that were wrought in the very *physical* body of Christ.

In our experience of both discipleship and mission, this makes a lot of sense. The fact is that humans suffer, and Christians who take seriously the lost and broken in our world will also suffer. This is the cost of discipleship; we are called to pick up our cross and follow Jesus (Matt. 16:24; Mark 8:34; Luke 9:23). Implicit in the cross is suffering. In fact, Jesus clearly states that anyone who fails to pick up and carry the cross cannot be his disciple (Luke 14:72).

This has significant implications for discipleship and mission. As disciples we need to ensure we have incorporated a theology of redemptive suffering into our understanding of God, for this helps make sense of what we ourselves, or others, may experience. We also need to cultivate a sense of empathy or compassion for the other. This, in our minds, squares with how Jesus responded to others. He not only identified by experiencing the limitation that humanity brought, but he extended himself to feel what the other was feeling. We have called this an *incarnation of the heart*, and believe it is essential if we are to embody what it is to be like Jesus and to offer this gift to the rest of humanity.

Identification on the level of the heart implies a certain intimacy with the people you are trying to reach. Identification, as we've said before, is understanding their stories, their heroes, their books, their take on things. To incarnate on the level of the heart means we begin to *feel* their stories, their lives, their pains. Our hearts and compassion are thereby activated.

If we are called to a particular people group or subculture, we need to understand the angst and pain the group may carry. A good example here is the Jewish community. It would be very hard indeed to launch a ministry to Jewish people without a basic knowledge of the Holocaust and a fairly solid apprecia-

Walking a mile in someone else's glasses.

tion of the pain that informs and motivates them. The GLBT community is another case in point; it will be hard to understand where they are coming from both socially and politically without knowing something of their personal and collective stories and the pain and marginalization they have experienced from the broader society—particularly the church.

Incarnation of the heart can be costly, so we often avoid it. However, it is too easy for us to just engage our minds or even bodies for the cause and sake of the gospel. Engaging the heart completes the picture. Jesus didn't fulfill his mission on earth through mere forced obedience to the Father's wishes; his heart was engaged, and he was moved with compassion to act on behalf of a lost humanity.

Maybe we are a tad weird, but whenever we visit a city we try to walk the red-light district. We recently did this in Amsterdam, and we took some people with us. Many of them were missionaries to that city but had never visited this important, if not very dark, aspect of that city's culture. Surely, loving a city requires that we feel its pain. The pain of the city can be a thermometer that connects us with the heart of God. To walk around and sense the lostness, despair, and longing can be difficult, but it is necessary if we are to make connections between God and the community.

Jesus puts himself in our situations because he loves us. "The people who sit in some black hole need no longer look upward to where a crack admits light and fresh air. They need only look down to the bottom of their abyss. There is Christ;

there where the border runs between despair and disintegration. Therefore we can trust Him. And therefore it is no empty phrase that He is there for us and that He is our brother."[8]

6. The Practice of Proclamation

Jesus came to proclaim the good news of the kingdom of God (Mark 1:14), and there is no question that we are called to the same task (2 Tim. 4:2). Aside from how we have individualized the proclamation—making it about personal salvation and narrowing the meaning of the gospel in the process—we have generally been quite good at this aspect of incarnational ministry. There is no doubt that the follower of Jesus must be both willing and able to share in the ministry of evangelism. We are, in the end, messengers: it is an essential part of our purpose in the world to deliver the message. But we must do it in ways that are entirely consistent with the message; otherwise our lives will discredit the very message we seek to deliver. This is where personal witness and evangelism must be yoked together. Jesus is the Word. His life and teaching are one and the same. He *is* his own message—he is the good news. We, however, being broken and sinful, do not have this level of integrity, so we have to learn to integrate life and message in order to legitimize what we say.

Following the logic of the incarnation itself, our message is heard properly only when we have gone through the process of identifying with people, hearing them, understanding the issues they face, humbly living with them, and knowing how they experience and express their search for meaning. If we do this, we will have earned the right to address the hearts of the people and bring salvation to them. If we don't do this, we will simply impose a cultural Christianity on them, and they could well end up in a worse situation than before (Luke 11: 24). This is what the Pharisees were guilty of in doing (Matt. 23:13, 15), and what we should be very wary of in our own lives as we seek to evangelize the lives of others. We therefore think that proclamation follows best after practicing the preceding "P's" of an incarnational lifestyle.

This is why discipleship plays such a crucial part in evangelism. Because discipleship is the process of increasingly becoming like Jesus, our lives will serve to legitimize what we say. Because we are appealing to people's deepest concerns, their existential issues known only to themselves and God, we stand on sacred ground; we must come into the relationship with personal integrity. When someone is not striving to be like his or her Lord and yet is calling others to give their lives over to God, it gives a very mixed message. It can even miscommunicate what God wants to do with people. Now, we are not saying that we should be perfect before we can share the gospel, but surely we should be on the journey of being transformed ourselves before we call others to this arduous task. We do well to remember that evangelism is witness. Daniel T. Niles sums this up beautifully when he says the disciple "does not offer out of his own bounty. He has no bounty. He is simply a guest at his master's table, and, as evangelist, he calls others too."[9]

We believe that engaging our world incarnationally is not an option. If we genuinely seek to be like Jesus, then incarnational discipleship and mission should be the norm. It is the way God has chosen to reach the world in Jesus. It will require that we patiently love a person, a community, even a whole culture, to the point that we spend ourselves on being little Jesuses to that community. Not only is the credibility of the people of God linked to incarnational expression, but the credibility of the gospel is at stake in it as well. As theologian Darrell Guder rightly says,

> The centrality of the community to the gospel means that the message is never disembodied. The word must always become flesh, embodied in the life of the called community. The gospel cannot be captured adequately in propositions,

249

or creeds, or theological systems, as crucial as all of these exercises are. The gospel dwells in and shapes the people who are called to be its witness. The message is inextricably linked with its messengers.[10]

Whatever our circumstance or context, understanding the implications of the incarnation and seeking to live them out will only make our lives more authentic, our love more tangible, and our light amidst the darkness shine more brightly.

Suggested Practices

- *Humanizing God, divinizing humanity*: Try to regularly factor the incarnation into your thinking. Not only does Jesus show us what God is like, but he also shows us a way to be truly human. It is therefore essential that we take seriously the doctrine of the incarnation.
- *Deal with fear and laziness*: According to M. Scott Peck, these two vices lay at the very heart of sin. Fear will keep us from practicing presence and proximity with non-Christian people, and laziness will keep us from regularly being in their world. Yet we need to draw near and be there in their world to communicate the love of God incarnationally.
- *Practice prevenience*: Trust the fact that God is already in any situation long before you arrive on the scene, and that if you have your eyes open, you can both see what he is doing and join with him.
- *Be intentional*: It is critical that we develop habits and practices that inculcate the incarnational impulse. We have to be very intentional about it because the current church default tends to negate this impulse. Get a copy of Alan's *The Forgotten Ways Handbook*: in it is a chapter dedicated to helping people engage incarnationally in a very practical way.

Discussion Starters

1. How does the fact that God became man change your perception of Christianity and discipleship?
2. Discuss the subversive nature of this aspect of biblical revelation.
3. What is the difference between presence and proximity? Articulate why you think they are both necessary.
4. Watch the movie *Slumdog Millionaire* and discuss how you can see the traces of God in the slums and in the poor. How would you reach these people?
5. "God is humble." Discuss the truth and implications of this statement.
6. How is "sharing in the sufferings of Christ" part of discipleship? How do you dodge suffering, and what does that do to your capacity to be an authentic disciple?

the last word

(conclusion)

Those that give up essential liberty to obtain a little temporary safety deserve neither liberty nor safety.

—Benjamin Franklin

To be unfree and in the power of something else, is perhaps the greatest of all suffering for a free being.

— Søren Kierkegaard

There is an exact equilibrium: The more security and guarantees we want against things, the less free we are. Tyrants are not to be feared today, but our own frantic need of security is. Freedom inevitably means insecurity and responsibility. But we moderns seek above all to be responsible for nothing.

—Jacques Ellul

One will not keep fear of insecurity from becoming a possessive demon by making oneself ever more secure. The hold of the god must be broken by flying in the very face of the drive for security.

—Gilbert Meilaender

252

A s we finish the initial drafts of this book, we are snowed in at a condo in Post Falls, Idaho. The presence of geese on the lake in such snowy conditions has reminded us of a parable told by Søren Kierkegaard.[1] Søren grew up in the countryside surrounded by farms that reared geese (among other animals). Each spring he would watch as a new gaggle of goslings hatched and grew. Over the course of their short lives, these geese would gorge themselves at constantly refilled troughs of grain until they were so fat they could hardly walk. He imagined that they believed their lives to be perfect, as every need they had was catered to in abundance.

When autumn came, the truth became apparent. The wild geese that had spent the warm summer months in Denmark would gather in preparation for their southerly migration. They would circle in the skies above the farms, calling out to any stragglers to join in their flight. At this point, the farmed geese would lift their heads from the feeding troughs and look into the skies, heeding the call of their untamed cousins. Listening to the call of the wild, they would become animated, running as best they could around their enclosures, emulating flight. Of course, their gluttonous diet and life of luxury meant they were far too fat to get airborne, and they probably didn't really want to join their untamed cousins on that perilous journey anyhow—but their instincts drove them at least to emulate flight on the ground. The wild geese would fly off and the fattened, domesticated geese would simply return to their barnyard existence, ignorant of the farmer's grim ultimate purpose—they were destined for the table.

Kierkegaard's parable goes on to tell of a wild goose who looked with dismay at his domesticated cousins. In the interest of food and relative luxury, they had given up flight for the mediocrity of the barnyard. With splendid motivation, he decided to spend some time with them in order to help them awaken to their true calling as geese and join the others in wild flight. Sadly, he lived there until he himself was tamed. Every year, when the wild geese would honk in flight overhead, he, like the others, would flutter his wings, rise a bit, and resolve to join them. But he never did. Instead, he finally became content to remain with the tamed and flightless—destined for the table. Kierkegaard ends his parable with a warning: while a wild goose can be tamed, seldom does a tame goose become wild again.

As disciples we are called to an untamed existence. Like the wild geese, we are meant to live wild and dangerous lives, flying above the heads of our generation, calling them to the authenticity of what they were created to do. Instead, we have allowed ourselves to be dulled into a life of mediocrity, where the only wild journeys we ever take are in our dreams.

We started this book with the parable of the skylark that sold its feathers for worms, and we end it with a parable that calls us to forgo a domesticated Christianity and adopt a life of untamed and risky discipleship. Clearly there are two common themes in the two parables. First, we should be aware of the surreptitious danger of domestication and other cultural encroachments on our discipleship. Second, the parables remind us that when we reach deep into ourselves, we realize that we are made for greater things and long to be all that Jesus wants us to be.

We don't for a moment think it is impossible to reactivate our discipleship once we have forsaken it. And while it will be hard to disentangle ourselves from the snares of idolatry, we already have all the resources we need to change the world. Jesus lives in us, we are bearers of the gospel of God, and we have the power and presence of the Holy Spirit. We have a community committed to the cause of the kingdom. But if we are going to recover discipleship in the way of Jesus, we will have to discard the things that keep us from fulfilling that destiny. We have to reclaim our feathers as well as the will to fly. We have some choices to make.

This book has explored some of the cultural, theological, and missiological hindrances that keep us from becoming the untamed people we are created to be in Jesus. We need to move beyond our many distorted understandings of Jesus, God, self, church, sexuality, money, status, family, and mission to rediscover the sheer liberating power of the biblical gospel.

We know you want it, because this is what every human being wants and is made for. Jesus sets us free! Now go and find it for yourself!

> It is for freedom that Christ has set us free. Stand firm, then, and do not let yourselves be burdened again by a yoke of slavery. (Gal. 5:1)

afterword

a call to an untamed adventure

In middle school, my brother and I went on an African safari. We were born less than a year apart and traveled in East Africa on the type of adventure most young boys only dream about. Anything but tame—this trip had close encounters with wild animals of every kind.

Our journey first took us to a hotel on stilts overlooking a water hole. The hotel is called Treetops. Wild animals would come from miles around to drink at the water hole, and tourists like us could observe them in their natural habitat from above. Of course, we were not the first ones to have had this view—the monkeys and baboons lived in the treetops before tourists ever came. The afternoon when we checked in to the hotel, we were warned to keep our windows closed so that these curious hosts wouldn't steal our possessions while we were asleep. The primates were so at home in the Treetops that they would actually mingle among the people, sometimes reaching right into their bags to take shiny objects such as cameras or purses. I learned not to consider these animals as tame simply because they were comfortable in close proximity to people.

I was on the top platform the next morning and saw a grey baboon reaching into a woman's purse to steal her camera (it seems crime is everywhere these days). He was close enough for me to reach out and touch, and I was foolish enough that I did. I actually grabbed his tail for just an instant. In a flash, the animal had spun around with a mouth wide open and screaming. I saw teeth that were longer than my second-period math class and sharper than Rachael Cohen in the first row who always raised the class curve! I quickly let go of the tail and froze with fear. The baboon took the camera and left. I'm actually surprised he didn't take a picture of the look on my face to show the rest of the troop for a good laugh.

Later that night I was not very hungry, so I decided to stay in our bungalow while my mother and brother went up to the lodge for dinner. Around dessert time I had a remarkable recovery and felt hungry, so I decided to join the meal, walking up to the lodge from our bungalow after dark. On the way to the lodge, I noticed something unusual, but since everything I was seeing was unusual to me, I didn't think much of it. Throughout the evening some zebra and impala would graze on the lawn, but this time there were none to be found. I kept walking up to the lodge and then noticed all the people inside watching me through the windows lit up from the interior lights. They were waving at me. Some seemed to be compelling me to return to my bungalow, others seemed to be telling me to hurry up and get inside. I had no clue as to why, but I hastened my step. Once I was inside I was told that a leopard was out on the grass *stalking me*. Fortunately, the sharpshooters had their rifles trained on her in case she wanted a little dessert herself. Wow, I thought, now there's a story that will impress my friends back at school. I remember thinking: how many kids at my school can boast a leopard has stalked them?

Within a couple weeks I had seen cheetahs, lions, giraffe, elephants, and hordes of wildebeest. I had been chased in a Land Rover by a rhinoceros and grunted at in a very threatening way by a bull. I had tried to catch foot-long lizards that lived in a palace (Prov. 30:28), and was eaten alive by more flies than Steven King could use in a horror movie.

I tell you this story of my adventures in untamed Africa because there is a lesson found there about life. There were two boys on this trip, both were the same age and of the same upbringing. I came home lucky to have all my fingers and lots of stories. My brother went on the same trip, but instead of recklessly living such an adventure, he spent most of his time reading a novel about adventures in Africa. We both had a great time, but one of us came home with stories to tell.

There are two kinds of people in the world: those who live the adventure, and those who only read about others living the adventure. I determined a long time ago that I wasn't going to be someone who only reads about the adventures of others—I would live a life of adventure. Full gusto, go-for-it faith that abandons all on the risk that God is indeed real and will carry me through.

In *Untamed*, Alan and Debra Hirsch have challenged us to live a life of reckless faith, a life worth telling stories about. They have dared us to abandon the domestic faith of suburban consumer "churchianity" in order to live a life of risk for the love of a Savior who left heaven to live among the poor and marginalized people of a backward and oppressed world.

The true Jesus is not safe and sterile, conflicted by a mission and a passive kindness—which Hollywood typically portrays and Christians are comfortable believing in. He said things that offended others regularly. He never carried the party line. Jesus shocked his foes, his friends, and his followers with equal doses.

The Hirsches wrote, "His was a wild holiness that calls to account all who refuse to deal with God, preferring instead to follow the lame dictates of a religion of ethical codes and pious rituals."

Alan and Debra went on to pose a revealing question and counter-question that opened our eyes to the tamed existence we have grown accustomed to: "What is it about the holiness of Jesus that caused 'sinners' to flock to him like a magnet and yet manages to seriously antagonize the religious people?

This question begs yet another, even more confronting question: Why does our more churchy form of holiness seem to get it the other way around?"

They went on to explain: "One of the greatest counterfeits for following the untamed Jesus comes from the substitution of morals and decency for Jesus's untamed kind of holiness. One of the standard attempts to stereotype, and therefore domesticate, Jesus is to make him into a moral teacher, someone who taught us how to live decent, rule-based lives."

As Spurgeon once commented: Morality may keep you out of jail, but it will not keep you out of hell. The holiness of God is much more than a tamed and moral existence. Jesus was on a mission to rescue not those who were moral, but those who were broken and imprisoned by evil. He was destined to reach into dark and sin-infested places to call out and redeem the beautiful image of God found in people that were enslaved by evil. He did not hang out in safe places. I imagine that today you would be more likely to find Jesus in a gay bar than a church service. If he went to a religious service, he would be likely to overturn the book tables and chase away the sales people. He risked his reputation to be with the people that needed saving and knew they did. This is our Savior. His mission has not altered or changed in two thousand years, and he bids us to join him. Are you willing to walk into some dangerous places with Jesus at your back? *Untamed* has told us what it means to follow such a wild and dangerous Messiah.

When I first heard that Alan and Debra were coming to live for a time in the States, I must admit to being very excited. My joy, actually, was as much (if not more) about Deb's coming as it was for Alan! You see, I have come to know these two and I truly believe that we need Debra's gifts and influence in these days as much as her genius of a husband. Yes, Alan is Debra Hirsch's husband, not the other way around! It is my honor in writing the afterword to this book to commend to you this incredible woman of God who has a needed message for us in these days.

My first introduction to Alan was at a coffee bar in Melbourne. I was given a copy of *The Shaping of Things to Come*, which I read on my long and uncomfortable flight home. It wasn't just the small and crowded economy seat that made me feel uncomfortable. As I arrived in Los Angeles, I found that there was one thing I didn't like about the book: *I didn't write it.*

Since then, I have been a close friend and fellow laborer with both Alan and Debra in trying to release a missional expression of church that takes Christ into the dangerous world. Alan has been teaching us all about the needed elements of an apostolic church movement. Each of his books has taken us closer to unlocking this reality in the West. This book is the perfect follow-up to *ReJesus*. In a sense, it discusses the essential part of a missional church, because it gets to the heart of the core ingredient of a missional movement—the follower of Jesus. We simply must have followers that abandon all to follow Jesus, or we are not growing his church but our own organization. Ultimately, our church is only as good as its disciples. Tamed disciples form tame churches. Adventurous disciples will form an untamed church that will change the world.

You may have found yourself uncomfortable with this book. If so, the Hirsches have succeeded. You see, an untamed life is not a comfortable one. Unpredictable, wild, exhilarating, and at times chaotic, yes; but comfortable, it is not. Get used to it if you want to live a life of real faith following a radical and revolutionary Savior who will take you on a white-knuckle ride way beyond your comfort zone. Abandon the safe and tame life of conservative religious morality. Live a life that has stories to tell. Be untamed in your faith and pursuit of the wild Savior, Jesus.

Neil Cole
Long Beach, CA
August 2009

notes

why write this book?

1. The Gay, Lesbian, Bisexual, and Transgender/Transsexual community, also referred to as the LGBT, or the LGBTQ (Q representing "queer" and/or "questioning") community.

the first word

1. Parable adapted from a version found in Jeffrey Satinover, *Homosexuality and the Politics of Truth* (Grand Rapids: Baker, 1996), 130.

2. Reggie McNeal, Neil Cole, Ed Stetzer, Michael Frost, Stanley Hauerwas, Rodney Clapp, Stuart Murray, Shane Claiborne, Dallas Willard, Howard Snyder, Richard Foster (to name but a few) all have written directly, as well as indirectly, on issues related to discipleship, and all acknowledge that discipleship is one of the most critical issues facing churches today.

3. Reggie McNeal, *The Present Future: Six Tough Questions for the Church* (San Francisco: Jossey-Bass, 2003), 1.

4. N. T. Wright, *Following Jesus: Biblical Reflections on Discipleship* (Grand Rapids: Eerdmans, 1974), preface.

chapter 1 jeebus made me do it

1. David Kinnaman and Gabe Lyons, *unChristian: What a New Generation Really Thinks about Christianity . . . and Why It Matters* (Grand Rapids: Baker, 2007).

2. Albert Nolan, *Jesus Before Christianity* (Maryknoll, NY: Orbis, 1978), 165–67.

3. N. T. Wright, *The Challenge of Jesus* (London: SPCK, 2000), 92.

4. Gregory Boyd, *Is God to Blame? Beyond Pat Answers to the Problem of Suffering* (Downers Grove, IL: InterVarsity, 2003), 16.

5. Quoted in John V. Taylor, *The Christlike God* (London: SCM, 1992).

6. Alan Hirsch and Michael Frost, *ReJesus: A Wild Messiah for a Missional Church* (Peabody: Hendrickson, 2009), 12–13.

7. For a thorough exploration of idolatry, image-making, and its consequences see Moshe Halbertal and Avishai Margalit, *Idolatry* (Cambridge, MA: Harvard University Press, 1992); and more recently G. K. Beale, *We Become What We Worship: A Biblical Theology of Idolatry* (Downers Grove, IL: InterVarsity, 2008).

8. Many would by now be concerned that we are somehow undermining all forms of religious art. And in some ways, and for the reasons above, we *do* believe that Scripture puts limits on attempts to represent God the Father, Jesus, and the Holy Spirit. But we also strongly believe in the validity of art and its attempt to symbolically portray truth in visual form. So in order to avoid image-making, we would suggest that Christian artists should direct their attention on events in the Bible and issues of the theological significance of texts, rather than on trying to image God in any way. And when trying to communicate understandings of God, that they use abstract and symbolic means, rather than attempts to capture him in images. In such cases, God ends up looking like an old, angry man, and Jesus ends up religious, spooky, racially defined, or culturally co-opted. And how can one adequately represent the Holy Spirit except symbolically? Such art cannot fully honor the revelation of God in Jesus. Besides, the way monotheistic believers are to reflect specifically on God is *not* through the image (for reasons explained above), but rather through the language/word and through remembrance and story. For instance, see Jacques Ellul, *The Humiliation of the Word* (Grand Rapids: Eerdmans, 1985) for a powerful example of this way of thinking.

9. Brandon O'Brien, "A Jesus for Real Men: What the New Masculinity Movement Gets Right and Wrong," *Christianity Today*, April 18, 2009, http://www.christianitytoday.com/ct/2008/april/27.48.html.

10. Hirsch and Frost, *ReJesus*, 12–13. Many representations of Jesus portray him as idealized humanity, highlighting the softer virtues—the more caring, gentle aspects of his nature. The wild-eyed Prophet seems to give way to either the overly cosmic Jesus or to the overly genteel vision of who he is.

11. O'Brien, "A Jesus for Real Men." O'Brien goes on to say, quite rightly, "Most importantly, Scripture gives no indication that Jesus came to earth to model masculinity. He is the 'image of the invisible God, the firstborn over all creation' (Col. 1:15). As such, he is not simply the perfect male; he is the perfect human being. Through his obedience to the Father, Christ exhibited the qualities that should characterize all believers, both male and female."

12. Ben Witherington III, quoted in Bruxy Cavey, *The End of Religion: Encountering the Subversive Spirituality of Jesus* (Colorado Springs: NavPress, 2007), 67.

13. Gregory Boyd, *Repenting of Religion, Turning from Judgment to the Love of God* (Grand Rapids: Baker, 2004), 97.

14. Stanley Hauerwas and William H. Willimon, *Resident Aliens: Life in the Christian Colony* (Nashville: Abingdon, 1989), 90.

15. Peter Vardy, *An Introduction to Kierkegaard* (Peabody, MA: Hendrickson, 2008), 50.

16. Ibid., 52–53.

17. *The Examen* is an ancient practice in the Church that draws upon and enacts the spiritual exercises of St. Ignatius of Loyola. For more information see: http://ignatianspirituality.com/ignatian-prayer/the-examen/.

18. You can find out more about the "six thinking hats" at http://en.wikipedia .org/wiki/De_Bono_Hats.

chapter 2   your god is too sick

1. Martin Buber, *Israel and the World* (New York: Schocken Books, 1973), 117.

2. C. S. Lewis, *Mere Christianity*, in Clyde Kilby, *A Mind Awake: An Anthology of C. S. Lewis* (London: Geoffrey Bles, 1968), 109–10.

3. William Temple, *Christian Faith and Life* (Harper & Brothers, 1931), 24.

4. C. S. Lewis, *Reflections on the Psalms*, quoted in Leanne Payne, *Restoring the Christian Soul* (London: Kingsway, 1992), 144.

5. See George Weigel, *Faith, Reason, and the War against Jihadism: A Call to Action* (New York: Doubleday, 2007), 13. For instance, the Cold War demonstrated, on a global scale, what is at stake regarding our fundamental ideas regarding human nature, human community, human aspirations, and human destiny. If we fought over ideas that relate to humanity, how much more do ideas about God have ramifications in society and in the human soul.

6. Ibid., 47.

7. If that is what radical Islamists believe, then at least in their own frame of reference, they are justified in believing that God can command anything, even the irrational. "And so contemporary Jihadists believe that the murder of innocents is not simply morally acceptable, but morally required, if such murders advance the cause of Islam. The same is true for lying—it is allowed in a Jihad if it advances its cause. And so we see that the origins of the lethal weapon of the 'homicide bomber' of our day are rooted in a defective, impassive concept of God" (ibid., 47, 50, 56).

8. See Alan Hirsch, *The Forgotten Ways: Reactivating the Missional Church* (Grand Rapids: Brazos, 2007), ch. 3 for a more thorough exploration of the lordship of Jesus—what Alan calls Christocentric monotheism.

9. Alan and Michael suggest that the true understanding of God comes from a combination of a number of factors, namely, the intersection between "orthopathy," orthopraxy, and orthodoxy. See Hirsch and Frost, *ReJesus*, ch. 6.

10. Leanne Payne, *Real Presence: The Christian Worldview of C. S. Lewis as Incarnational Reality* (Wheaton: Crossway, 1979), 24–25.

11. Søren Kierkegaard, *Concluding Unscientific Postscript* (Princeton: Princeton University Press, 1941).

12. The Bible is clear how critical it is to engage the heart when dealing with God (e.g., Ps. 101:4; Isa. 29:13; Matt. 15:8).

13. *The Cloud of Unknowing* (San Francisco: HarperSanFrancisco, 2004).

14. Jonathan Edwards, *On the Religious Affections* (Carlisle, PA: Banner of Truth, 1961), 11.

15. Quoted in Payne, *Real Presence*, 81

16. Vardy, *An Introduction to Kierkegaard*, 33.

17. Charles Williams, *Outlines of Romantic Theology* (Grand Rapids: Eerdmans, 1990), 101.

18. As Emile Durkheim shows, idols are in effect a projection of our social identity. God, who is beyond creation, cannot be limited to an image, an act of human creation or imagination. In fact, it is humans themselves who are made in the image and likeness of God. And "because idols estrange their servants from their own image of God, [they] lead them further from who they truly are into the void of falsehood" (Telford Work, *Deuteronomy*, Brazos Theological Commentary of the Bible [Grand Rapids: Brazos, 2009], 61).

19. Quoted in Carol Tavris and Elliot Aronson, *Mistakes Were Made, but Not by Me* (Orlando: Harvest, 2007), 65.

20. See "Cognitive Dissonance" at http://www.ethicsscoreboard.com/rb_defini tions.html. In other words, dissonance is the inherent discomfort resulting from experiencing two or more mental events (beliefs, attitudes, values, perceptions) that are incompatible with each other. This relates directly to the New Testament teaching on conscience: it's for good reason that the Bible talks about guarding the conscience and being careful not to sear it (e.g., Acts 23:1; 24:16; Rom. 9:1; 2 Cor. 1:12). Conscience is not always the best guide to the knowledge of God because it can be culturally conditioned, but going against conscience is almost always a bad idea (e.g., 1 Cor. 8:7, 10; 1 Tim. 1:19–20).

21. Payne, *Real Presence*, 81.

22. God's blessing is a promise in Scripture, but it should never be seen as "entitlement," nor in purely financial terms.

23. For an exploration of leader-crowd relationships, see Nikolai Berdyaev, *Slavery and Freedom* (New York: Scribners, 1972), 61–63.

24. M. Scott Peck, *People of the Lie: The Hope for Healing Human Evil* (New York: Touchstone, 1985).

25. C. S. Lewis, quoted in Wayne Martindale and Jerry Root, *The Quotable Lewis* (Wheaton: Tyndale, 1989), 411. See pages 209–411 for some of Lewis's thinking on this.

26. C. S. Lewis, in *A Mind Awake*, 142.

27. C. S. Lewis, quoted in Wayne Martindale, *Beyond the Shadowlands: C. S. Lewis on Heaven and Hell* (Wheaton: Crossway, 2005), 47.

28. In *The Forgotten Ways*, Alan suggests that the marks, or identifiers, of an authentic church include the following elements: (1) a covenant community (2) centered on Jesus as the Mediator, Savior, and Lord, (3) the encounter with Whom results in (4) worship (offering our worlds back to God through Jesus), (5) mission (extending the work of Jesus as agents of his Kingdom), and (6) discipleship (following Jesus and becoming like him).

29. Brennan Manning, *Lion and Lamb*, quoted in Michael Yaconelli, *Messy Spirituality: God's Annoying Love for Imperfect People* (Grand Rapids: Zondervan, 2002), 121–22.

30. Mark Labberton, *The Dangerous Act of Worship: Living God's Call to Justice* (Downers Grove, IL: InterVarsity, 2007), 13.

31. Lee Camp, *Mere Discipleship: Radical Christianity in a Rebellious World* (Grand Rapids: Brazos, 2008), 130–31.

32. Labberton, *The Dangerous Act of Worship*, 19–20.

33. Martindale, *Beyond the Shadowlands*, 161.

chapter 3 the spirit's edge

1. J. V. Taylor, *The Go-Between God: The Holy Spirit and the Christian Mission* (London: SCM Press, 2004), 45.

2. Lesslie Newbigin, *The Light Has Come: An Exposition of the Fourth Gospel* (Grand Rapids: Eerdmans, 1982), 161.

3. Gregory of Nyssa, *The Life of Moses*, trans. Abraham Malherbe and Everett Ferguson (New York: HarperCollins, 2006), 81.

4. James Jones, quoted in Steven J. Land, *Pentecostal Spirituality: A Passion for the Kingdom* (Sheffield: Sheffield Academic Press, 1993), 40.

5. J. V. Taylor, *The Go-Between God*, 48.

6. Hirsch, *The Forgotten Ways*, ch. 8.

7. Thomas Cahill, *How the Irish Saved Civilization* (New York: Anchor, 1996).

chapter 4 kultcha-schmultcha

1. Stephanie Rosenbloom, "Wal-Mart Worker Trampled to Death by Frenzied Black Friday Shoppers," *The Seattle Times*, November 29, 2008, http://seattletimes.nwsource.com/html/nationworld/2008448574_shop290.html.

2. Dick Staub, *The Culturally Savvy Christian: A Manifesto for Deepening Faith and Enriching Popular Culture in an Age of Christianity-Lite* (San Fransisco: Wiley, 2007), 5.

3. Greg Hawkins and Cally Parkinson, *Reveal: Where Are You?* (Chicago: Willow Creek Association, 2007).

4. Staub, *The Culturally Savvy Christian*, 27.

5. A cartoon by Thom Tapp, November 17, 2008, from http://blog.christianitytoday.com/outofur/upload/2008/11/cartoon_baptism.jpg.

6. Richard Foster, *Money, Sex, and Power: The Challenge of the Disciplined Life* (New York: Harper & Row, 1985), 19.

7. Susan Hope, *Mission-Shaped Spirituality: The Transforming Power of Mission* (London: Church House Publishing, 2007), 36.

8. Foster, *Money, Sex, and Power*, 25; and Jaques Ellul, *Money and Power* (Downers Grove, IL: InterVarsity, 1984), 44.

9. Foster, *Money, Sex, and Power*, 28.

10. Dr. Wesley White, "Poverty and Wealth after Rwanda," *Bulletin of St. John's, Nottingham*, September 16, 2008.

11. Ellul, *Money and Power*, 112.

12. Miroslav Volf, *Free of Charge: Giving and Forgiving in a Culture Stripped of Grace* (Grand Rapids: Zondervan, 2005), 54.

13. Ibid., 14.

14. Ibid., 28, 42–52. We are grateful to Dr. Wes White for his summary and for putting us onto Volf's excellent writings here.

15. Victor Lebeau, interviewed in *The Story of Stuff with Annie Leonard*, web-based film, directed by Louis Fox (Berkeley, CA: Free Range Studios, 2007), http://www.storyofstuff.com/.

16. Milton Friedman, quoted in Dick Staub, *The Culturally Savvy Christian*, 11.

17. Alan notes in *The Forgotten Ways*,

Much of that which goes by the name advertising is an explicit offer of a sense of identity, meaning, purpose, and community. Most ads now appeal to one or more of these religious dimensions of life. Take for instance a recent car ad targeting twenty-somethings in which we are introduced to a fantastic group of very cool people singing along in a car and generally having a great time. Throughout the ad, nothing is mentioned about the qualities of a car, its technical ingenuity, its availability, its price; rather the advert is an explicit appeal to the need for people to be accepted as cool people. The selling point on the ad is an offer of community, status, and acceptance by groovy people: if the consumer would just purchase this vehicle they will have achieved this. Analyzed in a religious way, we could see just about all advertising in this light. Buy this and you will be changed. The astute cultural commentator Douglas Rushkoff in his PBS documentary on consumerism, *The Persuaders*, has noted that advertisers and marketers are now learning from religion in order to sell products. Marketers have now co-opted the language and symbolism of all the major religions in order to sell the product because they know that religion offers the ultimate object of desire and that people will do just about anything to get it. If through advertising marketers can just link their products to this great unfilled void, they *will* sell. An advertising executive recently confessed to Alan that they are now deliberately stepping into the void that was left by the vacation of Christianity from Western culture. (107)

18. Hugh McLeod, *The Hughtrain Manifesto*, http://www.changethis.com/11.TheHughtrain.

19. Helen Trinca and Catherine Fox, quoted in Mark Sayers, *The Trouble With Paris* (Nashville: Thomas Nelson, 2008), 30–31.

20. Hirsch, *The Forgotten Ways*, 111. Cf. Sayers, *The Trouble With Paris*, pt. 3.

21. In their groundbreaking book *Affluenza,* economists Clive Hamilton and Richard Denniss detail how having more than ever before has made us unhappier than ever before. *Affluenza: When Too Much is Never Enough* (Crows Nest, New South Wales: Allen & Unwin, 2005).

22. Dick Staub, *The Culturally Savvy Christian*, 7.

23. Alain De Botton, *Status Anxiety* (London: Penguin, 2005).

24. Russell B. Goodman, *Wittgenstein and William James* (Cambridge: Cambridge University Press, 2002), 92.

25. Ibid., 21.

26. Juliet B. Schor, *The Overspent American: Why We Want What We Don't Need* (New York: HarperCollins, 1998), 51.

27. Hope, *Mission-Shaped Spirituality*, 36.

28. Manohla Dargis, "The Pursuit of Happyness (2006): Climbing Out of the Gutter With a 5-Year-Old in Tow," *New York Times*, December 15, 2006, http://movies.nytimes.com/2006/12/15/movies/15happ.html.

29. Lewis, *Screwtape Letters*, 143.

30. A. W. Tozer, *The Pursuit of God*, available at http://www.theboc.com/freestuff/awtozer/books/the_pursuit_of_god/bless_possess_nothing.html.

chapter 5 the church that jesus built

1. And actually, it's not as complex as one might think at first. For instance, the average reader of this book will have about ninety people in their orbit of meaningful relationships—some more, some less, depending on the amount of extroversion. When we come to Christ and become a disciple, it is not inconceivable that a certain percentage of those people will come to faith as well. Your relationships redeemed constitute an ecclesia as the Bible defines it. It doesn't need all the paraphernalia we've come to associate with the concept of "church."

2. Hirsch, *The Forgotten Ways*, chap. 1.

3. Hawkins and Parkinson, *Reveal: Where Are You?*

4. Drawn from 1 Peter 2:9.

5. http://en.wikipedia.org/wiki/Priesthood_of_all_believers , and the article on the peasants' war http://en.wikipedia.org/wiki/Peasants%27_War.

6. Hirsch, *The Forgotten Ways*, 171.

7. See *The Forgotten Ways*, 174–77 for a description of how we did this.

8. See Tony Dale, Felicity Dale, and George Barna, *The Rabbit and the Elephant: Why Small Is the New Big for Today's Church* (Wheaton: Tyndale, 2009), 159–60.

9. C. S. Lewis, *Mere Christianity*, quoted in Martindale and Root, *The Quotable Lewis*, 108.

10. See Hirsch, *The Forgotten Ways*, ch. 4; and Alan Kreider, *The Change of Conversion and the Origin of Christendom* (Eugene, OR: Wipf & Stock, 2007).

11. Alan Hirsch and Michael Frost, *The Shaping of Things to Come* (Peabody, MA: Hendrickson, 2003), 47, 210–12.

12. Michael Yaconelli, *Messy Spirituality*, 34.

13. Richard Neuhaus, *Freedom for Ministry* (Grand Rapids: Eerdmans, 1992), 33.

14. Darrel Guder, *The Incarnation and the Church's Witness* (Eugene, OR: Wipf & Stock, 1999), 48–49.

chapter 6 refocusing the family

1. E.g., Rodney Clapp, *Families at the Crossroads: Beyond Traditional and Modern Options* (Downers Grove, IL: InterVarsity Press, 1993); and Scott Bader-Saye, *Following Jesus in a Culture of Fear* (Grand Rapids: Brazos, 2007).

2. A term that combines two words to describe "teenagers who are online" and who are "always looking at the screen." See http://www.netlingo.com/word/screenagers.php.

3. Bader-Saye, *Following Jesus in a Culture of Fear*, chap. 2 and 102.

4. Janet Fishburn, *Confronting the Idolatry of Family: A New Vision for the Household of God* (Nashville: Abingdon, 1991).

5. Ibid.

6. Ibid.

7. Clapp, *Families at the Crossroads*, 67.

8. Ibid., 47.

9. Ibid., 46.

10. Fishburn, *Confronting the Idolatry of Family*.

11. For a great summary of the nature of first, second, and third places, see Micheol Frost, *Exiles: Living Missionally in a Post-Christian Culture* (Peabody, MA: Hendrickson, 2006), 56–63, as well as Hirsch, *The Forgotten Ways*, 145–46.

12. Clapp, *Families at the Crossroads*, 16.

chapter 7 the lying mirror

1. There are numerous books that deal with Kierkegaard's teaching in this regard. Good summaries can be found in David Gouwens, *Kierkegaard as Religious Thinker* (Cambridge: Cambridge University Press, 1996), ch. 3; and Frederic Sontag, *A Kierkegaard Handbook* (Atlanta: John Knox, 1989), 128–36. Kierkegaard's views of self and despair are echoed in almost all major Christian thinkers after him, including C. S. Lewis, Karl Barth, Dietrich Bonhoeffer, and Reinhold Niebuhr. For instance, consider this from C. S. Lewis: "From the moment a creature becomes aware of God as God and itself as self, the terrible alternative of choosing God or self for the center is opened to it. This sin is committed daily by young children and ignorant peasants as well as by sophisticated persons, by solitaries no less than by those who live in society; it is the fall in every individual life, and in each day of each individual life, the basics behind all particular sins; at this very moment you and I are either committing it, or about to commit it, or repenting it" (C. S. Lewis, *The Problem of Pain*, quoted in Clyde Kilby, *A Mind Awake*, 112).

2. Shirley Lyn Scott, "What Makes Serial Killers Tick? http://www.trutv.com/library/crime/serial_killers/notorious/tick/psych_6.html. The following are environmental factors, psychiatrists say, which can create a sociopath: studies show that sixty percent of psychopathic individuals had lost a parent; the child is deprived of love or nurturing; parents are detached or absent; inconsistent discipline—if father is stern and mother is soft, the child learns to hate authority and manipulate his or her mother; and hypocritical parents who privately belittle the child while publicly presenting the image of a "happy family."

3. Vardy, *An Introduction to Kierkegaard*, 56.

4. Hope, *Mission-Shaped Spirituality*, 16.

5. C. S. Lewis, *The Voyage of the Dawn Treader* (New York: Collier, 1971), ch. 7. We are also grateful to Leanne Payne's *Real Presence*, ch. 6, for the metaphor of "being un-dragoned."

6. Henri Nouwen, *The Way of the Heart* (New York: HarperCollins, 1981), 38.

7. C. S. Lewis, "The Weight of Glory," *Theology* 43 (Nov. 1941): 273–74.

8. Martin Buber, *I and Thou*, trans. Walter Kaufmann (New York: Free Press, 1971).

9. It is helpful here to remove the role of "discipling" from the confines of the church walls. In the Great Commission we are exhorted to go therefore and make disciples; we believe this to mean that we are called to disciple every person we encounter on the journey of life. Again, another way of looking at it is to "call forth the image of God" within every person. The role of "discipling" will, of course, vary from person to person, depending on our relationship with them and if they have accepted Jesus as their Lord and Savior. We have found the categories "pre-" and "post-conversion" discipleship helpful.

10. James R. Payton, Jr., "Keeping the End in View," *Christianity Today*, October 2008, 66.

11. C. S. Lewis, *Mere Christianity* (New York: Macmillan Company, 1952), 174–75.

12. C. S. Lewis, quoted in Leanne Payne, *Real Presence*, 25.

13. Gilbert Meilaender, *The Taste for the Other: The Social and Ethical Thought of C. S. Lewis* (Vancouver: Regent College Publishing, 2003), 46.

chapter 8 too sexy for the church?

1. Deb has spoken to thousands of young people over the years about sexuality. When she asks the question, "Where did you learn about sexuality?" only a small percentage ever respond with the church, parents, or the Bible.

2. Jonathon Kirsch, *Harlot by the Side of the Road* (London: Rider & Co, 1998), 1.

3. A. J. Jacobs, *The Year of Living Biblically: One Man's Humble Quest to Follow the Bible as Literally as Possible* (New York: Simon & Schuster, 2007), 10.

4. This was referred to as "concupiscence" and went from bad to worse.

5. While we affirm a place for healthy expressions of asceticism in Christian devotion (i.e., fasting on occasion) we reject the notion that pleasure comes from the devil.

6. Martin Buber, *Israel and the World* (New York: Schocken, 1973), 18.

7. Abraham Heschel, *A Passion for Truth* (London: Secker & Warburg, 1973), 52.

8. Paul K. Jewett and Marguerite Shuster, *Who We Are: Our Dignity As Human: A Neo-Evangelical Theology* (Grand Rapids: Eerdmans, 1996), 176.

9. Karl Barth, quoted in Richard Foster, *Money, Sex, and Power*, 91.

10. Stanley Grenz, *Sexual Ethics: A Biblical Perspective* (Dallas: Word, 1990), 35–38.

11. Rainer Maria Rilke, *Letters To A Young Poet*, http://www.sfgoth.com/~immanis/rilke/letter4.html.

12. The full quote is as follows: "Sexuality and spirituality are not, of course, exactly the same thing. They are not identical twins, but they are kissing cousins, and they arise out of the same kind of ground, not only in myth but in actual

human experience. The fact is that sex is the closest that many people ever come to a spiritual experience. Indeed, it is because it is a spiritual experience of sorts that so many chase after it with a repetitive, desperate kind of abandon. Often, whether they know it or not, they are searching for God. It is no accident that even atheists and agnostics will, at the moment of orgasm, routinely cry out, 'Oh God!'" (M. Scott Peck, *Further Along The Road Less Travelled* [New York: Touchstone, 1998], 220).

13. Christopher West, "God, Sex, & Babies: What the Church Really Teaches about Responsible Parenthood," Catholic Education Resource Center, http://www.catholiceducation.org/articles/sexuality/se0110.html.

14. We must understand "sexuality" in the broadest sense of the word, which includes our gender as well as social and physical longings.

15. Frederick Buechner, *Godric: A Novel* (New York: HarperOne, 1983), 153.

16. Robert Hicks, *The Masculine Journey: Understanding the Six Stages of Manhood* (Colorado Springs: NavPress, 1993), 55.

17. While recognizing the sameness of all human beings in both their existential and sexual longings, we also acknowledge that men and women often express their sexual needs in different ways.

18. Martin Buber, *The Origin and Meaning of Hasidism* (Atlantic Highlands, NJ: Humanities Press, 1960), 10.

19. C. S. Lewis, *The Great Divorce* (London: Geoffrey Bles, 1945).

20. The people interviewed were individuals who look at Christianity "from the outside in." Included in this group are atheists, agnostics, those from other faith perspectives, and other unchurched adults (Kinnaman and Lyons, *unChristian*, 249).

21. Kinnaman and Lyons, *unChristian*, 27.

22. Ed Stetzer, "LWR Releases Research on Homosexuality," June 12, 2008, http://blogs.lifeway.com/blog/edstetzer/2008/06/lifeway-research-reveals-a-cul.html.

23. Cavey, *The End of Religion*, 91.

24. See Branko Milanovic, "True World Income Distribution," available at http://econwpa.wustl.edu/eps/hew/papers/0305/0305002.pdf. The research also finds that assets of $2,200 per adult placed a household in the top half of the world wealth distribution in the year 2000. To be among the richest 10 percent of adults in the world required $61,000 in assets, and more than $500,000 was needed to belong to the richest 1 percent, a group which—with 37 million members worldwide—is far from an exclusive club. Most of us easily fit into the top 10 percent.

chapter 9 going out, going deep

1. Wright, *Following Jesus*, 34.

2. These categories draw upon and expand the 4 "P's" (presence, proximity, powerlessness, and proclamation) developed by our good friend Mike Frost in *Exiles*.

3. Frost, *Exiles*, 44.

4. Jeff and a number of others work together under the Uffizi Mission Project. If you want to find out more about what they are doing, you can visit the website http://www.uffizimission.org.

5. Dan Russ, *Flesh and Blood Jesus* (Grand Rapids: Baker, 2008), 19.

6. Søren Kierkegaard, quoted in Louis Dupre, *Kierkegaard as Theologian* (London: Sheed and Ward, 1963), 172.

7. "When he had received the drink, Jesus said, 'It is finished.' With that, he bowed his head and gave up his spirit" (John 19:30).

8. Helmut Thielicke, *I Believe: The Christian's Creed* (Philadelphia: Fortress, 1968), 101.

9. Words ascribed to Daniel T. Niles, *That They May Have Life* (New York: Harper, 1951).

10. Guder, *The Incarnation and the Church's Witness*, 22.

the last word

1. Kierkegaard, *Concluding Unscientific Postscript*, 30.

Alan Hirsch is the founding director of Forge Mission Training Network and co-founder of Shapevine. He is a sought-after speaker and trainer who travels the world extensively sharing his missional church experience. He is the author of *The Forgotten Ways* and coauthor of *ReJesus* and *The Shaping of Things to Come*.

Debra Hirsch is a minister at Tribe of Los Angeles, an eclectic bunch of missional artists and vagabonds in downtown L.A. She is also on the leadership team of Christian Associates International, a church-planting agency working on three continents.

The authors live in Los Angeles.